THEY CALLED HER THE BARONESS

The Life of Catherine de Hueck Doherty

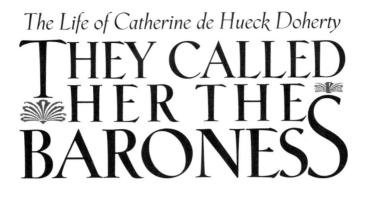

THEY CALLED HER THE BARONESS

Lorene Hanley Duquin

ALBA · HOUSE — NEW · YORK

SOCIETY OF ST. PAUL, 2187 VICTORY BLVD., STATEN ISLAND, NY 10314

Library of Congress Cataloging-in-Publication Data

Duquin, Lorene Hanley.
      They called her the baroness: the life of Catherine de Hueck
   Doherty / Lorene Hanley Duquin.
            p.   cm.
      Includes bibliographical references.
      ISBN 0-8189-0753-3
      1. Doherty, Catherine de Hueck, 1900-   2. Catholics —
   Biography.   I. Title.
   BX4705.D56D87   1995
   282'.092 — dc20   95-34825
   [B]   CIP

Produced and designed in the United States of America by the
Fathers and Brothers of the Society of St. Paul,
2187 Victory Boulevard, Staten Island, New York 10314,
as part of their communications apostolate.

ISBN: 0-8189-0753-3

Printing Information:

Current Printing - first digit   1   2   3   4   5   6   7   8   9   10

Year of Current Printing - first year shown

1995   1996   1997   1998   1999   2000

DEDICATION

To George de Hueck and Father Emile Briere,
whose desire for truth in spite of the pain,
taught me that truth does set you free.

Table of Contents

Acknowledgments

I met Catherine de Hueck Doherty in 1971. She was 74 years old, and had survived the Bolshevik Revolution, two World Wars, the Great Depression, and the battle for racial justice in the United States.

I was 20, and had survived three years at a Jesuit college.

If anyone had suggested that someday I would write her biography, we both would have laughed out loud.

It wasn't until the summer of 1988 that I began to wonder what had happened to this strange baroness. A few months later, the idea that I should write the story of Catherine's life stopped me cold. I started digging for facts, and before long, I began to sense that Catherine's experiences as a single parent, a working woman, a social reformer, a partner in a mid-life romance would speak to people today. But there was also something in her story that scared me. Her life carried a strong spiritual message: <u>To love without counting the cost and to preach the Gospel without compromise.</u>

I was a marginal Catholic with shallow beliefs and casual connections to the Church. I had also written enough magazine profiles to know that you can't step into another person's life and walk away unchanged. I decided that I didn't want to write this book, and I tried to push the idea out of my mind, but the idea would not go away.

In March 1989, I drove to Madonna House, fully expecting that they would politely tell me to leave. To my complete astonishment, they told me the Holy Spirit had instilled this idea in me, and if I decided to write this book God would take care of everything.

"How do you know that?" I demanded.

"You'll never know it in your head," one of the directors replied. "You'll only know it in your heart."

And so began my journey into the life of Catherine de Hueck Doherty.

I would like to acknowledge that this book would not have been possible without the support and encouragement from the Madonna House directors Jean Fox, Albert Osterberger, and Fr. Robert Pelton, who gave me access to Catherine's diaries and personal papers. I will never be able to find the words to adequately thank one of Catherine's closest friends, Father Emile Briere, who walked with me spiritually every step of the way. I am also immensely grateful to Madonna House Archivist, Bonnie Staib, who worked side by side with me in sorting through Catherine's unprocessed correspondence, artifacts, and photos.

Equally important was the support and assistance from the de Hueck family. Catherine's son, George de Hueck, gave me access to his personal papers, supplied me with valuable sources, and spent hours dredging up painful memories. I am also grateful to his lovely wife, Ilinca, and his daughter, Sharon Castelin and her family, who were most gracious to me on trips to Mobile, Alabama. I want to thank Paul de Hueck, Mary Davern, Ian de Hueck, and Peter de Hueck for their openness to this project. I am especially grateful to Tony and Doris de Hueck, who provided valuable insights about Boris and Claudia.

For background information on Catherine's childhood and family life in Russia, I am indebted to the Kolyschkine* family, including Catherine's brother, André Kolychkine of Havana, Cuba; her sister-in-law, Joan Kolychkine of Brussels; her nieces, Catherine de Perlinghi of Brussels, Marianna Wright and her husband, Tony, of Toronto, Natasha Butler of London, England; and Catherine's great-nieces, Marina Kollar and Inna Strukow of Nutley, New Jersey.

I am also grateful to Eddie Doherty's brother and sister, Tom

---

* See the chapter note on page 10 for an explanation of the various spellings of the family name.

and Eileen, who so willingly shared stories about Catherine and Eddie.

Noted historian, Fr. James Hennesey, SJ, author of *American Catholics: The History of the Catholic Church in the United States*, was both a friend and a source of valuable historical insights and research tips throughout the past six years.

I extend special thanks to Fr. Tom Zoeller, who arranged for historian, Sister Elizabeth Louise Sharum, OSB, to send me the raw research and transcripts of interviews from her 1975 dissertation on Friendship House. Sister Louise's generosity saved me years of work, and she became a treasured friend in the process.

I am thankful for the work of Catherine's former secretary, Jan Thompson, who oversaw the typing and organization of Catherine's diaries; for Madonna House librarian, Raandi King, who made copies of tapes whenever I needed them; and for the support of Linda Lambeth, who heads up Madonna House Publications. I am most grateful, however, to all of the men, women and priests at Madonna House for prayers, love, and encouragement, but especially Fr. Bob Wild and Fr. Paul Bechard.

Location research for this book proved to be formidable because of the number of places Catherine lived throughout her lifetime, and yet constantly crossing my path were people willing to check facts, pick up documents, and make personal contacts with various sources that I missed during my own travels.

The European research would have been incomplete without the help of American Airlines flight attendant Suzanne Flynn, who took photos and visited archives on lay-overs in London and Brussels. I also want to thank Sue for her gracious hospitality and help during research trips to New York, but mostly, I am grateful for her friendship.

In London, I would like to thank Fr. Ian Dickie at Westminster Diocesan Archives; the Friars of the Atonement at the Catholic Central Library; Veronica Marchbanks of the British Red Cross; Geoffrey Palmer, YMCA historian; Sr. Brenda St. Lawrence of the Sisters of Sion; Leonard Sullivan of the Catholic Evidence Guild; Edmund Swinglehurst, Archivist at Thomas Cook Group Ltd.;

Father H.J. Tennant of Oblates of St. Charles; and Fr. A. Whitehead, CRL, Provincial Historian at Christ Church Priory.

Several people unearthed valuable data during trips abroad, including Marysia Kowalchyk, Mark Schlingerman, and Sushi Horwitz, who brought home helpful background information from an extensive trip through Russia, and Jeannine Biron, who uncovered background information in Paris. Kelley Russell Mariano taped preliminary interviews with Joan Kolychkine in Brussels; Irma Zaleski dug up important information about the Kolyschkine family history in Warsaw, Poland; and Mary Kay Rowland and Bonnie Staib located the school Catherine attended in Ramleh, Egypt.

At Graymoor, I am indebted to Br. Denis Sennett, SA, at the Friars of Atonement Archives for his help, hospitality, and good humor.

For important leads and background, I would like to thank Alfreda Locke Irwin, Historian-in-Residence, at the Chautauqua Institution.

For insights into the mystery of Michel d'Herbigny, I extend thanks to historian Léon Tretjakewitsch of Toronto; David Murphy of the Catholic Truth Society in London; Miriam Stulberg for weeding through correspondence at the Bibliothèque Nationale in Paris; and Fr. James L. Dugan, SJ, former librarian at the Pontifical Oriental Institute in Rome.

Dr. Frank Barbarossa, M.D., and Dr. Joseph McKenna, M.D., provided important medical information, and I could always count on Marianne Hanley and Rich Sullivan for legal advice.

I wish to acknowledge D.W. Wright, Registrar & Archivist at The Pierpont Morgan Library, New York City for background information on J.P. Morgan's trips to Russia. Charles M. Knoll of Sonoma, California supplied fascinating information on Russian railroads.

In Toronto, I would like to thank historians Jeanne M. Beck and Fr. Joseph O'Neill for their encouragement and insights. I am also grateful to Canadian Jesuits Edward J. Dowling and Patrick Boyle for information on Fr. John Milway Filion. At St. Michael's

Hospital, I wish to acknowledge the assistance of Peter A. Kopplin, M.D.; Barbara Ann Trubic, Training & Development Director; and Marina Englesakis, Librarian/ Archivist. At Sheridan Nurseries, I am most grateful for the efforts of Elaine Tonge and Howard Stensson, who supplied information about the Dunnington-Grubbs.

In Montreal, the assistance of Mr. and Mrs. Maurice Coupey and Thelma Sherman was invaluable. I also appreciate the efforts of Father Cyril Bulshevich of St. Peter & St. Paul Russian Orthodox Cathedral; and Joseph Cosette, SJ, Archiviste, Archives de la Compagnie de Jésus in Québec. I also want to acknowledge Sr. Margaret M. Gargan, FMM, of Montreal, and Sister Huguette Richard, FMM, of Ottawa for information about the Franciscaines Missionnaires de Marie.

In Chicago, I extend special thanks to Betty Schneider, who connected me to important Friendship House people, and also shared her own memories and personal papers. My gratitude also goes to Al Schorsh, who provided insights on Ann Harrigan; and Msgr. John S. Quinn, who gave me the grand tour of Bishop Sheil's former residence.

To Fr. Nick Ayo at Notre Dame, a warm thank you for his hospitality.

In Combermere, the presence of Mary Davis during interviews with local people was absolutely essential, and I would like to recognize one local person in particular, Shirley McLean, who has become a dear friend.

Special thanks also go out to the staffs at various archives and libraries, including the Archives of the Roman Catholic Archdiocese of Toronto, the Archives of the University of Notre Dame, the Archives of the Archdiocese of Chicago, the Chicago Historical Society, McGill University Library, the Toronto Research Library, St. Michael's College Library, Canisius College Library, the New York Public Library, the Buffalo & Erie County Public Library, and particularly to Fr. Bonaventure Hayes, OFM, Librarian at Christ the King Seminary in East Aurora, New York.

At the heart of this book was information, documents, and

memories shared by various people, many of whom knew Catherine at various stages of her life. They include: Anatole Avtzine, Fr. Paul Bechard, Betty (Hatting) Britton, Msgr. Daniel Cantwell, Rita Perrier Chapeskie, Olga (LaPlante) Charlton, Msgr. James F. Coffey, Alma Coffman, Trudi Cortens, Ava and Maurice Coupey, Patty Crowley, Fr. Henry Culkin, Fr. Gene Cullinane, Dmitri Danchich, Mary Davis, Theresa Davis, Joanne DeGidio, Irene DeRoché, Catherine and José de Vinck, Nina (Youmatoff) Doull, Eileen and Tom Doherty, Msgr. Ed Dugan, Genevieve Enoe, Dorothy (Harrison) Ennis, Michael Fagan, Joyce Field, Sadie Fletcher, Fr. Paul Hanly Furfey, Carol Ann Gieske, Jim Guinan, Josephine Halfman, Barry Hayes, Noreen Hickey, Rosemary Horan, David and Mary (Galloway) James, Andrew James, Marie Javora, Marité Langlois, Phil Larkin, Gloria Lawton, Mamie Legris, Blanche (Scholes) Lepinskie, Sylvia and Bill Lynch, Ronnie MacDonnell, Romeo and Betty (Welling) Maione, George and Tanya Markow, Basil Markow, Theresa Marsey, Kathy McVady, Mary Beth Mitchell, Cathy Mitchell, Dr. Frederick Moes, Nina (Polcyn) Moore, Belle (Bates) Mullen, Joe Newman, Kathleen O'Herin, Fr. Joseph O'Neill, Anna Pashkoff, Laurette Patenaude, Joe and Evelyn Peplinskie, Dorothy Phillips, Shirley (DeWitt) Poore, Irene Posnoff, Bishop William Power, Archbishop Joseph Raya, Thérèse Richaud, Kathy Rodman, Mary Kay Rowland, Mary Ruth, Bill Ryan, Margaret Ryan, Betty Schneider, Al Schorsh, Thelma Sherman, Kathy Skipper, Fr. Michael Smith, OMI, Fr. Steven Somerville, Fr. Ric Starks, Ellen Tarry, Fr. Andrei Urusov, Blanche (Harrison) Wells, Elsie Whitty, Bishop Joseph Windle, Mayme (Mayhew) Yantha, and George Youmatoff.

I am especially grateful to Brother Aloysius Milella, SSP, and Father Edmund Lane, SSP, of Alba House, who have been solidly behind this project.

There were also people throughout the past six years, whose support and friendship sustained me. To my good friend, Father John Catoir, I hold an enormous debt of gratitude. To Margery Facklam and Ann Blask, I extend thanks for their enthusiasm, encouragement, advice, and friendship. I am also grateful to

Chuck O'Connor and José de Vinck for their careful reading of the manuscript; to Christopher de Vinck for his good advice; to Catherine de Vinck for her love, to my brothers, Jack and Pat, for working on my humility, and to Tom and Dorothy Flynn for just being there.

A special note of thanks goes to Father Paul Nogaro, who helped me discern in the very beginning whether or not to take on this project, and to Beth Gorman Colon, who dragged me up to Madonna House in 1971.

My deepest thanks go to my parents, John and Virginia Hanley, to my husband, Dick, and to my children, Christopher, Tom, Betsy, and Maggie, who lived through six years of turmoil, but survived intact.

Lorene Hanley Duquin
October, 1995

Introduction

by John T. Catoir
Director of The Christophers

I n every century there are a few individuals whose lives seem to boggle the imagination. Catherine de Hueck Doherty was such a person.

As the daughter of Russian nobility, she traveled all over Russia, Europe, and Egypt before she was a teenager, learning six languages in the process. She was an aristocrat who became a pauper for Christ, a pillar of moral strength, who suffered from severe bouts of fear and insecurity. She was a woman who could charm an audience, but she preferred solitude. The story you are about to read records the agony and the ecstasy of her spiritual journey.

The Baroness was not actually a baroness because Russia did not follow the European feudal system, but she was from a wealthy family with an equivalent station in society. She was called the "B" by those closest to her because it was a diminutive form of the "Baroness." Later, a group of children from Harlem dubbed her "The Bee who brings us honey."

Overnight, her life in Russia turned from that of a "fairy tale princess" to "hunted fugitive." After being arrested and condemned to death by starvation in the wake of the Bolshevik Revolution of 1917, she managed to escape and make her way to Canada. Straddled with a sick husband and without money, she worked at first as a waitress, eventually becoming a star on the lecture circuit. Before television there were traveling tours that entertained under tents, drawing large crowds night after night. It meant time away from her husband and son, but she had no choice if they were to survive.

Motivated by a promise she made to God to do something worthwhile with her life if she were saved from the jaws of death, she started Friendship House in Toronto. The Toronto clergy became disenchanted with the idea of a lay person, a woman at that, taking the initiative and beginning her own private apostolate. In the early 1930's, "Catholic Action" was defined as, "Church-work delegated by the bishop or the local pastor." It usually took the form of raising money to fix a leak in the convent basement, or some such thing. God help anyone who performed the corporal works of mercy without permission.

Crushed by rejection, but undaunted, Catherine followed her heart and opened a Friendship House for Black Catholics in Harlem, and she was received warmly by Cardinal Spellman and the New York clergy. Eventually, she opened a third Friendship House in Chicago at the request of Bishop Bernard Sheil.

Her marriage to Eddie Doherty created new tensions among the staff members, and the Baroness — still determined to pursue a life dedicated to the Gospel — decided to go back to Canada where she established Madonna House. Originally (this was intended to be a rural apostolate among the poor in Combermere, a township in one of Ontario's most economically depressed areas) but in time it became headquarters for an international movement.

It was in Combermere that I first met Catherine de Hueck Doherty nearly thirty years ago. By the time I arrived, she had already attracted many followers who joined her in dedicating themselves to "living the Gospel without compromise."

They came from all over the world and stayed through austere Canadian winters. She called them staff workers, and prepared them to take promises of poverty, chastity and obedience. One of their main tasks was taking care of the countless young adults who flocked to Madonna House year after year. The community became a port in the storm of life for many kids, some of whom arrived exhausted and battered by abuse of one kind or another. They came for spiritual and psychological help, and received both.

Madonna House is a spiritual community of celibate men and women, living together in peace and harmony. The men work the farms, build the barns, and repair the machinery, while the women do the cooking, the sewing, the laundry and innumerable tasks that create an atmosphere of emotional comfort. One of the things that intrigued me about Madonna House was the relative absence of sexual tension. No doubt it exists, but there seems to be grace in abundance to deal with it. Only a few couples in thirty years went off to marry.

The center-piece of each day is the Holy Sacrifice of the Mass, which is offered alternately by one of the many priest members of the community. Madonna House has matured to the point where it is now sending out priests and staff workers to missions all over the world. At this writing they have 23 houses established on five continents. Catherine made the rule that they would only go to countries where they were invited by the local bishops to serve in various capacities at the bishop's direction. Most of the houses they open today are "listening houses," as the B called them, places where people can come to talk and pray in a quasi-contemplative setting.

When I first came to Madonna House I was deeply moved by the spirit of love and holiness I found there, especially among the staff workers. I made up my mind to return the next summer and I have been coming back each summer for 28 years. Eventually I bought a small piece of property on the river about a mile away from the main house, and had a log cabin built on it. I love the area not only for its natural beauty, but for the people who enrich the place with their special vitality. Each year I stay for about three weeks and come away rested and spiritually renewed.

The people at Madonna House are serious about holiness. They are masters of the art of hospitality, even when they are strained to the breaking point trying to accommodate unexpected guests. The youngsters who flock to them season after season, many of whom are wounded by the devastating effects of drugs, child abuse, and divorce, are allowed to stay free of charge, as long as they work and obey the rules./They are expected to call first/ since there are limits even to heroic charity. Madonna House has become a spiritual hospital as well as a house of hospitality, but those who come must agree to take responsibility for their actions, keeping the common good in mind.

The spirituality of Catherine de Hueck Doherty is the inspiration behind this amazing community. And yet there are those who think she was a fraud, while others without hesitation call her a saint. The story you are about to read attempts to unfold the mystery of her life in such a way as to allow you to answer that question for yourself. I'm a bit prejudiced in her favor.

It was Jesus who said, "By their fruits you will know them." My own opinion is based on the fact that Catherine's life is still bearing rich and abundant fruit, and will probably continue to do so for many years to come. That tells me something about God's part in all this. Madonna House is getting more vocations than many large dioceses in the US and Canada.

In the past I had mixed feelings about the B. She could be like a Sherman tank if you got in her way. She had a powerful looking build though I'd guess she was only 5'6". Her booming voice and heavy Russian accent gave her an authority that could be chilling. And yet she could make herself small and charming at will. When she flashed her smile she could warm your heart. There was a tenderness about her, and when she wasn't being the Czarina, she could be quite docile.

Many years ago I invited her to be a guest on my television show. I was the director of The Christophers at the time. Knowing how she could wax eloquent, going on and on when asked a question, I suggested that she keep her answers short. To my amazement she took that request literally and began giving me one word answers. It went something like this:

"You wrote a book entitled, *The Gospel Without Compromise.* Do you think there are many people who live the Gospel without compromise?"

"NO."

"Why did you choose Combermere, Ontario as the place to begin your apostolate?"

"GOD."

And so it went until I stopped the tape and told her she could elaborate a bit more on her answers. She was fine after that.

In March 1991, a young woman from upstate New York named Lorie Duquin came to see me. She was a magazine writer for publications like *McCall's*, *Redbook*, and *Ladies' Home Journal*. She explained that she had been working on a biography of Catherine for the past two years, and Father Emile Briere, a Madonna House priest, who had been a close friend and spiritual advisor to the B, had asked her to visit me the next time she was in New York City.

When Lorie first got the idea to write this biography of Catherine, she was fascinated by the fact that Catherine was a divorcee with a Church annulment, a single parent, a working mother. She thought Catherine's story might speak to women today, but her literary agent advised her not to write the book. "It will ruin your career; it's too religious," she was told. Lorie also worried about the loss of revenue while she was doing the necessary research, but she was drawn from within by a strange desire to write the book anyway, a desire that would not go away.

There was a moment when she actually thought she might do it without bringing God into the picture, a naive thought, which now seems utterly ludicrous to her. Finally, she decided she would do the book only if Madonna House would give her access to Catherine's personal journals and correspondence. Almost hoping they would reject her demand, she was stunned to find them perfectly willing to go along.

When Lorie started the research, she was a lukewarm Catholic and something of a skeptic when it came to stories about saints. When she came to my office that morning, she was on the verge of quitting. She had uncovered a quagmire of conflicting views about Catherine. Some people loved her and thought she was the Mother Teresa of Canada. Others saw her as a mad Russian, who bulldozed her way to a position of power and control. Lorie was tired, discouraged, and saw little hope of ever finding a publisher for the project. She desperately wanted to walk away from the research and forget she had ever heard the name Catherine Doherty.

We talked for nearly two hours, and she impressed me as an honest person caught up in a mystery beyond her comprehension. She wondered if God was urging her to go forward against her own inclinations. It was a distinct possibility, I told her. The Madonna House people had already discerned that Divine Providence was involved. I encouraged her to follow her heart and forget all about the other questions, particularly the one about a future publisher.

Lorie left the office that day determined to accept the challenge and follow her own inner light. The book you are about to read is the product of six long years of research, writing and rewriting. It was really a labor of love, as she separated myth from fact.

Lorie's family, her husband, Dick, and four children, Maggie, Betsy, Tom and Chris, ranging in age from 12 to 19, made many sacrifices along the way. For this we are most grateful.

The B's life is now carefully recorded with professional objectivity. I'm sure you'll find that Catherine de Hueck Doherty led an extraordinary life, one filled with miracles of grace and love. I hope you enjoy this book as much as I did. God bless you.

Father John Catoir
September 8, 1995

1

Combermere, Ontario Canada

1985

At a quarter past five on the morning of December 14, a Catholic priest hurried through the darkness of the Canadian woods. The north wind roared across the Madawaska River and through the Laurentian foothills, rocking the white birches and ravaging the soft boughs of the fir trees, but the 68-year-old priest ignored the icy chill. His eyes were fixed on the soft light that glowed through the windows of a small cottage. From a distance, the cabin looked like a gingerbread house, hand-crafted from pine logs with a steep, snow-covered roof. Catherine de Hueck Doherty, known to many as "The Baroness," had lived in that one-room cottage for nearly 30 years.

The priest climbed the steps and pushed open the heavy oak door. Inside, an oil stove radiated penetrating warmth. The furnishings were sparse: a large wooden desk, a small chest of drawers, an antique rocker with a multicolored afghan folded over the back, a worn oriental carpet, a half-finished hooked rug abandoned in a corner. Russian icons with strange faces and haunting eyes hung on the walls. And in a bed by the fireplace, 89-year-old Catherine lay dying.

The two younger women, who attended the frail baroness, deferred to the priest. He gave Catherine final absolution for all the sins of her life, and placed a tiny piece of consecrated bread on her tongue, food for her journey through the darkness of death to everlasting light. Then he gathered her in his arms, and whispered, "Katia, we love you and we thank you for everything."

Catherine had already stopped breathing, but the priest believed she heard him. A few moments later, he felt life leave her body.

"Death is one of my favorite subjects only I seldom talk about it because everybody is afraid," Catherine once remarked. "One day, one moment, I hope soon, but it's up to God, I shall wake up, and I shall realize that I lived in a splendor the like of which I never understood. I shall understand that which my heart yearned for all my life. I shall understand love! Doesn't that excite you? Don't you want to jump? Don't you want to dance? Don't you want to be happy that you really will know what love is about? I mean the love of everybody. . . the love of God for man, mine for you, for everybody!"

Later that afternoon, an obituary writer for *The New York Times* tried to sort out the details of Catherine's life, finally referring to her as a "Roman Catholic social worker," founder of "the now-defunct Friendship House in Harlem, which distributed food and clothes to the needy," and founder of "Madonna House, an organization of men, women and priests affiliated with the Roman Catholic Church."

Catherine would have hated the description.

Born into the wealth and luxury of Russian nobility, she envisioned herself as a woman of destiny. During World War I, she nursed dying soldiers. During the Russian Revolution, she escaped Communists, who condemned her to death as an enemy of the people. As an émigré in North America, she endured the taunts of people who called her "Katie the Polack," until a chance encounter with a talent scout propelled her into a career as a celebrated lecturer.

In her youth, Catherine glowed with passion and beauty. Blond and blue-eyed, with a sharp intellect, she captivated Irish novelist Liam O'Flaherty and enticed British philosopher Bertrand Russell. She knew the heartbreak of an unhappy marriage, the pain of divorce, the struggle of single parenthood, the agony of a run-away child, and the joy of a mid-life romance in the 1940's with America's highest paid reporter, who gave up everything to make her his wife.

She was a woman of courage, who fought for the rights of immigrants, and was accused of being "a Communist spy."

She was a woman of uncompromising principle, who dared to live the Gospel message of love. When a Catholic priest lashed out at her, destroying her reputation and driving her out of the city, she forgave him.

A forerunner of the Civil Rights Movement, she earned the respect of an oppressed race and withstood the verbal and physical abuse of Christian people who called her "nigger lover."

"I am a woman in love with God," she insisted. "Men think of me as a stranger and a fool. They do not know that I am a song, a dancer, a woman in love with God."

In 1947, her friends and followers rejected her leadership, and Catherine retired in humiliating defeat to the Canadian woods. By the early 1950's, however, a new group formed around her, and Catherine's vision of living the Gospel without compromise became reality when she founded Madonna House, a religious community that has grown to over 200 staff workers, who serve the poor on five continents.

Catherine believed in God on a personal and profound level. She claims to have heard God's voice leading her into the hearts of people all over the world. Some call her a modern-day saint, and have started a movement for her canonization by the Catholic Church. Others insist she was a charlatan. By some standards, her life was a shining success, and by other standards, a folly, a failure. Yet no one can deny that the story of her life and her constant struggle with joy and sorrow, passion and pain, doubts, loneliness, and rejection are anything less than extraordinary.

Chapter Notes

oblivious to the icy chill: Emile Briere, *Katia, A Personal Vision of Catherine de Hueck Doherty*, p. 166. (Hereafter *Katia*).

"Katia, we love you...": Ibid., p. 167.

he felt life leave her body: Interview, Fr. Emile Briere.

"Death is one of my favorite subjects...": "The Lady They Call the B," *World Religions*, produced by Mike McManus, TVOntario, Dec. 7, 1973.

Later that afternoon...: Fr. Tom Zoeller, "Pass it On," *RES*, Feb-Mar., 1986.

"A Roman Catholic Social Worker," and f.: "Catherine de Hueck Doherty, Charity Worker, Is Dead at 89," *The New York Times*, Dec. 15, 1985.

"I am a woman in love with God...": "A Woman in Love with God," *RES*, Feb-Mar. 1986.

2

The Great Fair
Nizhny-Novgorod, Russia
1896

C atherine was born at the Great Fair in the ancient city of
Nizhny-Novgorod. Her father, a Russian nobleman, had
business to conduct at the fair, and his wife, pregnant
with their first child, decided to accompany him. "My mother
miscalculated," Catherine later explained. Yet, even if Emma
Kolyschkine had known the baby would be born at the fair, she
probably would have gone anyway. Strong-willed, smart, and
remarkably independent for a woman of her day, the prospect of
an extended stay at the fair would have been too enticing for
Emma to refuse.

The Great Fair at Nizhny-Novgorod opened every summer
where the Oka River flows into the Volga. It was the largest fair in
all of Russia, with goods valued at over 250 million rubles, the
equivalent of 125 million dollars. Peasants arrived in horse-drawn
carts filled with flowers, fruit, vegetables and handicrafts. Merchants and traders traveled in caravans, on barges, and in trains
loaded with Persian carpets, oriental silks, Moroccan leathers,
wool from Cashmere, and black tea from China. Sultans, khans,
and princes, even Tsar Nicholas II and the Tsarina Alexandra
visited the Great Fair in the summer of 1896.

Theodore and Emma Kolyschkine arrived in May, because
Rossia, an international insurance company, had asked Theodore
to open a temporary office there. For the duration of their stay,
Theodore rented a private railroad car that was sidetracked at the

main station on the south side of the fairgrounds. The car had electric lights, hot water, comfortable beds, and a lounge with thick carpets and velvet arm chairs. The station restaurant offered catering services, and for four rubles a day, Theodore and Emma could hire a horse-drawn carriage and explore the narrow streets lined with 8,000 open air stalls.

The fair was a wonderland for the senses with ringing bells, flapping flags, steamboat whistles and merchants hawking their goods. From one street drifted the sweet aroma of cinnamon and spice; from another the fresh smell of soap; from a third, the seductive scent of exotic perfumes. There were bolts of satin, soft leathers, and thick sable pelts to stroke. Roving vendors sold icy sherbets and slices of juicy watermelon, while peddlers presided over kegs of caviar, barrels of crisp pickles, and sacks of salted sunflower seeds. Peasants sat on benches watching dancing bears and daredevils. Gypsies whirled to the jangle of tambourines, and fortune tellers predicted the future from the lines on the hand or tea leaves in the bottom of a cup.

It was in the midst of this paradise of pleasure and profit that Emma felt the first pains of childbirth. The granddaughter of a physician, Emma had delivered babies and felt no fear of nature's ways. The ordeal must have been heart-wrenching for Theodore, however, whose first wife, the lovely Catherine Kondratova, had died 16 years before after giving birth to their only child, a son named Vsevolod. Grief-stricken, Theodore left the infant in the care of his sister, Olga, and accepted a commission with the Hussars of Grodno where he distinguished himself as a man of courage and principle. Tsar Alexander III called him "an officer we shall not forget." Over six feet tall, with blue eyes and light curly hair, women found him irresistible, but Theodore rejected the possibility of remarriage until the summer of 1895, when he met Emma during a hunting trip in the country.

Theodore had barely noticed the long-haired girl in a white caftan picking wild flowers at the top of the hill until a sun shower soaked the earth and the girl ran for shelter. Fascinated at the way her wet clothes clung to her body, Theodore followed, and when he caught up, the expression in her eyes startled him. Emma had the same haunting eyes as his first wife.

Emma Thomson was not a peasant; in fact, she had no Russian blood at all. Her ancestors included members of French nobility, who fled to St. Petersburg after the French Revolution, a few wealthy Germans, and a Scottish physician brought to Russia by Tsar Nicholas I in the early 1800's to westernize Russian medicine. Her family adopted the Russian language and customs, and the Tsar elevated them to the ranks of Russian nobility. Emma's father held a government position in St. Petersburg, equal in status to an army captain. Emma studied music at the Smolny Institute, an exclusive school for daughters of the nobility founded by Catherine the Great. According to official records, Emma was Lutheran, but in practice she followed the mystical ways of Russian Orthodoxy. As a young woman, she made pilgrimages, walking barefoot to Russian shrines where she would "pray in front of a miraculous Icon." She lived by intuitions, feelings, and an intimate understanding of the ways of God and nature, which compelled her to reach out to the less fortunate.

During summer holidays from Smolny, Emma would "go to the people," a Russian movement that began in 1874, when young intellectuals traveled deep into the countryside to work as farm hands or servant girls, nursing the sick, teaching children to read, and trying to improve the lot of peasants. The custom waned after a few years, but revived during the famine of 1891-92 that killed millions. Hundreds of young people, like Emma, dressed in peasant garb and lived with poor families in crude one-room log houses with dirt floors and thatched roofs.

Emma milked cows, fed chickens, washed clothes in the river, gathered wild herbs for folk medicines, and found peasant life far different from the idyllic scenes in Russian art. A few wealthy peasants owned land, but the masses worked in grain fields controlled by village communes. Most earned enough to pay taxes with little left over. Tiny vegetable gardens provided food in summer, with cabbage soup and dark bread a staple in winter. Smallpox, scarlet fever, and diphtheria ravaged villages.

Infants died because malnourished mothers lost their milk. Yet Emma looked beyond the dirt and disease, and she found herself entering the hearts of the people.

Few in St. Petersburg understood her altruistic bent. Teachers scolded her because manual labor made her hands rough and callused. "Wait a minute and listen," Emma insisted, and when she played the piano, "her experience of having gone to the poor, the deep cries of peasants that nobody heard, was in her music."

It was during one of Emma's summers in the country that she and Theodore Kolyschkine decided to marry. Their families wanted the wedding to take place in St. Petersburg, but Emma insisted on being married in Oksoscha, a tiny village on the banks of the river Msta, where she could "share the happiest day of her life with simple peasants, whom she loved and who loved her."

They set the date for Monday, October 29, 1895. Father Fedor Nikolaevsky, an Orthodox priest, performed the ceremony and prayed for "a peaceful life, length of days, chastity, mutual love in the bond of peace, long-lived offspring, gratitude from their children, and a crown of glory that does not fade away."

Nine months later, on Saturday, August 2 in the Russian year, which was 13 days behind Western calendars, Emma gave birth to their first child, and named the baby, Catherine, in memory of Theodore's first wife.

Catherine was "a big, lovely baby, full of health, blond with big blue eyes," but Emma's first words to her infant daughter were disturbing: "You are born," she said, "under the shadow of the cross." Catherine later wondered if her mother's words reflected the trials of childbirth, or whether Emma had a dark vision of her own, a grim foreshadowing of the pain that would follow Catherine through life.

When the Great Fair closed at the end of August, Theodore and Emma brought their infant daughter back to St. Petersburg for a private baptism by a Russian Orthodox priest in the Kolyschkine home. The ceremony began with an ancient ritual that places the soul on a spiritual battleground face to face with the power of Satan. The priest raised Catherine toward the West — "unclad, unshod, with hands uplifted" — in a symbolic gesture of facing darkness and evil. Three times the priest asked the infant to renounce Satan. Three times, her uncle Konstantin responded for her, "I do."

Allowing no margin of doubt, the priest asked one more time: "Hast thou renounced Satan?"

"I have," her uncle replied.

"Breathe and spit upon him!" the priest commanded.

Then he lowered Catherine's hands in a gesture of peace and surrender. Turning her to the East, a symbolic conversion to the source of light that destroys darkness and overcomes evil, he asked the child three times to unite herself to Christ. Three times, her uncle responded for her, "I do."

"Dost thou believe in Him?" the priest asked.

"I believe in Him as King and God," her uncle replied.

After blessing the baptismal waters and anointing Catherine with oil, the priest held her upright and exclaimed: "The servant of God, Catherine Fedorovna, is baptized in the name of the Father, Amen. And of the Son, Amen. And of the Holy Spirit. Amen."

With each invocation, he immersed Catherine in the water and raised her triumphantly. When it was over, she was clothed in a white gown, a robe of righteousness, a garment of immortality, that symbolized the purity of her tiny soul as she embarked on the journey through life, a journey that would lead her into the thick of the battle between forces of darkness and light.

Chapter Notes

pregnant with their first child...: The year 1900 is often cited as the date of Catherine's birth, but childhood passports and other documents record her actual date of birth as 1896. Accounts also vary regarding the birth order of Catherine and a sister, Natasha, who died in infancy. Family documents establish the date of Theodore and Emma's wedding as Oct. 29, 1895, and Catherine, as their first child. There are no records of Natasha's birth date. She was probably born around the turn of the century, and died from a malformed renal canal.

"My mother miscalculated": C de H, *Fragments of My Life*, p. 9. (Hereafter *Fragments*).

Goods valued at more than 250 million rubles: Karl Baedeker, *Russia, A Handbook for Travelers*, A facsimile of the original 1914 edition, p. 344. [At the turn of the century, one ruble was worth approximately 50 cents.]

"an officer we shall not forget": Interview, André Kolychkine. [Catherine's brothers adopted a French spelling of the name Kolyschkine by dropping the "s" after they settled in Belgium.]

the expression in her eyes: Interview, Marina Kollar.

"pray in front of a miraculous Icon": Serge Kolychkine, unpublished family history, MHA.

"go to the people": W. Bruce Lincoln, *In War's Dark Shadow, The Russians Before the Great War*, pp. 40-41.

"Wait a minute...": *Fragments*, p. 181.

"her experience of having gone to the poor...": *Ibid.*, p. 182.

"share the happiest day of her life": Serge Kolychkine, *op. cit.*

on August 2: Russia retained the Julian calendar which was 13 days behind Gregorian calendars used throughout the western world. In 1918, the Russian calendar was updated and Catherine's date of birth changed to Aug. 15.

"a big, lovely baby": Serge Kolychkine, *op. cit.*

"You are born under the shadow of the cross": CD, "Little Mandate — How It Came To Be," Apr. 27, 1968, MHA. (Hereafter *Little Mandate*).

baptized by a Russian Orthodox priest...: In her memoirs, Catherine wrote that she was baptized on the day of her birth, but family documents establish that the baptism was performed by a Russian Orthodox priest in the Kolyschkine home in St. Petersburg on or about Sept. 2, 1896 old style, Sept. 15, 1896 new style. MHA.

The ceremony began... and f.: Alexander Schmemann, *Of Water and the Spirit*, pp. 27-71.

3

Ekaterinoslav, Russia

1897

Catherine was still an infant when Theodore and Emma moved to Ekaterinoslav, a Ukrainian city in the heart of Russia's largest coal mining district. By the end of the century, French and Belgian businesses had invested heavily in factories, mines, and railroads, causing the population of the city to soar as peasants left the country seeking jobs. The move to Ekaterinoslav was a major promotion for Theodore, offering a salary and commission for selling commercial accident and fire insurance. The Kolyschkines settled into a large house on Potemkin Street, and before long, Theodore built a profitable account base. A Belgian associate described him as:

> a man with a tremendous personality and charm. *C'etait un grand Seigneur!* Extremely intelligent. He had a quick grasp of the situation and an art of handling people. His perfect knowledge of French and Western Europe, made him very popular in Franco-Belgian circles and gave him the possibility of concluding large transactions for Rossia.

The rapid industrialization from which Theodore profited spawned a dark side, however, as greedy factory owners exploited workers, and peasants discovered a different kind of poverty than they had experienced in the country. A typical work day lasted fourteen hours with hazardous conditions, frequent accidents, and shamefully low wages. Signs in factories read:

IN THE EVENT OF AN ACCIDENT, THE OWNER
AND DIRECTOR OF THE FACTORY ASSUME NO
RESPONSIBILITY.

Nearly half of all workers lived in factory-owned barracks
where they slept on wooden platforms with only their coats to
cover them. "The plank platforms were infested with bedbugs
and lice," one worker recalled. "Sometimes when I returned there
from the factory at two or so in the morning, I almost choked from
the foul stench."

Theodore must have been aware of these conditions, but he
faced problems of his own in those years. Emma gave birth to a
daughter, Natasha, who died in infancy from a malformed renal
canal. Two miscarriages followed. "My parents, of course, were
sad at their deaths, and wept over them very much," Catherine
later wrote.

Catherine was too young to understand other family tensions that centered on Vsevolod, Theodore's 17-year-old son from
his first marriage, who became embroiled in a passionate love
affair with Lusia, a 15-year-old girl in Ekaterinoslav. Theodore
tried to separate the young lovers by cutting off Vsevolod's
allowance, but the relationship continued, and Lusia gave birth to
several illegitimate children. While Theodore's sense of honor
impelled him to provide financial support for Lusia and the
children, he refused to accept them socially. "She was an outcast,"
one family member recalled. "She was never invited to any of the
family celebrations." Lusia did not disappear from the scene,
however, and her role in the family drama became more intricate
as Catherine grew older.

Catherine's first memory of Ekaterinoslav was watching a
large gold leaf float through the air and land on a pond in the park
near their home.

> I wanted to capture it, hold it, and keep it. I put out my
> hand half-way extended toward the water. . . [but] . . .
> more marvelous than the leaf, was this strange thing

that was my hand. It led me to discover myself. I bent
over the waters and saw my face, and was astounded at
the sight. Looking down, I beheld my whole self, and
laughed loud for the joy of the discovery.

The incident made such an impression on Catherine that she
had recurring dreams of her outstretched hand reaching for a
golden leaf. "Somehow even yet it seems the most extraordinary
moment of my life."

If Catherine's quest for the unattainable became a lifelong
characteristic, so too did her strong-willed determination. At one
moment she could be a dreamy child, the picture of innocence in
white frocks, large brimmed hats, and high button shoes, but she
could also be curious and impulsive with a stubborn streak —
traits she inherited from Emma — that periodically erupted into
a war of wills between mother and daughter. It required tremendous patience on Emma's part to restrain this child without
destroying her spirit. The tack she took was to channel Catherine's
energy in the direction of love. "Without love," Emma told
Catherine, "there is no happiness."

Emma's words did not become real, however, until the day
five-year-old Catherine decided to run away. Emma followed at
a distance as Catherine stomped down the street. "I did not cry,
though with every step I felt sadder and sadder," Catherine later
admitted. What Emma allowed Catherine to experience was the
absence of love, a condition Catherine brought on herself as a
consequence of her decision to run away. The experience forged
in Catherine an understanding that she had the power to make
choices in her life, choices her mother kept telling her to measure
on a scale of love. "Love is the law," Emma insisted. "And love is
the goal."

Some of Catherine's most deeply embedded childhood
memories centered on visits to the family estate in the rural
province of Tambov, south of Moscow, where she and Emma
gathered mushrooms and berries in the woods. "She seemed to
me to be so wise," Catherine recalled, "so well learned in all the old

folk ways of Russia. She knew every tree, every herb, every flower, every root in the forest."

Yet Emma's way of raising natural experiences to a supernatural level made the most profound impression on Catherine. Once, when Catherine thought they were lost, Emma told her, "No one is ever lost who believes in God, for God is always near."

God was not only near, Emma told Catherine, he was present in all life. The wind, Emma said, was God's way of teaching the tall trees humility. "See how they bend low!" Friends, according to Emma, were special gifts from God. Emma described her own experiences of having worked with peasants as "dreams dreamed in God" — not dreams that come during sleep — but dreams God places into your mind during waking moments. Filled with wonder, Catherine told her mother that she wanted to touch God. Emma stretched out her hand and said, "Touch me," permanently fusing into Catherine's consciousness the idea that God is present, not just in nature or on a supernatural plane, but in every person. Emma told Catherine that she could find God's face in all human faces, hear his voice in every human tongue, and discover God's footprints on the paths people walk through life.

Theodore expanded Catherine's ideas about the universe. He traveled often in those years, and frequently took Emma and Catherine with him to foreign countries where they stayed in an embassy or in palatial homes of prominent people. Theodore told Catherine legends about the native people. He insisted Catherine eat the food of the country, follow the customs, and under no circumstances, he warned, should she say, "But in Russia we do it thus and so."

Catherine toured Istanbul on the shoulders of a Russian embassy staff worker and marveled at sights and sounds of the marketplace. In Athens, she played on the crumbling marble steps that led to ancient temples. By age six, she possessed an unquestioning acceptance of people unlike herself and a childlike faith in a God who ruled the universe with love.

In 1902, Theodore traveled alone to St. Petersburg to discuss with the Rossia Insurance Company his future assignment to

Egypt. It was a good time to leave Russia. The economy had plunged into a depression. Peasants, who wanted more land and lower taxes, rampaged through the countryside, burning manor houses and murdering wealthy landowners. In cities, workers went on strike demanding shorter hours, improved working conditions and increased pay. Anti-Semitism exploded with Russian mobs vandalizing synagogues and storming through Jewish sections of towns and cities to rape, loot and kill Jews.

Reports of assassination attempts against local officials led to the shocking news that revolutionary terrorists murdered D.S. Sipyagin, Minister of the Interior. Secret police pursued political agitators, and sent an estimated 60,000 dissenters into exile during the first two years of the century. At all levels of society, people groped for solutions. Vladimir Lenin offered one answer. In 1902, he published a pamphlet entitled "What Is To Be Done?" which advocated a party of professional revolutionaries, tightly organized, dedicated, and disciplined, who could lead the working class into revolt. By the time Theodore, Emma, and Catherine left for Egypt in 1903, Russia was like an enormous heap of dynamite just waiting for a spark.

Chapter Notes

"*a man with tremendous personality...*": Serge Kolychkine, *op. cit.*

"*IN THE EVENT OF AN ACCIDENT...*": Lincoln, p. 113.

"*The plank platforms were infested...*": *Ibid.*, p. 117.

"*My parents, of course...*": *Fragments*, p. 9.

"*She was an outcast.*": Interview, Marina Kollar.

"*I wanted to capture it...*": "I remember," *RES*, Feb. 1965.

"*Somehow even yet...*": *Ibid.*

"*Without love...*": "Journey Inward," *RES*, May 1962.

"*I did not cry...*": "Journey Inward," *RES*, Aug. 1958.

"*Love is the law...*": "Journey Inward," *RES*, May 1962.

"*She seemed to me to be so wise...*": "Journey Inward," *RES*, July 1962.

"*No one is ever lost...*": *Ibid.*

"See how they bend low!": "Journey Inward," *RES*, Sept. 1958.

"dreams dreamed in God...": "Journey Inward," *RES*, Jan. 1960.

"Touch me...": CD, *Dearly Beloved, Letters to the Children of My Spirit*, Vol. III, p. 95. (Hereafter *Dearly Beloved*).

"But in Russia we do it...": *Fragments*, p. 48.

4

Ramleh, Egypt

1903

The Kolyschkines settled into a seaside villa in the resort community of Ramleh, on the outskirts of Alexandria. "The House," as Catherine called it, had airy rooms with marble balconies overlooking the Mediterranean Sea. Theodore hired an Arab boy to give Catherine a ride on a donkey every morning to Notre Dame de Sion, the exclusive girls' school in Ramleh, where Roman Catholic nuns practiced Christianity in a much different way than Russian Orthodoxy. Her first playmates were an English boy and a Greek girl, and Catherine, who already spoke fluent French and Russian, learned two new languages.

Over 100,000 Europeans lived in Egypt at the turn of the century. The British arrived in 1882 to settle a dispute over the Suez Canal, and formed a "veiled protectorate," which gave the appearance of an Egyptian government while real power rested in the hands of a British consul. European investors built irrigation dams, expanded railroads, and modernized harbors. Land value skyrocketed. "We are making money hand over fist," a Frenchman noted. "Everyone is in the swim."

Everyone, that is, except the 10 million Egyptian natives, whom Europeans looked down upon as an uneducated mass of humanity that lived in squalor, prayed in public, and bartered shamelessly at street bazaars. To shield themselves, the Europeans built isolated communities, like the one where the Kolyschkines lived, and held afternoon tea parties on manicured lawns with formal dinners and gala balls in the evenings. Occasionally, a

Pasha appeared on a guest list, but typically, natives remained in roles of servants and laborers.

These imperialistic attitudes reeked of racial superiority and divided Egypt into two different worlds. Catherine lived in the world of the Europeans, but ventured often into the world of the natives. Theodore and Emma allowed her to play with an Egyptian boy and she learned to speak Arabic. She attended the Moslem wedding of their cook, and visited the harem of a nearby Pasha. Catherine delighted in the Egyptian culture and had no idea that others did not share her enthusiasm. One unforgettable incident was an impromptu belly dance Catherine performed at an afternoon tea party that Emma hosted. She learned the dance by watching Bedouins at the market. "The different parts of their bodies seemed to be unconnected. They could move each breast separately, move their 'behinds' separately, and move their bellies like undulating waves on the surface of the ocean."

Catherine's awkward attempts to imitate the Arabs shocked Emma's guests, and afterward, Catherine noticed similar attitudes in the way Europeans treated beggars. In Russia, Catherine had seen her parents invite poor people into their home, and they told her that when you give to a pauper you are giving to Christ himself. In the streets of Ramleh, however, beggars of all ages cried out, "*bakshish, bakshish, ya khawageh*" — (oh, sir! a gift!), and the Europeans replied, "*ma fish, ma fish*" (I have nothing) or "*Allah ya tik*" (may God give thee!). It made such a deep impression on Catherine that she wrote a school essay about an Arab boy, who died because no one gave him money or food. "Do you know what happened to all the people who didn't give him anything? A terrible thing happened. All their wares were destroyed. Worms came into their food and it was ruined."

Only later did Catherine realize these incidents in her early life were a preparation for her own suffering that lay ahead. Her first recollection of pain occurred at age seven when she gashed her leg while walking on the beach. Theodore broke her barrage of tears by saying, "If you can't bear physical pain, child, how will you bear the pain of the heart and of the mind that will certainly come to you?" Catherine did not understand, "but so earnest was his voice and so tender that I stopped crying."

Another time she asked why some days were gray and others sunny. Theodore replied that life is a succession of darkness and light. "God makes it that way so we should know pain and joy."

In school, the nuns talked about the pain of Christ, and Catherine, who was accustomed to seeing Christ's crucifixion in the symbolism of Russian icons, was so moved at the realism of a crucifix that she pried the corpus off every cross she could find, placing the figures in her doll's bed in an attempt to take away the pain. One day she scraped the red paint off the wounds on a life size crucifix in the school corridor, an effort that did not please the nuns. When Emma explained that the only way to ease the pain of Christ was to love him, Catherine began kissing crucifixes in the devout way Russians kiss icons, and people wondered if this pious child would someday be a nun.

A convent would never claim Catherine, however. She had a different road to travel, a road filled with physical, mental, and emotional pain. It was Theodore, who taught her that the only way to cope with suffering is through prayer. Catherine was eight or nine years old at the time, and her brother, Serge, who was born in August 1904, was still a baby. Emma had cholera, and the doctors had given up hope. Theodore brought Catherine and Serge to Emma's bedside, and Catherine watched as her father anointed Emma with blessed oil from olives grown in the Garden of Gethsemane. "Lord have mercy," he prayed. "Lord have mercy." Then he took the children's hands and asked them to pray with him. "I still get goose flesh when I think of this scene," she later wrote.

The next morning Emma regained consciousness, and a link formed in Catherine's mind connecting everything her father had told her about pain: light followed darkness, joy followed pain, and it was all joined in some mysterious way to God. When Emma felt well enough to travel, Theodore took the family to a desert resort where Emma regained her strength. The family traveled often. Photos show Theodore, Emma, and Catherine on horses at the start of a safari. They made annual pilgrimages to the Holy Land at Easter, and Theodore planned an exotic trip up the Nile to the Sudan in a flat bottomed boat with sails called a *dehabeah*.

During hot Egyptian summers the Kolyschkines returned to Russia to visit the family estate in Tambov. A peasant taught Catherine how to handle a horse — a skill that would one day save her life. Another peasant gave Catherine her first ecology lesson when he told Theodore one of the fields was sick because no one scattered hay on the land after the harvest the year before. "Sometimes," Theodore told Catherine, "it takes four generations to restore soil that has been hurt by one generation."

In Tambov, Catherine and Emma took food and medicine to local peasants. Catherine's memory of walking to a Russian shrine with Emma occurred during this time, but her favorite memories of Tambov centered around the kitchen with its shiny copper kettles and wooden dishes. She loved the smell of bread baking and the scent of herbs drying in the rafters. "I remember an old shepherd who used to come and play his tunes in the kitchen. When I asked him where he got them, he answered: 'from the wind and the trees and the song of the grass and the talks of the flowers and the song of the brooks. . . .'"

Pilgrims traveling to shrines knocked at the kitchen door, and in return for food and a place to sleep, they sat at the wood table telling stories of their adventures. One pilgrim told of meeting a runaway child whose abusive stepfather caught up with her in the night and kicked the little girl unmercifully. Suddenly, the pilgrim said, a light appeared, and took the form of a woman, who gathered the battered child in her arms. Awestruck, the stepfather knelt in the road weeping and begging for forgiveness.

Years later, in recounting these tales, Catherine wrote: "Did they actually happen? Again I can only say that this is how they were told to me. They flow from the lives and adventures of people pilgrimaging around Russia in search of God." Catherine believed there was truth in the stories, and this quest for the essence of goodness and truth colored her childhood memories. "For me personally, my childhood is a place where I can hide in a world that was normal, a world where nature and man were in harmony, a world where man took from nature only what God wanted him to take."

If Catherine saw the darker side of Russian life, she never mentioned it. Yet, during these years, Russia suffered humiliating defeats in a war against Japan, and hostility among peasants and workers increased. On the morning of January 9, 1905, a Russian Orthodox priest led a peaceful march to the Winter Palace to ask the Tsar to hear workers' pleas for higher wages, lower taxes, public education, a representative assembly and an end to war. As the marchers neared the palace, Imperial guards opened fire, killing 200 and wounding nearly 800. The massacre, recorded in Russian history as Bloody Sunday, heralded a year of strikes, mutiny in the army and navy, political assassinations, and peasant uprisings.

In Egypt, political problems of a different nature erupted after British soldiers went pigeon shooting for sport in Denshawai, a small village near Tanta in June 1906. The natives, who raised pigeons for a living, attacked the soldiers with wooden sticks. The British retaliated by arresting 52 villagers, and condemning four to death by hanging, eight to prison terms, and the rest to fifty lashes. The executions and floggings took place in the village with the natives forced to watch. Theodore must have been aware of the animosity caused by the Denshawai incident. A short time later three unrelated incidents convinced him it was time to leave Egypt.

The first was a financial setback, possibly linked to international insurance holdings paid to policy holders after fire destroyed San Francisco in the earthquake of 1906. Theodore came home one evening with a diamond necklace for Emma. It was the last gift for a while, he told her. "God has given. God has taken away. The will of God be done."

The second incident involved an Egyptian Pasha, who wanted to make 12-year-old Catherine his fourth wife. Using Catherine as an interpreter, Theodore instructed her to tell the Pasha that he planned to prepare her for marriage, and when ready, she would be as lovely as her sister Natasha.

"Natasha is dead!" Catherine exclaimed.

"Exactly," Theodore replied.

The third incident erupted when Catherine, who had become attracted to the spirituality of the nuns at the convent school, wanted to convert to Roman Catholicism. Theodore flatly refused, and immediately sent Catherine and her governess to Paris where Catherine was enrolled in a secular school run by Mlle. Milliard on the Avenue de la Grande Armée. She later remarked that it seemed as if her parents purposely placed her "in surroundings well calculated to drive far from her thoughts any leanings toward 'Romanism.'" She remembers wishing that someday there could be unity between Catholics and Orthodox, and that desire became implanted in her heart like a tiny seed.

The family eventually followed Catherine to Paris where they settled into a six-room apartment on Rue Chalgrin in one of the most fashionable districts of the city. Catherine recalls being "poor" during this time, but the Kolyschkines were far from poverty levels. Theodore accepted a position as superintendent of agencies for an international insurance company in Belgium, and he traveled to places as remote as India and China. "Occasionally, I was left in some school for a month or so when father was traveling," Catherine recalled.

In 1910, Theodore moved the family back to St. Petersburg, where he secured a post as district manager of Russki Loyd, an international insurance office affiliated with the Belgians and the Equitable Insurance Company of New York. The family lived in an elegant apartment at 25 Morskaya, not far from the Winter Palace and St. Isaac's Cathedral. Their neighbors included the German Ambassador and the master jeweler, Peter Carl Fabergé.

Founded by Peter the Great only 200 years before as a window between the East and the West, St. Petersburg had broad avenues, grassy squares, and buildings that blazed with gold, silver, bright reds, yellows, and turquoise. Roving vendors sold *kvas, pirogi,* and mint-flavored cakes along the Nevsky Prospect where Catherine and Emma shopped for leather from London and the latest fashions from Paris. At the Princess Obolensky School for daughters of the nobility, Catherine excelled in academics and tennis. Strong and healthy, her young body had matured early in the Egyptian sun. By age 13, she was physically developed and strikingly beautiful, but her emotional maturity had not kept pace. Catherine was still a child, and completely unprepared for the whirlwind she was about to fall into.

Chapter Notes

"We are making money...": Larry Henderson, *Egypt and the Sudan,* p. 110.

"The different parts of their bodies...": *Fragments,* p. 20.

"bakshish, bakshish, ya khawageh...": Karl Baedeker, *Egypt, Handbook for Travelers 1902,* p. xxi.

"Do you know what happened...": *Fragments,* p. 17.

"If you can't bear physical pain...": *Ibid.,* p. 43.

"But so earnest was his voice...": "Journey Inward," *RES,* Nov. 1961.

"God makes it that way...": "Journey Inward," *RES,* Oct. 1959.

destined to enter a convent: CD, *My Heart and I,* p. 44.

"I still get goose flesh...": *Fragments,* p. 22.

"Sometimes it takes four generations...": "The Earth is Angry," RES, July, 1959.

"I remember an old shepherd...": *Ibid.*

"one pilgrim told...": CD, *Not Without Parables,* pp. 27-31.

"Did they actually happen...": *Ibid.,* p. 10.

"For me, personally...": *Fragments,* p. 46.

"God has given...": *Ibid.*, p. 30.

"Natasha is dead": ED, *Tumbleweed*, p. 50. (Hereafter *Tumbleweed*).

wanted to convert to Catholicism, and f.: "Near East Relief Speaker at Mt. St. Joseph," unidentified news clip, MHA.

"Occasionally, I was left in some school...": *Fragments*, p. 47.

5

St. Petersburg, Russia
1910

In the spring of 1910, Halley's Comet appeared over St. Petersburg, and those who sensed the discontent that rumbled through Russia's capital insisted it was a bad omen. The dazzling social structure of St. Petersburg had changed after Bloody Sunday, when the Tsar moved his family to a country palace at Tsarskoe Selo about 14 miles outside the city. Court functions no longer governed the social calendar. Midnight suppers after an evening at the theater or the opera became the fashion.

Theodore and Emma moved easily into St. Petersburg society, and hosted elegant soirées. American financier, J.P. Morgan, and Russian artist, Ilya Repin, were guests in the Kolyschkine home. Relatives also visited, and family controversies erupted when Theodore's son, Vsevolod, moved his mistress, Lusia, and their five children to St. Petersburg. The ill-fated couple eventually married to make the children legitimate, but marriage did not tame Vsevolod. Like many young noblemen, he fell into "an attitude of utter, mindless debauchery that pervaded segments of Russia's educated youth, who shrugged off all concerns for society, morality, or justice with the phrase, *"tryn-trava"* — 'It makes no difference. Who cares? Why bother?'" These wealthy young aristocrats pursued pleasure with no fear of consequences, and the sensualist art and literature of the day glamorized them with graphic accounts of lust and seduction. Private sex clubs emerged. Prostitution exploded into a booming business.

Catherine never noticed this side of her dashing stepbrother. "I actually venerated Vsevolod," she admitted.

One of Vsevolod's frequent companions during this time was his first cousin, Boris de Hueck, a wealthy young nobleman, who had inherited an annual income of 25,000 rubles — the equivalent of $13,000 a year — from his paternal grandmother. Boris was the son of Theodore Kolyschkine's youngest and favorite sister, Vera, an attractive woman with delicate features. "Her conversation was flowing, in a purely feminine way — jumping from one subject to another, a lot about nothing. Frocks, fashions, society news."

Vera married twice, the first time in 1888, to the wealthy industrialist, Guido de Hueck, "a well-educated, stable man with a rather cold, calculating, mathematical, and domineering mind. His aim was money, the social standing and power it gives." Boris was their only child.

One morning in 1901, when Boris was 12 years old, Guido kissed Vera good-bye as he left for work and never came home, choosing instead to live with his mistress. Vera, who had tolerated Guido's infidelity for years, became distraught, and a bitter feud broke out between Guido de Hueck and Theodore Kolyschkine, who was outraged over the way Guido treated Vera. The hostility grew so intense that the two men would dine in the same room at the St. Petersburg Yacht Club and never acknowledge each other's presence.

Guido eventually married his mistress, and Vera married a childhood admirer named Nicolai Petrovitch Evreinoff, an eccentric nobleman, who could not tolerate children, noise, or stupidity. They sent Boris to board at the Military Cadet School of Tsar Alexander II.

Boris was a paradox: Highly intelligent like his father, he excelled in mathematics and logic, but his sketchbooks also reveal a delicate sensitivity to the physical beauty of people and places. In 1907, he entered the Riga Polytechnical Institute where he studied engineering and architecture. He spent vacations cavorting with his cousin, Vsevolod.

Boris was smaller than Vsevolod with a wiry build, darker hair, and more angular facial features. Photos show a roguish character with a smirk beneath a neatly trimmed mustache, ears too large for his head, and dark eyes. He dressed impeccably with an air of aristocratic arrogance. "If he passed you on the street you would stop and gasp. You would almost feel like bowing. He walked like a king."

Boris was the kind of man who could make a woman tingle with excitement and tremble with fear, a man who held the potential to inflict both pleasure and pain, adulation and insults. He was compulsive, conceited, manipulative, and incredibly charming. Sometime in 1910, after Lusia married Vsevolod, Boris took her as a mistress. When Lusia discovered she was pregnant with Boris' child, they ran away to Riga. Lusia gave birth to a baby boy, but the baby died within days, and the ill-fated couple returned to St. Petersburg, where Lusia reunited with Vsevolod, and Boris discovered Catherine.

Catherine had no knowledge of Boris' and Lusia's affair. She was busy with school and domestic training because Emma believed that one should never ask a servant to do something that had not been mastered oneself. On weekends and vacations, Catherine worked with the household staff. "I learned all the fine arts of being a woman," she recalled, "and I learned them with a certain amount of discipline because periodically I would rebel!"

In the laundry, she scrubbed clothes and pressed table linens. In the kitchen, she kept "utensils clean, knives sharp, and floors and tables scrubbed until their white pine wood rivaled snow." For special dinners, she molded butter, cut carrots and turnips into flowers, braided asparagus, and stuffed cabbage leaves. The cook rejected anything that wasn't perfect, and Catherine would cry in frustration. After dinner, she polished the copper pots with old pieces of black bread that had fermented into a soft mush. She mended clothes, darned socks, and patched lace and linens. She learned to knit, crochet, weave, spin, embroider and bind books.

Family trips to Tambov were rare during those years because of the distance. Instead, the family spent summers on their 1,000-acre estate in Antrea, Finland, only a little over 100 miles by train from St. Petersburg. "I loved its old sprawling house, its herb room and work room, its milk cellars and pantries, its old barns, and its orchards and fields," Catherine recalled. They had tennis courts, a swimming pond, and a leafy tree where Catherine perched herself to daydream or read. At Antrea, she learned to milk a cow, churn butter, and make cheeses, breads, and jams.

Catherine also learned to work on herself "inside." Several times during the year, Russians examined their consciences, asked forgiveness of everyone in the household, and went to church to confess their sins to a priest. "Be not ashamed that you come before God and before me, for you do not declare to me, but to God, who is present here," the priest whispered. In her diary, Catherine listed her faults as: "exaggeration, love of praise, doing good not for good's sake but for the pleasure it gives, gluttony, I love food, good food."

Her social conscience also developed at this age. "As I look around and see the poor of Russia, so poor, and so many illiterate, I wonder if I could not do something about it." She described how she gave a beggar woman diamond earrings that had been a gift from a family friend. Spontaneous generosity sprang from Catherine's impulsive nature, but her impulsiveness also had a negative side, which exploded when a romance blossomed between 14-year-old Catherine and her 21-year-old cousin, Boris. Teetering on the ridge that separates children and adults, Catherine's hormones raged and her jumbled emotions produced a fervent desire to pull away from family along with an intense fear of letting go. In Russia, strict rules kept girls, like Catherine, away from young men unless guarded by a duenna or chaperon, but as family members later explained, "Complete informality and freedom of movement existed only between related families where young people were constantly thrown together, moving in and out of each other's homes."

Theodore and Emma tried to halt the relationship, and family members recall heated discussions about Catherine's behavior. There were "kisses behind the door," and rumors that Boris planned to run away with Catherine, rumors Theodore could hardly ignore after Boris and Lusia ran away the year before. "My sister did not know what she was doing," her brother insisted. "She was not in love with him. She was in love with the idea of love."

When gossip spread that Catherine and Boris were lovers, family members recall Theodore throwing his hands up in the air, and saying, "Now you will marry," trapping Catherine in the web she had woven, a web more complicated than her adolescent mind could comprehend. While family members insist Catherine wanted to wed, she later felt she had been "railroaded into a marriage," claiming that at 15, she had no understanding of what she was doing. She often said, "My life can be divided into two parts: Up to my marriage, it was heaven. After my marriage, it was hell."

Guido de Hueck opposed the marriage and none of the de Huecks attended the ceremony performed by Father Dimitri Padalka at St. Isaac's Cathedral on January 25, 1912. Catherine wore a white satin gown with a cathedral-length lace veil. She and Boris held lighted candles, and on their heads two golden crowns symbolized the respect they owed one another as they began their own small kingdom. At the end of the ceremony, the priest led them around the altar three times as a prelude to the eternal journey married couples walk, a journey Catherine and Boris would never complete.

Nearly 300 friends and relatives attended a reception in the Kolyschkine apartment. "I circulated among the guests and tried to attend to everything as befits a new bride. Then I dressed for travel. I wore a very beautiful blue moire dress and blouse, made out of China silk, with a little blue beret. . . My husband's wedding gift to me consisted of a necklace of beautifully matched pearls and earrings. (Everyone said I was unlucky to receive pearls, which are connected with tears.)"

Even more disturbing were Emma's words to her daughter. "Don't expect Boris to be faithful to you," she said.

Catherine and Boris spent their first months of marriage in a small apartment in Riga while Boris finished school. Catherine later referred to this time as her "slavery days." Relatives from both sides of the family visited, and stories emerged of Boris' explosive anger at Catherine. In one instance, the de Hueck relatives discovered that Catherine brought dolls with her, and their mocking laughter irritated Boris, but instead of defending his young wife, Boris blamed Catherine for the embarrassment he felt, and his anger spewed out at her. Humiliated, she ran from the room in tears.

It was a pattern of verbal and emotional abuse in the marriage that submerged Catherine into a pool of misery. She clung to moments when Boris behaved as if he loved her, but something inevitably triggered his rage. Catherine blamed herself for his mood swings and depressions. When it became clear that he was unfaithful to her, she came to the distorted conclusion that her inadequacy caused his compulsive desire for other women. Catherine became obsessed with pleasing Boris so as not to trigger another angry outburst, but her attempts at control were an illusion. In reality, Boris controlled and manipulated her. No matter what she said or did, she could never live up to his ever-changing demands and expectations. She could never satisfy his moods or sate his sexual desires.

In the fall of 1912, Catherine and Boris returned to St. Petersburg, and moved into an apartment building owned by Guido de Hueck on Geslerovsky Street. Boris finished his graduate projects, and after receiving his diploma in May 1913, he started his own architectural firm. Catherine settled into the role of a society matron. She made her debut at the Bal Rose, which was held at the Winter Palace each year to honor young married couples of the nobility. She wore a white gown, with her blond hair piled high on her head. She was under the tutelage of Boris' mother, whom she continued to call Aunt Vera. Unlike Emma who had worked with peasants, Vera organized philanthropic balls and fund drives. The contrast must have been striking for Catherine, but she forayed along Vera's path in the early years of her marriage, and before long, Vera had Catherine selling trinkets at charity bazaars. At one of these events, Vera presented Catherine to the Tsarina Alexandra. Catherine remembered the Tsarina's sorrowful eyes, and the longing look of her daughter, the Grand Duchess Tatiana, who said, "I wish I could sell, too."

On the surface, Catherine's life did seem enviable. Married to a successful young nobleman, she pursued her own studies at the university with no financial worries, no obvious problems. Beneath the surface, however, there stirred in Catherine the same restlessness that pervaded St. Petersburg society. "It was as if something was in the air hovering over each and every one of us," one Russian recalled. "People hurried and rushed about, never understanding why they did so, not knowing what to do with themselves."

Unrest among the lower classes was less subtle. Workers went on strike and peasants clamored for land. People talked of ridding Russia of Jews through exile or extermination. In Europe, revolutionaries, like Vladimir Lenin, published radical theories for a new social order, and waited in bitter anticipation for the chance to make those theories a reality.

In March 1913, Emma gave birth to her last child, a boy named André, and Catherine later admitted that rumors spread that "this was my child." Nothing ever came of the senseless gossip because the end of St. Petersburg society as Catherine and Emma knew it was very near.

On June 28, 1914, a member of a Serb nationalist terrorist group called the Black Hand assassinated the Austrian heir to the throne, Archduke Franz Ferdinand, and his wife in Sarajevo. Austria held Serbia responsible for the murder, and Russia warned that she would mobilize her troops if Austria retaliated. Ignoring the threat, Austria declared war against Serbia on July 28. The next day Tsar Nicholas II ordered his armies to mobilize. Germany's Kaiser Wilhelm countered with an ultimatum for the Tsar: Demobilize or face war. At noon on August 1, the ultimatum ran out. The next day in St. Petersburg, Tsar Nicholas II announced that Russia was at war with Germany. Crowds in front of the Winter Palace shouted hurrahs and *"Bozhe Tsaria!"* — God save the Tsar. Two days later, the Russian Horse Guards left the city in trucks, wagons, and railroad cars with trumpets signaling their departure. World War I had started, and Catherine — still young, still beautiful — was about to enter a horror beyond her wildest imagination.

Chapter Notes

The dazzling social structure...: For descriptions of Pre-Revolution Russian culture and society see Suzanne Massie, *Land of the Firebird: The Beauty of Old Russia*, New York: Simon and Schuster, 1980.

"an attitude of utter, mindless debauchery...": Lincoln, p. 379.

"I actually venerated Vsevolod...": *Tumbleweed*, p. 53.

"Her conversation was flowing...": Serge Kolychkine, *op. cit.*

"a well-educated, stable man...": *Ibid.*

"If he passed you on the street...": Interview, Ava Coupey.

"I learned all the fine arts...": *Fragments*, p. 45.

"utensils clean...": *Yesterdays*, p. 10.

"I loved its old sprawling house...": *Ibid.*, p. 12. [Until 1917, Finland was part of the Russian Empire.]

"Be not ashamed...": Adrian Fortescue, *The Orthodox Eastern Church*, p. 422.

"exaggeration, love of praise...": On Jan. 11, 1938, Catherine copied into Diary #17 an excerpt from a diary she wrote at age 12, MHA.

"As I look around...": *Ibid.*

"Complete informality...": "The Relationship Between the Hueck and Kolychkine Families," *Family Notes*, Vol. 1, p. 6, MHA.

"kisses behind the door": Interview, André Kolychkine.

"My sister did not know what she was doing...": *Ibid.*

When gossip spread...: CD to G de H, Nov. 27, 1967, MHA.

"Now you will marry...": Interview, André Kolychkine. [To circumvent Russian laws prohibiting marriages between first cousins, Theodore Kolyschkine paid an official $25 to have Catherine's age recorded as sixteen, and to omit the maiden name of the groom's mother on the marriage documents, and thereby hiding the fact that Catherine and Boris were blood relatives.]

"railroaded into a marriage": Interview, Fr. Emile Briere.

"My life can be divided into two parts...": *Ibid.*

"I circulated among the guests...": *Fragments*, p. 50.

"Don't expect Boris to be faithful...": Interview, Fr. Emile Briere.

"slavery days": Diary #64, May 16, 1945, MHA.

"I wish I could sell, too...": Diary #4, Oct. 6, 1928, MHA.

"It was as if something was in the air...": Lincoln, p. 381.

"this was my child": CD to G de H, Nov. 27, 1967, MHA.

6

The Russian Front
World War I
1915

Boris accepted a commission as a Major with the Imperial Engineers in the First Russian Army on the northern front between Minsk and Riga. Eighteen-year-old Catherine, still impetuous, still naive, decided to follow him. She enlisted in the Red Cross, and after an eight-week training course in St. Petersburg where she learned to dress wounds, roll bandages, empty bedpans, and change sheets, she boarded a medical supply train bound for the front.

Catherine never spoke of her life with Boris during the war years, but a subtle incongruity must have existed between them with Boris engineering ways to destroy lives, while she fought to save them. They lived in a small house near division headquarters, but underwent long periods of separation because of their individual duties. Catherine worked as a nurse's aide in a field hospital, which also served as a transfer station for soldiers going to the front. She wore the Red Cross uniform — a long gray dress with a white apron, and a white veil covering her hair. She scrubbed dirt, blood, and vomit off floors, cut away the vermin-infested uniforms of wounded soldiers, and washed the bodies of the dead. "In World War I, I dipped into the sea of pain," she confessed.

Catherine saw men with holes in their lungs gasping for air, men without faces, men whose brains throbbed through cracked skulls. She breathed the stench of decaying flesh, and her head

reverberated with the agonizing wails of men in pain. After one
siege, she carried amputated limbs out of the operating room. "I
don't know if you understand what that means," she later wrote.

> Three doctors cutting arms, legs, and handing them to
> me — still warm and one part of them bleeding. They
> covered me with a sort of poncho, if you want to call it,
> made out of rubber so the blood did not stain my
> uniform. It stained my shoes and ran down my legs. In
> fact you slip eventually on the blood because... well,
> there were so many dead limbs. And the nurse directed
> me to put them to the right side of the building where
> there was a sort of big hole. Well, this is what I did and
> slowly watched the hole stop being a hole. The legs, the
> hands, the arms leveled themselves with the earth and
> then they began to mound...This went on for 68 hours....

Chlorine gas, which the Germans used against the Russians
for the first time in May 1915, left soldiers writhing in agony as the
deadly gas formed an acid in their lungs and stomach that ate
holes through the membranes. Dumdum bullets filled with par-
ticles of rusty metal and dirt turned the smallest surface wound
into tetanus, and men died with their bodies wracked in spasms.
The first year of the war claimed two million Russians. Replace-
ment forces sent to the front had only four weeks training, and
some of these new recruits had never fired a gun.

Catherine later recalled with horror how emergency orders
to retreat forced medical personnel to abandon first aid stations
and field hospitals leaving behind patients too weak to transport.
The Russian Military Command added to the chaos by ordering
Cossack troops to evict Jews from areas near the front for fear they
would act as spies. Soldiers pillaged farmlands and burned villages leaving thousands of peasants homeless. Swarms of flies
covered dead horses. Farm animals rotted in fields. Thirteen
million refugees took to the road and the rush of wagons crushed
anyone who fell. Wounded men grabbed at the skirts of the nurses
and begged for help. Some shouted dreadful curses. "I have seen

children slowly dying of hunger, while their mothers lost their reason over the tragedy," Catherine recalled. "I have seen a field green with grass one day and literally stripped of every blade the next by people who had nothing else to eat. I have seen towns without a single roof on the houses because the straw of the thatching was taken to be boiled and eaten."

During one retreat, fear seized Catherine as she sat in a transport wagon filled with wounded soldiers, and something in the depths of her soul cried out:

> Why should these young people in their youth die, be killed, or maimed? Why? I ask God loudly and clearly, "Why?" and the echo brings my why back to me. I am shaken, shaken in the corner of a covered wagon in which lie about ten, or maybe less, wounded people. I who sit on the very corner of it, I am shaken, not so much with the horrible road we travel, but I am shaken as with a fever. . .
>
> God who promised to look after the poor, the sick, the lonely, is false to his promise. How can it be? God cannot be false to anything because he is God. And suddenly I find my face wet with tears. I am encircled with those doubts. They come closer and closer and closer. It is as if now, any minute, I shall die in the arms of my doubts.

Somewhere, in the darkness of Catherine's doubts, a tiny shaft of light flickered, and it brought the understanding that God did not cause or condone war. ". . . it is we who have brought about the wounding of our soldiers, the widows, the orphans, by entering into another war. We always enter into another war. It is our will that does it, not God's."

By the late fall of 1915, Russians halted the German advance, and troops dug in for winter. When fighting resumed the following spring, Catherine received a promotion to supervisor in charge of a canteen unit that delivered bread, tea, and soup to the trenches in horse-drawn wagons. Earlier in the war, she received a medal for bravery under fire when a piece of shrapnel fell into a cauldron of fish soup and soaked her. By 1916, however, food supplies dwindled, and Catherine cut rations so severely that she nearly panicked one day when she found maggots in the meat for her unit. She soaked the meat in vinegar until the white worms rose to the surface. Then she rinsed the meat and boiled it with potatoes. "I ate only potatoes," she recalled. "I couldn't stomach the maggots at that time. I wasn't hungry enough yet."

It was during this bitter time that Catherine met a wounded officer named Nicholas Makletzoff. Tall and handsome, with a long, lean face, dark bushy eyebrows, and green eyes, Nicholas had the aura of an aristocrat, but beneath the surface, Catherine saw that Nicholas knew a deeper pain than physical wounds. Three years before, he lost his wife when she gave birth to their first child. The baby girl lived with relatives while Nicholas finished his engineering degree at the prestigious Institute of Civil Engineering in Moscow. In 1915, he received his commission in the Russian army.

Catherine's vibrant personality, her beauty, and her own understanding of pain captivated Nicholas. He treated her with the kindness and respect that Boris had never shown. "My golden woman with eyes of blue azure," he called her. She called him Kolya, a nickname for Nicholas, and she admitted that she could be completely honest with him. "I do not need a mask with you," she once told him. During the day, they walked in the forest, and on clear, cool evenings they sat and talked in the moonlight. Before long, they fell in love, but they both knew it was just a wartime romance, an impossible fantasy.

Catherine's friendship with Nicholas sustained her through the autumn of 1916, when heavy frosts and freezing rain plunged the Russian army into deep depression. Nearly six million men had already died in a war that had no meaning for them. Regular deliveries of ammunition and food stopped. Supplies of morphine and anesthetics ran out. Catherine recalled "how soldiers were treated only with cold water, and their injuries bandaged only with poor rags." Doctors performed amputations and surgeries with bare hands because there were no more rubber gloves. "I used to think that it would be an act of mercy to be allowed to kill some of the poor patients who were brought to us having half their faces blown away and limbs hanging off," Catherine confessed, but she changed her mind when she saw how these men "showed dauntless bravery in their sufferings."

Only cowards tried to avoid pain. They came to the hospital with self-inflicted flesh wounds and begged for a release from duties. Catherine knew that she could not condemn the cowards any more than she could end the pain of the wounded, and she later admitted that during this time, she struggled with her own fear of being wounded, a fear that soon became real.

It happened one night in the aftermath of a German attack. The first aid tents needed help, and shortly before dawn, Catherine's supervisor asked her to report to the front lines. Catherine left on horseback, and along the way, her horse reared. Catherine fell, and the horse's hoof hit her chest. Pain seared through her, but relying on the knowledge of horses she gained as a child in Tambov, she calmed the animal, and pulled herself into the saddle. She arrived at the post with blood trickling from her mouth, and the doctors suspected internal bleeding from a torn lung.

After regaining enough strength to travel, Catherine requested sick leave, and boarded a train for St. Petersburg. The Tsar had renamed the city Petrograd in an attempt to give the capital a stronger Russian identity, but Catherine discovered a city in despair with tattered men and women standing in long lines to buy bread. Hostility consumed the workers. Patriotism vanished. She walked from the station to her parents' apartment on Morskaya, and when Theodore saw how weak she was, he suggested that they spend Christmas at their estate in Finland. The warm smells of cakes and breads, and the quiet sounds of the Finnish countryside soothed Catherine. Boris stayed at the front, but Nicholas Makletzoff followed her, and the family invited him to join in the holiday celebration. Catherine's brother, Serge, remembered how Nicholas spent hours reading Gogol to her. "I always loved

Nicholas," Serge admitted. "He was an extremely honest and good man. A man with a big heart. Kind. Quiet. Complete — without any compromises. Very, very Russian by character, breeding, mentality. . . with two big loves in his heart — Russia and you."

On the twelfth day of Christmas, the day commemorating the visit of the Wise Men to the Infant Jesus, Catherine asked Nicholas to leave. The next morning she wrote in her diary:

> God, why did I tell him to go? Why this urge toward him? Because I love him and I know he loves me. Kolya, please come back. No. Because I would never make anyone happy. Please, God, why did you make me like I am with the spirit and the body always in opposition?

Catherine had just begun to learn about life.

Chapter Notes

"In World War I, I dipped...": CD, *The Gospel of a Poor Woman*, p. 36. (Hereafter *Gospel of a Poor Woman*).

"I don't know if you understand...": CD, *Stories for Staff Workers that go..."IN ONE EAR AND OUT ANOTHER"*, MHA, pp. 149-150. (Hereafter *IN ONE EAR*).

Chlorine gas...: See Stanley Washburn, *On the Russian Front in World War I, Memoirs of an American War Correspondent*, p. 143.

"I have seen children slowly dying...": "Horrors of Red Terror Days," *Rochester Democrat and Chronicle*, Apr. 24, 1927.

"Why should these young people in their youth die...": CD, *Doubts, Loneliness, Rejection*, pp. 23-24. (Hereafter *Doubts*).

"it is we...": *Ibid.*

"I ate only potatoes...": *IN ONE EAR*, pp. 151-52.

"My golden woman...": NM correspondence, MHA.

"I do not need a mask with you...": *Ibid.*

"how soldiers were treated only with cold water...": "Baroness Lectures at Town Hall," *Guide*, Feb. 27, 1925, Port Hope, Ontario.

"I used to think that it would be an act of mercy...": "Lecture Well Attended," unidentified news clip, n.d., MHA.

"I always loved Nicholas...": Serge Kolychkine to CD, Mar. 2, 1970, MHA.

"God, why did I tell him to go?": Diary excerpt, Jan. 7, 1917, NM correspondence, MHA.

7

Petrograd

1917

As Catherine hurried to a doctor's appointment that February, a burst of gunfire sent people screaming in all directions. She fell to the ground and crawled into the doorway of a hotel. The police found no reason for the shooting. A few days later, women textile workers, who were celebrating International Women Worker's Day, joined striking men in a street march that erupted into minor scuffles and looting in the late afternoon. The following day, nearly half of the city's workers poured into streets crying, "Bread!" "Down with Autocracy!" "Down with war!" By Saturday, February 25, over 240,000 people joined the protest. Factories and businesses closed. Newspapers suspended publication. Derailed streetcars lay sideways on the tracks. People hurled rocks, bottles, and chunks of ice. Mounted police fired shots into the crowd.

"We watched all of these events, crowds, street fighting, from our balcony," Catherine's brother recalled.

That evening the Tsar sent a telegram to General Khabalov ordering an end to the disturbances, but it was too late. On Sunday morning, an army regiment joined the protesters, and by late Sunday afternoon, the entire Petrograd garrison went into mutiny. Mobs stole guns from arsenals, freed prisoners, sealed off government buildings, and set fire to police stations. Tsarist troops in the fortress of Peter and Paul surrendered. By sundown on Monday, February 27, insurgents held the city. Three days later, Tsar Nicholas II abdicated the throne to his brother, Michael, who renounced the crown the following morning.

As news of the revolution spread, elated messages of support from cities, towns and villages flooded into Petrograd where two rival powers emerged: In one wing of the elegant Tauride Palace, the Soviet of Workers and Soldiers declared itself the ruling body of the proletariat. In the other wing, the president of the Senate, which aligned itself with the bourgeois class, announced the formation of a Provisional Government.

Boris was on furlough in Petrograd during these tense days for the funeral of his stepfather, the eccentric Nicolai Evreinoff, who died from a stroke. Boris wanted Catherine to return to the front with him, but she refused. Still suffering from the chest injury, she insisted on staying at the Kolyschkine estate at Antrea with her mother, who was organizing shipments of household goods that Theodore sent from the apartment on Morskaya. Like most wealthy noblemen, Theodore Kolyschkine believed the revolution was "a temporary aberration that could not survive," but as a precaution, he moved furniture, oriental carpets, jewelry, heirlooms, and books to Antrea. At the same time wealthy noblemen, like Theodore, moved their treasures out of Russia, Vladimir Lenin moved in with a hunger, not for wealth, but for power.

Lenin's train steamed into Petrograd's Finland Station on April 3, and a crowd of cheering soldiers and workers greeted him. Holding a bouquet of flowers, Lenin proclaimed that the time had come to turn against capitalist exploiters. "The Russian revolution achieved by you has opened a new epoch. Long live the world-wide socialist revolution!"

Catherine saw Lenin speak. He was dynamic, with a calm, clear logic and simple directness that ignited crowds to fever pitch. She described it as "the mellifluous, powerful voice of Lenin," and she had recurring visions of mobs "whose shouts penetrate like nails."

Later that spring, Catherine returned to the front for the last Russian offensive. At first, Russian troops advanced, but a strong

German counterattack forced the Russians into retreat. Morale dissolved and Bolshevik infiltrators increased dissension in the trenches. "They simply said to the soldiers, 'Why don't you go back to your villages, seize the estates of the landlords, and divide them among yourselves!'" Catherine recalled. "That was the one thing the Russian peasant always wanted more of — land. So they left the front, took the train, and went home."

The soldiers that stayed terrorized officers. "During this period, one would hear shots every morning at sunrise, and would know that some officer was being put to death," Catherine recalled. Boris hid in a basement at headquarters from his own men, who wanted to kill him. Catherine forged Red Cross passes for officers trying to escape. Late one night, a young soldier came to warn her that the soldiers' soviet knew about the falsified passes, and slated her for arrest. She set out immediately on horseback for the nearest field hospital where friends gave her peasant clothes and food. The next morning Catherine began her journey back to Petrograd on roads congested with soldiers carrying boxes of loot they had stolen from homes and shops. The trip that would normally have taken 11 hours, took days, and Catherine, who had always traveled first class, slept on floors in railway stations.

"A Revolution is always distinguished by impoliteness, probably because the ruling classes did not take the trouble in good season to teach the people fine manners," Leon Trotsky reflected sarcastically. Something in Catherine's soul would one day lead her beneath those bitter words to a deeper truth, but for the present, every ounce of her strength focused on survival.

Theodore and Emma were at the apartment on Morskaya when Catherine arrived. She was thin and pale, with a raspy cough that left her breathless and weak. A few days later, a doctor confirmed that she had tuberculosis. Catherine wrote in her diary that she didn't care if she died. She checked into the Imperial Sanitarium for Tubercular Patients in Finland, but left when she realized she could receive better care at home.

There is no record of where Catherine was after midnight on October 25, when Red Guards in Petrograd took over the post office, the power station, the telephone and telegraph agency, the State Bank, railway stations, bridges, and key office buildings. By daybreak, Bolsheviks surrounded the Winter Palace where the Provisional Government had moved their headquarters. That evening, pro-Bolshevik sailors on the battleship *Aurora* fired a blank shot at the Winter Palace, and during the next few hours, random shots struck the palace walls and windows. Shortly before 2:00 a.m. on October 26, Red Guards entered the Malachite Chamber where they arrested the officials of the Provisional Government.

The next morning shops opened and people hurried to work as usual. That afternoon, Trotsky announced that power had passed into the hands of the Petrograd Soviet. "The bourgeois class had expected barricades, flaming conflagrations, looting, rivers of blood," he later wrote. "In reality a silence reigned more terrible than all the thunders of the world. The social ground shifted noiselessly like a revolving stage, bringing forward the popular masses, carrying away to limbo the rulers of yesterday."

Later that evening, Lenin read a proclamation abolishing private ownership of land. Mass looting of stores and apartments in exclusive sections of Petrograd began. Windows in the Kolyschkine apartment were "shattered by the bullets of the reds." In the weeks that followed, a Bolshevik decree abolished class distinctions, and Catherine noted that ". . . everybody is a *tovarisch* (comrade)." Anti-Bolshevik newspapers closed, and the court system collapsed as workers and peasants formed revolutionary tribunals to dispense justice. Red Guards searched bourgeois homes for firearms and fur coats.

Concerned for the safety of Emma and four-year-old André, Theodore took them back to Antrea. "It was a cold day," Catherine's brother, Serge, recalled. "Snow in the streets. Soldiers were looting the wine cellars of Schmit, the biggest wine dealers in Petrograd. Trams were not running. There was machine gun fire in the streets. My brother Vsevolod offered to help. Father, mother, and

Vsevolod walked from our flat to the Finland Station. Vsevolod was carrying André in his arms."

Theodore and 12-year-old Serge returned to Petrograd a few days later. "Nobody believed that the Communists would last," Serge explained.

> I carried on with The Imperial School of Law (it was my last term 1917-1918) and father with The Russian Loyd. We lived at the same address Morskaya 25, but this time occupied only 2-3 rooms. Other rooms were empty and closed. Our old maid, Macha, lived with us. Conditions were very difficult. Rationing. Hunger started. Cholera (a few hundred deaths per day). Hardly any fuel for heating. We suffered from cold.

Catherine stayed in Petrograd with Boris, who had returned from the front. Food was scarce and the black market flourished. "At home my eyes fell on a sterling silver tea set," Catherine later wrote. "I grabbed it, and made my way to the street where I had seen other people barter like valuables for food. Five minutes later I had exchanged $800 worth of silver for two herrings and a few potatoes."

Hucksters sold hunks of wood baked in a thin coating of dough. People ate horse meat, cats, dogs, and rodents. Women scrounged through garbage cans looking for potato peels and cabbage leaves. One day, as Catherine searched for food, drunken soldiers pinned her against a wall.

> I put my hand against my forehead and someone shot a revolver at me and the blood came into my face and I fainted. They decided that I was dead and went their merry way around the corner. I came to and there was I — bloody as can be and nobody ever stopped to help anybody because they were afraid. I had something to wipe my face with and I discovered my face was okay but my hand was a mess. Even to this day I have a scar of the bullet wound.

Another time, Catherine froze in horror as two men shot a woman. They asked Catherine if she wanted the woman's fur coat. "I can't, I can't," she screamed and ran away.

In his newspaper column, Maxim Gorky despaired over the loss of human dignity. He denounced the burning of libraries, the chopping of pianos with axes, and the destruction of valuable paintings. "Thievery is spreading, robberies are increasing, shameless people engage in bribery just as cleverly as the officials of the Tsarist regime."

Catherine later claimed that during this time Boris was sick from gas and shell-shock in the war, but it eventually became apparent that her use of the word "sick" often alluded to Boris' infidelities. "It is very sad," she wrote in her diary.

> It is night. The wind is howling. I am not sleeping. God be praised. Boris is not here. Beginning with the moment I came back to him my joy and tranquillity are gone. I am so unhappy.

Memories of Nicholas became a dream world for Catherine where ". . . each thought of him is a little piece of happiness for me." For the next ten years, the fantasy of Nicholas rescuing her provided a mental and emotional escape, a coping mechanism to help her survive in a marriage that was demeaning and destructive.

In December, Catherine, Boris, Theodore, Vera and Serge took the train to Antrea to spend Christmas with Emma and André. Conditions in Finland had deteriorated. Russian army deserters instigated massive strikes and rioting by telling Finnish workers that the upper classes exploited the poor. The Finnish government organized a Civic Guard to oust the Russians, but workers countered by forming a Red Guard made up of vagrants and criminals. Throughout the countryside, Finnish Bolsheviks urged local peasants to loot estates and murder land owners. Travel between Russia and Finland was treacherous, but the borders remained open, and the train carrying the Kolyschkine family arrived safely. It must have been a bittersweet reunion, filled with memories of the past and fears about the future. They had no idea this was the last Christmas they would all spend together.

Chapter Notes

"We watched all of these events...": Serge Kolychkine, "Details Concerning: Chapter 1917," MHA.

"a temporary aberration...": G de H, "Huecks Settle in St. Petersburg," *Family Notes*, Vol. VII, p. 12, MHA.

"The Russian revolution achieved by you...": Leon Trotsky, *The Russian Revolution*, pp. 222-223.

"the mellifluous, powerful voice of Lenin": CD, *Urodivoi*, p. 82.

"They simply said...": *Fragments*, p. 53.

"During this period, one would hear...": "40,000 Reds in Dominion Says Speaker," unidentified news clip, Mar. 4, 1925, MHA.

"Boris took refuge in a basement...": "Says Russian Trade Pact is Only Political Dodge," *Toronto Globe*, Apr. 4, 1921.

"her long journey back to Petrograd...": In some sources, Catherine claims that she met Boris along the road and they returned to Petrograd together. In most accounts, however, she claims to have made the journey back to Petrograd alone, which seems to be substantiated by excerpts from her 1917 diary and other sources.

"A Revolution is always distinguished...": Trotsky, p. 128.

she didn't care if she died: NM correspondence, MHA.

"The bourgeois class had expected...": Trotsky, p. 368.

"shattered by bullets of the reds": "Had Adventurous Time Dodging The Russian Reds," *Toronto Daily Star*, July 7, 1922.

"everybody is a tovarisch (comrade)": Diary #1, Jan. 15, 1918, MHA.

"It was a cold day...": Serge Kolychkine, "Details Concerning: Chapter 1917," MHA. [Serge also noted, "It was probably this event, which by oral family transmission took a legendary form — That my father had to carry me (a boy of 13 years) through the snows to Finland! Anyhow, Father, Mother and André arrived safely back to Antrea."]

"Nobody believed that the communists would last...": *Ibid.*

"At home my eyes fell...": C de H, *Friendship House*, p. 10. (Hereafter *Friendship House*).

"I put my hand against my forehead...": *IN ONE EAR*, pp. 70-71.

"I can't, I can't...": *Fragments*, p. 55.

"Thievery is spreading...": Maxim Gorky, *Untimely Thoughts*, pp. 100-102.

"It is very sad...": NM correspondence, MHA.

"each thought of him...": *Ibid.*

8

Antrea, Finland
1918

On January 1, 1918, Catherine opened the diary Boris gave her. His inscription made no effort to conceal his attempts to control her:

> In this book you will write day by day what has happened to you. As you know I have affection for what is mine, whether it be much or little.
>
> You will hide no bad things or even thoughts from me and I hope I will never find them, in this year, in which you start your diary.
>
> Your Boris

Catherine kept the journal as Boris instructed, but it contains none of the deep introspection in other diaries. It records events, with occasional remarks about Boris. Some of the comments are negative: "Boris is in an awful mood and he spoiled mine altogether." Others are positive: "Today is the anniversary of our marriage. With all my soul I am happy and satisfied." Some comments illustrate her attempts to appease him: "Boris is in a bad mood despite my approaches." Others reveal her frustration: "My poor Boris is tired and exhausted and I as well. However, I am silent and endure it."

"There were many difficult days between Boris and me," Catherine later confessed. "My life with him was very strange. I always tried to forgive and forget. It was like a refrain, "forgive, forget, forgive, forget.""

In early January, Boris had orders to return to the front, and he insisted that Catherine accompany him. Emma wept when they left. They took the train to their summer home (*dacha* in Russian) near the tiny village of Kiskile, about 30 miles from Antrea, which Catherine had named *Merri-Lokki*, meaning Sea Gull, because it perched on a rocky ledge overlooking a small lake. They stayed in Kiskile for two days stocking firewood and supplies in case they would need the house as a refuge. On January 12, they arrived in Petrograd, and found Vera had moved boxes of her belongings into their apartment. "It is simply dreadful," Catherine wrote, "but who cares. It is so bad now that it isn't worth speaking about such insignificant things."

Dead horses from the October uprising lay along curbsides like massive frozen heaps. Newspapers warned of robberies. Rounds of gunfire rang out. "When there are revolutions, all normal activities are at a standstill," Catherine later wrote. "And one spends an accumulation of time trying to keep alive, wondering all the while when death or prison will call."

One terrifying night Catherine and Boris heard men's voices in the stairway, followed by a scuffle and a woman's agonizing scream. The *Tcheka*, a secret police force formed to rout enemies of the revolution, had seized the man in the apartment across the hall.

As members of the nobility, Catherine and Boris did not qualify for food rations, and the nationalization of banks limited withdrawals. Catherine later recalled the humiliation of facing a teller who laughed in her face. "We are very hungry and there is nothing to eat," she wrote. "I do not know what to do. I want to eat very much. Real hunger."

On the morning of January 15, they pushed their way through the railway station, and squeezed into a third-class carriage that would take them to the front. The Bolsheviks had signed an armistice with the Germans on December 2, and were negotiating a peace treaty. There was no fighting at the front, no terrors in the night. Boris received a two month extension on his furlough with a final discharge date of June 20, and Colonel

Bastrakoff presented Catherine and Boris with the St. George Cross for acts of bravery during the war. "What joy!" wrote Catherine. It was Russia's highest military honor, but Catherine's excitement dissolved when they returned to Petrograd and discovered that civil war had broken out in Finland. Trapped in Petrograd, tension took its toll. "I am again tired with a headache and dizziness," she wrote. "I am hungry and sleepy but neither is possible. Good Lord, when will all this end."

Catherine's patience with Aunt Vera also waned. Vera could not comprehend the dangers Catherine faced in trying to find food on the streets, and she criticized Catherine because her hands were rough and red. Catherine later admitted that Vera's arrogance saved their lives one afternoon when the two women set out for the summer home Vera owned near the Smolny Institute, where the Bolsheviks had their headquarters. A Red Guard asked where they were going, and Vera snapped, "To Smolny." Catherine braced herself for arrest, but the soldier assumed they were on their way to Bolshevik headquarters and let them pass.

By mid-February, Russian peace talks with the Germans broke down, and German troops advanced within one hundred miles of Petrograd. Boris insisted that they had to risk an escape to Finland. Vera refused to go. "Oh, Lord," Catherine prayed, "let me and mine be in your hands. Guard and save us."

The next morning, Catherine and Boris dressed in peasant clothes, and left without Vera. They traveled to Bjelo Ostrow, a small village on the border where they planned to stay with friends until a local peasant could smuggle them into Finland. For two weeks they waited, hiding in a pig sty when local Communists made routine searches for members of the nobility. "It's difficult to explain what pain you feel when you're up to your neck in mire made by swine," Catherine recalled. "That's another kind of pain — the fear of the way you're reduced to the state of an animal."

At dusk one night, a peasant led them to a gully where a mountain stream separated the two countries. Shots rang out as they slid down the frozen embankment, splashed through the icy water, and scrambled up the Finnish cliff. They paused briefly in a thicket to catch their breath and then ran through the forest to a nearby railway station where they learned that Finnish Communists held the southern part of the country. Catherine felt like a fugitive, unable to return to Russia and uncertain of what they would face in Finland. They hid at their *dacha* in Kiskile. "It's funny how you can go someplace, and yet your heart is in another place. And so we were out there in our *dacha* in Finland, but Boris was worried about his mother, and I was worried about my father and Serge."

Catherine turned to the Bible as a source of comfort and strength. "It is a wonderful book," she wrote in her diary. "God give me your cross and let me follow you! But I am not worthy enough to be chosen."

Catherine never elaborated on her little prayer, but a heavy cross entered her life a short time later when Finnish Red Guards discovered the young aristocrats and arrested Boris on charges of concealing weapons. "His body will be returned to you in a coffin," they told Catherine, and left her alone in the *dacha* while a local tribunal tried Boris as an enemy of the people. The tribunal condemned both Catherine and Boris to a slow death by starvation in the hope that under duress the young couple might confess to burying money or jewels on their property. The guards brought Boris back to the *dacha*, confiscated their horses and food, tormented them with slaps and ridicule, and left, promising that they would return unexpectedly. Over the next few days, Catherine and Boris found a few frozen potatoes in the cellar and they caught fish in the lake, but it wasn't enough to sustain them. As hunger pains set in, Catherine gnawed on firewood. Red guards came regularly to taunt them. One day, they brought a dog and jeered as Catherine and Boris pounced on the animal, wresting the bone out of the dog's jaws, and fighting with each other until they realized that the bone was bare.

Their torment lasted three months. Toward the end, Catherine and Boris slept most of the day. She dreamed of pastries with cheese fillings, steaming stacks of pancakes, heaps of fried potatoes, and plump *pirogies* stuffed with chopped spinach and mush-rooms. "They were so real I could taste them or almost pick them up. It was like a mirage... There are no words to describe this kind of hunger."

Catherine's body swelled, her teeth loosened, and her hair fell out in clumps. Shivering from cold, she lay close to the stove. Thoughts of closing the flue and ending the pain by asphyxiation tormented her. "All you need is a slight movement of your arm, and you have death, which now becomes a friend and merciful," she kept thinking. In a final moment of desperation, Catherine stared into the flames and promised God: "If you save me from this, in some sort of way I will offer my life to you." Then, she lapsed into unconsciousness. She had no recollection of how much time passed, but she remembered waking to the shouts of Finnish White Guards, who defeated the Bolsheviks in Helsinki and were routing Communists from the countryside. The White Finns took Catherine and Boris to a hospital in Vyborg, where nurses spoon fed them until they regained their strength. In the late summer of 1918, Catherine and Boris arrived at Antrea.

"Mama," Catherine sobbed. "Don't you know me. . ."

"Katia, Oh, horror! Katia," Emma cried.

Emma had lost hope of seeing anyone from the family alive. Months before, she received news that Theodore and Serge had gone into hiding in Petrograd after the *Tcheka* slated Theodore for arrest, but she had heard nothing since. That fall, Catherine and Boris bribed a border guard, who let them cross into Russia and search for missing family members. In Petrograd, they found Vera still in their apartment. "But father had vanished, and so did Serge my brother. We couldn't find them anywhere."

Catherine and Boris stayed only a few days in Petrograd. They never found Theodore and Serge, and Vera still refused to leave. Catherine's step-brother, Vsevolod, and his wife, Lusia, also insisted on staying. Later that fall, Theodore and Serge finally escaped to Finland after paying a 10,000 ruble bribe. Serge never forgot the raw emotion as Theodore and Emma clung to each other after a year of separation.

Catherine and Boris lived with her parents at Antrea throughout the winter. Boris found a job as an architect in Vyborg. Serge and André attended a Finnish school with Guido de Hueck's sons by his second wife. "Once, in the school, my father met Guido de Hueck," Serge recalled. "Compared to the big storm which happened in Russia and which swept away so many lives, how small seemed our family quarrels. Both men understood it at once and without any words shook hands."

By November 1918, the war with Germany had ended, but in Russia, a savage civil war erupted with armies of White Russians fighting the Bolsheviks. In early 1919, a call went out for veteran officers to enlist with the White Forces. "Boris said we have to go and fight the Communists," Catherine recalled. It was their only hope of reclaiming their country.

That spring, Catherine and Boris traveled to Helsinki where Boris received his commission as a Major in the White Russian Army in Murmansk, a seaport in northern Russia. Since Bolsheviks controlled the connecting railroads, the young couple took an alternate route, traveling by train to Narvik, Norway, where they boarded a coastal steamer that carried them around the tip of Norway and into the choppy waters of the Arctic Ocean. As their ship approached the wide mouth of the Tuloma River they caught their first glimpse of smoke from the tiny town of Murmansk. They were 150 miles above the Arctic Circle.

Chapter Notes

"In this book you will write..." and f.: Diary #1, p. 1., MHA.

"There were many difficult days...": Fragments, p. 89.

"It is simply dreadful...": Diary #1, Jan. 12, 1918, MHA. [For descriptions of Petrograd after the Revolution see Marie, Grand Duchess of Russia, Education of a Princess, A Memoir, New York: The Viking Press, 1930.]

"When there are revolutions...": C de H, Friendship House, p. 150.

"We are very hungry...": Diary #1, Jan. 13, 1918, MHA.

"What joy!": Diary #1, Jan. 29, 1918.

"I am again tired...": Diary #1, Feb. 4, 1918.

"To Smolny..." and f.: CD to G de H, Nov. 27, 1967, MHA.

"It's difficult to explain...": "The Lady They Call the B," *World Religions*, produced by Mike McManus, TVOntario, Dec. 7, 1973.

"It's funny how you can go someplace...": CD, *The Gospel of a Poor Woman*, p. 32. (Hereafter *Gospel of a Poor Woman*).

"It is a wonderful book...": Diary #1, Mar. 22, 1918, MHA.

"His body will be returned...": "Russian Refugee Tells of Harrowing Trials," *The Kitchener Ontario Record*, Oct. 14, 1924, MHA.

The torment lasted three months: "Went Through Terror of Russia's Red Revolution," *The Daily Gleaner*, Nov. 26, 1932, MHA.

"They were so real...": *Fragments*, p. 57.

"All you need is a slight movement...": CD, "The Immaculate in Russia," *Immaculata*, September, 1961, p. 16.

"If you save me from this...": *Little Mandate*, MHA.

"Mama...": *Tumbleweed*, p. 86.

"But Father had vanished...": *Gospel of a Poor Woman*, p. 32.

"Once, in school...": Serge Kolychkine, unpublished family history, MHA.

"Boris said we have to go...": *IN ONE EAR*, p. 151-160.

9

Murmansk, Russia
1919

Catherine and Boris stepped off the ship into what looked like a junkyard strewn with boxcars, military trucks, and mounds of iron and steel. An unpaved road led to a cluster of log cabins that served as homes, stores, and offices. Beyond the village, long rows of corrugated metal army barracks bulged on flat barren fields. Only the Orthodox church with its onion dome gave the appearance of lasting worth.

"Having mushroomed too fast to carry an imprint of permanence, the town of Murmansk was raw," a Swedish nurse observed.

The air smelled of tar, smoke, and sawdust. Springtime temperatures hovered near freezing. The sun, Catherine noted "never set for months. It would go down to the far rim of the ocean, and then begin to rise."

For centuries, Murmansk existed as a sparsely populated fishing village where weather-beaten natives ate raw minnows. During World War I, the Tsar transformed the town into a military supply depot, and Allied countries shipped arms and ammunition into the port to bolster the fight against the Germans. By the time Catherine and Boris arrived in the late spring of 1919, the war with Germany had ended, but Allied troops from eleven countries stayed to fight the Bolsheviks under British command.

"My husband and I were billeted in a small house," Catherine recalled, "but we rarely saw each other. He worked with the English Royal Engineers and used to go out on frequent forays."

Boris was assigned to a special-duty transportation unit that repaired railroad tracks, installed telegraph lines, and rebuilt bridges destroyed by the retreating Bolsheviks. Catherine volunteered as an aide with the "Syren" Force of the British Red Cross under Lt. Col. E.L. Moss. A hospital ship docked in the Murmansk harbor served as the central supply station for field hospitals scattered throughout the northern territory. Catherine worked at a field hospital about ten miles from Murmansk, and it was in this hospital that she first encountered Americans. "Shake a leg and make it snappy," a delirious American officer kept shouting.

> So I took his leg and shook and shook and shook! I shook it 20 times a night! I entered all this in the night book. It had one wonderful result: It made the matron break down and laugh. All the American nurses and doctors laughed, too. And for the rest of my days in Murmansk, everybody laughed when they saw me and said, "Shake a leg, Nurse, and make it snappy."

Catherine also saw the dark side of hospital work in Murmansk with atrocities more repulsive than anything she had encountered in World War I. Patrols found bodies of soldiers tied to trees with their stomachs sliced open and intestines hanging out. Some had been castrated; some had arms and legs severed. Bags stuffed with body parts would arrive at Allied hospitals in driverless horse-drawn sleighs.

"That is the kind of enemy you're fighting," an American officer warned.

Lenin insisted, however, that violence was an essential part of the dictatorship of the proletariat and the most efficient way to purge the new society of bourgeois values. "The people who protest against acts of terrorism committed by the Communists entirely forget what the term dictatorship means," he explained. "Revolution is in itself an act of terrorism. The word dictatorship in all languages means simply the rule of terror. It is likewise evident that when the revolution is most in danger the dictatorship must be most pitiless."

The savage brutality distressed Allied soldiers, who had no understanding of how they ended up in Murmansk. "As I see it, this is not our war," a Canadian pilot observed.

"The average United States Soldier would rather be quartered in hell," an American wrote.

Catherine tried to comfort the soldiers, not just in her hospital work, but also as a volunteer at the YMCA canteen in Murmansk. The canteen showed movies, offered library books, and supplied candy, cigarettes, and hot chocolate free of charge. Bible classes and lectures were also part of the Y's commitment "to unite those young men who, regarding Jesus Christ as their God and Savior according to the Holy Scriptures, desire to be His disciples in their doctrine and in their life, and to associate their efforts for the extension of His Kingdom amongst young men."

Catherine's experiences with the YMCA in Murmansk left a lasting impression on her. It was her first exposure to a strictly lay organization that focused on meeting the soldiers' spiritual needs along with their physical, social, and educational needs. She translated letters and documents for the English-speaking soldiers. In gratitude, the Americans gave her a box of what appeared to be peppermint sticks. "I chewed one for about an hour," she recalled. "It wouldn't melt. I tried another. Nothing."

She finally called to ask what kind of candy this was, and was told it was chewing gum.

"What do you do with it?" she asked.

"You chew it," one of the Americans laughed.

The easy way Catherine and the Americans poked fun at each other's cultural differences was not typical. Heated disagreements over military strategies, the treatment of soldiers, the condition of equipment, salary levels, and living conditions resulted in British and American officers looking down on the Russians as a crude race, while the Russians considered the British patronizing and arrogant. Hostility festered, but Catherine didn't share those feelings. Her ability to speak English and her childhood experiences of meeting people from other cultures helped her form new friendships. Photos show her as a radiant 22-year-old with long blond hair tied in a loose bun and little wisps falling softly around her face. She had deep blue eyes, high aristocratic cheekbones, and a quick smile. She had regained enough weight to appear healthy and strong, and whether she wore her long-skirted Red Cross uniform and apron or her military uniform with its fitted wool jacket, dark skirt, boots, and wide-brimmed hat, a strong mix of vitality and sex appeal radiated from her. She was the kind of woman that men felt comfortable with, and she maintained an easy, and at times flirtatious relationship with men of all ages.

When the British learned her linguistic abilities included Finnish, French, and a little Polish, as well as Russian and English, they asked her to work part time as an interpreter, a rank few women of her day ever hoped to attain. She later remarked that she needed "all the diplomacy I had learned from my father."

Catherine also continued her work as a nurse's aide, commuting daily by train from British headquarters to the field hospital on the outskirts of Murmansk. One day she overheard two Bolsheviks conversing in Finnish about a consignment of dynamite they had stolen from the Allied headquarters. When the train pulled into the station, she waited until the men boarded, and then sat within earshot. "They didn't suspect that I could understand Finnish. They continued to talk." Later that day, the Allies hailed Catherine as a heroine when she reported the location of the dynamite and the identities of the men.

The incident that left the most profound impression on Catherine, however, was a pilgrimage she and Boris made to one of Russia's most famous monasteries on the island of Solovetsky in the White Sea, which lay within Allied territory. Before the revolution, 10,000 people journeyed every summer to this "singing island," founded in 1429 by Saints Hermann and Sabbatius, who claimed the Mother of God told them to find a place where they could live simply and pray. Wise men, called *staretzi*, stayed in tiny cottages hidden deep in the woods and visited the monastery once a month to celebrate the Orthodox liturgy.

When Catherine and Boris walked through the Holy Gate in

the summer of 1919, a bearded monk told them a *staretz*, who had lived as a hermit for more than 30 years, was receiving pilgrims. The monk led them to a small cell where a frail old man sat on a wooden bench. He had a long white beard and deep blue eyes. "I have never seen, in an old man, the eyes of a child until I looked into these eyes," Catherine recalled.

> We chatted a while and then asked for his blessing. The first one to be blessed was Boris. And then the *staretz* blessed him, beautifully, wonderfully, but didn't say anything out of the way. When I knelt, his dry, warm hands gave warmth to my whole body and my heart jumped with joy. I felt happy with his hands on my head. He lifted my chin, looked into my eyes and said, "Child, you are predestined by God to do great works for Him. You will suffer much but don't be afraid. Follow where He leads. Go in His footsteps." And then he blessed me with the usual long blessing. We walked out of there, Boris and I, wondering what the words of this holy man meant to me.

By the time Catherine and Boris returned to Murmansk, the British had announced plans to evacuate Northern Russia, and the Allies had already started shipping troops home. The British government offered political asylum to Russian military personnel and civilians, but after days of bitter debate, General E.K. Miller, commander of the White Forces, decided the Russians should stay to fight the Bolsheviks. A few weeks later, Boris was wounded in a Bolshevik raid at a railroad installation, and the British medical staff urged Catherine to leave Murmansk. "Your husband is sick," Lt. Col. Moss told her. "I can put you on the international ship to nurse the Bulgarians and Slavs, and then I can send your husband with you."

Months later, Catherine thanked Moss for saving their lives, but at the time, the choice was not clear. About 6,000 Russians had applied for evacuation, most of them war brides, businessmen, and members of the nobility, who had enough money to begin life again in England, but they incurred the scorn of their countrymen, who accused them of betrayal and cowardice.

In late August, General Miller made a final plea for the British to stay, but the decision remained irrevocable, and less than three weeks later, the last Allied ships steamed out of the Murmansk harbor. Catherine and Boris sailed on an earlier transport, and her photo album became a bittersweet reminder of Murmansk. Tiny black and white snapshots tell the story of rustic log cabins, muddy dirt roads, army barracks, warehouses, and the Russian Orthodox church with its haunting icons and flickering candles. Catherine captured two little boys asleep in a rowboat, native fishermen casting their nets, and village women washing clothes in the river. She snapped photos of a Bolshevik prisoner of war with his head shaved, a peasant woman stooped on a railroad track as a British doctor bandaged her foot, Boris at the reins of a one-horse carriage, and a Russian supply train inching its way across the barren countryside.

The final pages of her photo album show people of all ages, some in uniform, others in civilian clothes, gathered on the deck of a ship. A few are smiling, but most appear dejected as they look back at Russia for the last time. As the ship steamed out of the harbor, she took photos of the choppy waters, the lighthouse, the long wooden piers, and the dockyard with the tall hoisting cranes, smoke stacks, and piles of debris. She believed with all her heart that she would one day return to Russia, but she never again set foot on Russian soil.

Less than five months after the Allied withdrawal, the Red Army advanced into the northern territory with a vengeance so fierce that the war-weary White forces dissolved within weeks. Those lucky enough to escape fled to Finland. The rest faced imprisonment or execution. By March 13, 1920, a Bolshevik Revolutionary Committee had seized control of Murmansk. The monastery on the island of Solovetsky became a concentration camp.

Chapter Notes

"Having mushroomed too fast...": Louise de Kiriline Lawrence, *Another Winter, Another Spring*, p. 87.

"the sun never set...": *Tumbleweed*, p. 89.

"My husband and I were billeted...": *Fragments*, p. 61.

"the 'Syren' Force...": Veronica Marchbanks, British Red Cross, to the author, Feb. 19, 1992.

"Shake a leg...": *Fragments*, p. 62.

"That is the kind of enemy...": Dennis Gordon, *Quartered in Hell*, p. 291-294.

"The people who protest...": "Talk with Bolshevik Head," *New York Times*, Apr. 23, 1919.

"As I see it...": Frank J. Shrive, *Observations of a P.B.O. (Poor Bloody Observer)*, p. 81.

"The average United States soldier...": Gordon, p. 302.

"to unite those young men...": Kenneth Scott Latourette, *World Service*, p. 22.

"I chewed one for about an hour...": *Fragments*, p. 62.

"all the diplomacy I had learned...": *Tumbleweed*, p. 89.

"They didn't suspect...": *Fragments*, p. 63.

"I have never seen in an old man...": *Little Mandate*, MHA.

"Boris was wounded": "Went Through Terror of Russia's Red Revolution," *The Daily Gleaner*, Nov. 26, 1932, MHA.

"Your husband is sick...": *Fragments*, p. 63.

About 6,000 Russians had appealed...: David Footman, *Civil War in Russia*, p. 201.

10

Great Britain

1919

The journey from Murmansk was heart wrenching. "One leaves his country," Catherine wrote.

> He becomes a refugee. . . He flees the fatherland, the one he loves, the one that means so much to him. He was born in it; he absorbed everything about its customs and ways. Suddenly he is compelled to enter a strange and foreign land.

The ship's destination was London, but when Boris' condition deteriorated, medical personnel removed him at the Port of Leith in Edinburgh and transferred him to a military hospital. The rubles Catherine brought from Russia were practically worthless, so she sold a few pieces of jewelry that she had stashed in her luggage. Realizing that it would be foolish to squander the jewels on daily living expenses, she found a job as a nurse's aide in the hospital where Boris was, and each week, she set aside money for train tickets that would eventually take them to London. She later recalled that they stayed in Edinburgh six months. It was probably six weeks or less.

London in the fall of 1919 bustled with cyclists, horse-driven carts, trams, taxis, and steam-lorries. Chimneys spewed out soot, and dense fog created dark shadows and chilling dampness. Wartime rationing remained in effect, and a severe housing shortage left Catherine and Boris homeless. Catherine turned to friends she had met through the YMCA in Murmansk, and they offered temporary lodging in servants' quarters on the top floor of a YMCA hostel on Bedford Place. "When I arrived in England, my life was such a hell that I almost drowned myself," she later confessed.

While Boris recuperated, Catherine searched for work. Her broken English branded her an immigrant, and lack of experience barred her from the most menial jobs. She eventually found work at the Russian Red Cross where she sewed underwear for the White Russian Army. It was a depressing existence. London newspapers carried harrowing stories about Bolsheviks roasting White Russians alive, raping young women to death, and stamping sacred icons into the mud. Nightmares plagued Catherine and she developed the compulsion to hide food in secret places. Her only moments of peace came after work when she stopped at the Catholic church she passed on her way home. "One time," she admitted, "in a moment of total desperation, I prayed to heaven to take my life or give me some reason for living."

Catherine believed God answered her prayer when she discovered that the Sisters of Sion, who ran the school she had attended in Egypt, had a convent on Chepstow Villas in the Bayswater section of London. Catherine visited the nuns, and to her astonishment, she met one of her former teachers. Childhood memories rushed back: What happened to the little girl who scrubbed the red pain off the crucifix? What happened to her sense of awe at stories a young nun told about the Blessed Mother and St. Francis of Assisi? What happened to her promise to offer her life for priests? Or her desire to become part of the Catholic Church? At age 12, Catherine had not understood the schism between Orthodoxy and Roman Catholicism, and her parents deliberately steered her back to Orthodoxy. Now, the choice was hers. Drawn by a spiritual force she could never adequately describe other than to say it was a movement of God in her soul, Catherine chose Roman Catholicism. "I always had the intuition that there was something God wanted me to do," she insisted.

Her compatriots found Catherine's decision incomprehensible. Historically, Russians held deep animosity toward Catholics, Jesuits, and the Papacy. Russian national identity and Orthodoxy were so intertwined on a political, cultural, and intellectual level that many Russians considered Catherine's alliance with the Catholic Church a betrayal. "You change your religion, that meant you are disloyal to your own people," explained a Russian friend. "It is not a question of just religion. It is your family, your education. You can't just throw it all away and say forget it."

Yet, on Thursday, November 27, 1919, in the chapel of the Sisters of Sion, Catherine knelt before 70-year-old Father Gilbert Higgins, CRL, a gentle Irish priest with white hair and deep blue eyes. Placing her hand on the book of the Gospels, she pledged obedience to the Roman Pontiff and belief in the doctrines of the Roman Catholic Church, admitting that she had erred in the past "inasmuch as I have held and believed doctrines opposed to her teaching."

Despite the strong abjuration, Catherine never felt as if she had renounced Orthodoxy. She saw herself as a blend of Eastern and Western spirituality. "Pursued by the good Lord from the banks of the Nile to the banks of the Neva, and from the banks of the Neva to those of the Thames, the happy convert wishes now to work with all her strength for the reunion of the Russian Church with the Roman Church," Father Higgins proclaimed during the ceremony.

Catherine later acknowledged the influence of the 19th century Russian philosopher, Vladimir Soloviev, who regarded Orthodoxy and Catholicism as an equal and inseparable part of what he called "the Universal Church." The Church had divided over human and political factors, Soloviev insisted, but a spiritual bond remained. "I would say that I am simply a product of Soloviev," Catherine confessed. She recalled how her parents discussed Soloviev's philosophy, and how Theodore read aloud from Soloviev's works. Soloviev believed the East and West would reunite, not through the conversion of one side to the other, but through mutual acceptance. It was a subtle distinction that few in either Church recognized or understood at the time.

Catherine told Father Higgins that she wanted to translate

Catholic doctrines into Russian. She believed that her compatriots would overcome political and social prejudices if they saw the spiritual side of Catholicism as she had. Through Father Higgins and the Sisters of Sion, Catherine started transcribing material from French to Russian for Father Michel d'Herbigny, the controversial French Jesuit, who would soon become a Bishop and advisor to Pope Pius XI.

Boris did not share Catherine's commitment to Catholicism. He wanted to return to Russia and join the White Army under General Wrangel. When he inquired at the Russian Embassy about travel permits, a member of the diplomatic staff noticed the de Hueck family crest on his ring. In a dramatic gesture, the official slammed his hand on the table to show that his ring and Boris' were identical. Identifying himself as Walter de Hueck, a distant uncle from Riga, he persuaded Boris to stay in London and work at the Embassy as an assistant to the Financial Attaché, who was organizing supplies in England for the White Russian Armies. Walter de Hueck also promised Catherine a job if she learned secretarial skills. In January 1920, she enrolled in correspondence courses at Pitman's Secretarial School, and within a few months, the Embassy hired her.

Catherine and Boris lived comfortably on their combined incomes. They moved into a furnished flat at 28 Pembridge Gardens in Notting Hill, and hired a Russian girl, named Dunia Vassova, who had emigrated with them from Murmansk, as a live-in maid. Walter de Hueck drew them into the social life of the Russian community. They sold Russian war bonds to support the White Russian Armies, raised money for the Russian Red Cross, and assisted Russian émigrés, who had fled the Bolsheviks with only the clothes on their backs.

One of Catherine's closest friends during this time was Maria da Luz, a young Portuguese woman, who had come to London after the death of her father the year before. Together, they frequented the Jesuit church at Farm Street, where rousing sermons on society's ills by the famous Father Bernard Vaughan, SJ, moved wealthy men and women to put expensive jewelry and large bills into the collection plate.

The fledgling Catholic Evidence Guild also made a lasting impression on Catherine. Trained as street orators, Guild members proclaimed the Catholic faith to crowds peppered with drunks, bigots, and skeptics near the Marble Arch in Hyde Park. "Our lectures usually took around fifteen minutes," recalled Frank Sheed, one of the most talented Guild members. "In the rest of the hour the crowd questioned us. Upon the papacy and Church history generally we had week after week, year after year, as unsparing a viva voce examination as has been known in the world — every charge ever brought against a Pope was leered at us, sneered at us. And from the beginning we were bound to the strictest honesty — there must be no bluffing or sidestepping."

If Catherine had any illusions about Catholicism, the speeches in the park dispelled them. Guild speakers admitted to the distressingly human side of the Church, acknowledging the Spanish Inquisition and other scandals throughout Church history. They pointed out that every Catholic, including the Pope, publicly confesses at Mass that he or she has sinned. "Our aim," Sheed explained, "was to show why we, knowing the worst — knowing indeed a worse worst than they themselves knew — still knew ourselves in union with Christ. However ill he might be served by his representative at any time, we could still find in his Church, as no where else, life and truth and the possibility of union with him to the limit of our willingness."

During this time, Catherine also met the Nobel prize winning Indian poet, Rabindranath Tagore, whose arrival in London that May prompted a round of teas, dinners, and social gatherings. Rich in spiritual imagery, Tagore's poetry portrayed God as a living reality, a friend, a father, and sometimes as a passionate lover. He believed that one discovered God through prayer, through nature, and through the performance of ordinary duties and service to others. Tagore's ideas reflected all Catherine had learned about God from her parents and the nuns, and in her naive enthusiasm, she impulsively asked, "How it is possible that you are not a Christian?"

"Child," Tagore replied, "I am waiting for you to become one."

The words stung, but it remained a lesson in real Christianity that Catherine never forgot.

Catherine's involvement with Catholicism gradually influenced Boris, and on June 11, 1920, he knelt before Father Henry Blake, OSC, in Our Lady of Sorrows church to make the same profession of faith Catherine had made six months before.

Catherine and Boris' lives had changed, not only in a spiritual sense, but also in the revitalization of their marriage. Photos show them entertaining friends in their apartment, playing board games, walking in the park and sight-seeing in London. Street shots of Boris with a bowler hat, vested suit and cane make him look more British than Russian. Catherine appears ravishing in brimmed hats, veiled hats, and stylish coats and dresses. The only thing missing from their lives was a baby, but doctors assured Catherine that only a miracle could undo damage caused by tuberculosis and starvation, which left her sterile. Catherine prayed for a miracle, and promised that if she did become pregnant, she would consecrate the child to the Blessed Virgin.

That summer, the Bolsheviks defeated General Deniken's White forces and the remnants of Wrangel's army retreated further south. By September, Catherine and Boris lost their jobs when the White Russian Embassy closed. They moved to a smaller flat at 52 Tregunter, and tried to find work in an economy that had plunged downward. Their Russian maid, Dunia, found outside jobs, and gave her wages to Catherine to help pay the rent. By November, Boris was still unemployed and Catherine worked in a laundry. She felt constantly nauseous and so tired that she could barely function, but her doctor attributed it to nervous tension. When the strange symptoms did not go away, her astonished physician finally confirmed that she was pregnant. "Evidently things that cannot happen, do happen to you," he exclaimed.

The news forced Catherine and Boris to make a decision

about their future. They had no hope of ever returning to Russia. Catherine's father and Guido de Hueck both wanted them to return to Finland, where Theodore had re-established his insurance business and Guido had opened new cotton mills. Neither Catherine nor Boris wanted to go. Boris also had a job offer in India, but Catherine ruled it out because of the heat. In December, a chance encounter with H.B. Dunnington-Grubb and his wife, Lorrie Alfreda, opened another option. The Dunnington-Grubbs were highly acclaimed landscape architects, who had emigrated to Toronto in 1911, and launched a successful gardening and landscape business there. They had returned to London for the Royal horticultural shows, and noticed Boris sketching some of the displays. Impressed with his work, they offered him a position in Toronto as a draftsman.

The geography and climate of Canada with its vast plains, mountains and rivers seemed similar to Russia. "Houses are usually heated by a furnace, which does away with a large number of fires," *The Times* reported, "and modern kitchen stoves, washing machines, and similar household conveniences are much more in general use than they are over here." The cost of living was low, and the Dunnington-Grubbs promised to pay their passage. When Catherine insisted that under no circumstances would she leave London without Dunia, the Dunnington-Grubbs agreed to pay Dunia's passage, too.

Plans were set for them to sail for Canada in March, but with only a few weeks until their departure, Catherine tripped while shopping at Selfridges and fell down a flight of stairs. Fearing a miscarriage, her doctor ordered bed rest and questioned whether Catherine could endure an ocean voyage. Catherine remained adamant, however, that they proceed with their plans. On March 19, 1921, Dunia and Boris followed as seamen carried Catherine aboard the S.S. *Minnedosa* on a stretcher. The crossing was uneventful, and after seven days at sea, Catherine, Boris, and Dunia watched from the deck as the North American shoreline appeared on the horizon. They all had great hopes for a new life, hopes that would gradually crumble and decay.

Chapter Notes

"One leaves his country...": *Doubts*, p. 91-92.

Chimneys spewed out...: "London Air Dirtiest in England," *New York Times*, Sept. 15, 1919.

Wartime rationing remained in effect...: "Cost of Living Still Rising," *The Times*, London, Oct. 16, 1919.

"When I arrived in England...": NM correspondence, MHA.

"One time, in a moment of total desperation...": *Ibid.*

"I always had the intuition...": *Fragments*, p. 66.

"You change your religion...": Interview, Anatole Avtzine.

"on Thursday, November 27...": "House Journal," Nov. 27, 1919, Sisters of Sion Archives, Bayswater, London. [Note: Catherine's reception into the Catholic Church was recorded in the Diocesan Convert Register on Dec. 31, 1919. Westminster Diocesan Archives, London.]

"inasmuch as I have held and believed...": Ethelred Taunton, *The Law of the Church: Cyclopaedia of Canon Law for English-speaking Countries*, pp. 256-257. Cf. Instruction by the Sacred Congregation of the Holy Office on July 20, 1859.

"Pursued by the good Lord...": "Newsletter," Nov. 1919, Sisters of Sion Archives, Bayswater, London.

"I would say that I am simply a product of Soloviev": Panel Discussion on Soloviev by Dr. Karl Stern, Helene Iswolsky, and Catherine Doherty, Aug. 24, 1964, transcribed tape, MHA.

Father Michel d'Herbigny...: In 1919, d'Herbigny was on the faculty at a Belgian seminary. He also organized Catholic aid programs for Russian refugees in France and Belgium with the hope of bringing Russian converts into the Catholic Church. He visited London occasionally to give retreats to the Sisters of Sion. In 1921, d'Herbigny moved to Rome, and became an advisor to Pope Pius XI, who named him President of the Pontifical Oriental Institute in 1922. He was ordained a bishop and traveled to Russia on a secret mission in 1926 to ordain priests. D'Herbigny viewed Orthodoxy as a dying religion, and formulated for Pius XI a policy of spiritual conquest in dealing with Russian émigrés. This policy further strained relations between Catholics and Orthodox over the next 50 years. See Léon Tretjakewitsch, *Bishop Michel d'Herbigny SJ and Russia, A Pre-Ecumenical Approach to Christian Unity*. (Hereafter *Bishop Michel d'Herbigny*).

organizing supplies in England: "Experience and Qualifications of Baron Boris de Hueck," MHA.

"Our lectures usually took...": Frank Sheed, *The Church and I*, p. 46.

"Our aim...": *Ibid.*, p. 63.

Tagore believed ...: B.C. Charkravorty, *Rabindranath Tagore: His Mind and Art*, pp. 40-64.

"How is it possible..." and f.: *IN ONE EAR*, p. 102.

"On June 10, 1920...": "1920 Convert Register," Westminster Diocesan Archives, London.

"but doctors assured Catherine...": NM correspondence, MHA. [Tuberculosis can cause blockage of the fallopian tubes. Interview, Frank Barbarossa, M.D.]

"Evidently things that cannot happen...": *Tumbleweed*, p. 100.

"Houses are usually heated...": "Lack of Women in Canada," *The Times*, London, Mar. 30, 1920.

"set sail on March 19...": Employment and Immigration Canada to Emile Briere, Dec. 13, 1990.

11

The Dominion of Canada

1921

As the S.S. *Minnedosa* inched its way into the harbor at St. John, New Brunswick, Boris penned a post card to Catherine's brother:

Dear Serge, Today we safely reached [North] America. In an hour we will feel it under our feet. We will stop in St. John for a day or two for Catherine, then we will carry on.

The ship docked at Sand Point on the west side of the city where large sheds served as immigration centers. Father George Daly, CSSR, waited on the pier to welcome the Catholics on board. Newspaper reporters, alerted by the steamship company that the passenger list included Russian nobility, also waited to interview Catherine and Boris. The intricacies of Russia's Tchin system of nobility must have confused the reporters. Unlike European feudal nobility that uses titles, the Russians had numerical ranks. Although both the de Hueck and Kolyschkine families held hereditary nobility, neither had a title. Yet according to Catherine, when she and Boris disembarked: "Every newspaper man was around like a bee and everybody called us Baron and Baroness."

By the time the train carrying Catherine and Boris steamed into Toronto's Union Station, Boris had decided to use the title "Baron." Catherine resisted and used the name Mrs. C. Hook for several months until she finally succumbed. "As far as I am concerned, it was Boris who organized the whole thing," she insisted.

Boris eventually claimed that Peter the Great bestowed the title on his family in the 18th century, a story that left Walter de Hueck completely astounded:

> I don't understand your explanations about legalizing the title and obtaining legal papers for it! About which "Title" are you talking? Guido told us that newspapers are calling Katia "Baroness." Is it possible that Boris legalized this title in an official way? If so, my congratulations!

While the title was probably not legitimate, it served them well in Toronto, a city that derived its name from an Indian word meaning "place of meeting," but a city not known for warmth or hospitality. The staunchly conservative Protestants in Toronto society held Catholics in disdain. The Irish Catholics in the city held equally negative views toward Protestants. "They called it the Belfast of Canada," one Torontonian recalled, "because it had the same close, bitterness toward others."

Catholics and Protestants shared one common view: a mutual dislike of immigrants, particularly Slavic immigrants, who emigrated to Canada in the early 1900's to escape persecution by the Tsar. By 1921, over 10,000 Russians and Ukrainians lived in the Toronto slums, where they eagerly consumed pamphlets smuggled into Canada by the newly formed Communist Party in New York City. While Catherine claimed she and Boris were the first Russians in Toronto, she meant the first members of the nobility. Within days of their arrival, *The Toronto Globe* reported:

> A Russian Baron with lively recollections of the overthrow of the Czars, the paralysis of the Russian army, the uprising of the Bolsheviks, and the terrors of the "White" regime in Finland has just come to this city. Here he hopes to improve his fortunes, which received a hard blow at the hands of the "Reds." Baron Boris de Hueck, who crossed the Atlantic from London on the *Minnedosa*, is a member of the Russian Academy of Architecture and of the British Association of Archi-

tects, and has associated himself here with Mr. H.B. Dunnington-Grubb, the garden architect.

Engraved invitations to dinners and teas started arriving at their apartment on Glen Road, and Catherine discovered that she could hold people spellbound with stories about Russia, the war, and the revolution. While she appreciated the invitations, she also sensed that she and Boris were in the same positions as the Pashas in Egypt, whose names appeared on guest lists because they served as a diversion, a curiosity from another culture, an entertainment, but she knew that Toronto society would never really accept them. "To reject means not to accept," she later wrote.

> It is an amazing thing how rejection can hurt beyond any other state or emotion. To be rejected, not to be accepted, is to enter a dark, tragic garden that appears to be all evil. There is nothing about it that appears to be normal. No, it is all surrealistic.

Mrs. Harris McPhedran, the wife of a prominent Toronto physician, known as "a friend of the friendless," proved to be a remarkable exception. A member of St. Paul's Anglican Church, Mrs. McPhedran did not fit the rigid mold of society matron, and she helped Catherine ease the transition into a new life in a new country. "When I first came to Canada, her house was my other home," Catherine recalled.

Within two weeks of their arrival, Catherine also arranged for a private meeting with Archbishop Neil McNeil, the 70-year-old Roman Catholic prelate, who had, like Mrs. McPhedran, cut through Toronto's prejudice barrier. Known as "the best Presbyterian in Toronto," McNeil never refused a person in need no matter what their creed or nationality. Catherine poured out her soul to McNeil. She depended upon him as a spiritual father, and he recognized in her a deepening spirituality that she did not comprehend herself at that early stage.

In late May, Catherine and Boris bought a brick bungalow with a large front porch and a small grassy yard at 60 Nairn

Avenue, a new development on the northern edge of the city that bordered farmland. Maple saplings lined the street, and they could walk to St. Clare's Catholic church a few blocks away. "The price was $2,500, and we could buy it for $20 a month," Catherine recalled. "We couldn't buy furniture, but people were very generous and donated some."

Six weeks later, on July 17, 1921, Catherine gave birth to a nine pound baby boy in Toronto General Hospital. Father Edward McCabe, pastor at St. Clare's Catholic church, baptized George Theodore Mario de Hueck on August 14, and as promised, Catherine consecrated the infant to the Blessed Virgin. Henry Baldwin, a prominent Toronto political figure served as godfather. Catherine's Portuguese friend from London, Maria da Luz Caupers, was godmother by proxy.

Photos of Catherine during this time show a radiant young mother, a little heavier than in Russia, but still beautiful with her long blond hair cut in curls around her face and pulled into a bun. Her happiness evaporated when Boris lost his job with the Dunnington-Grubbs, and they plunged into a financial crisis so severe that the bank threatened to repossess the house. Dunia, who was restricted under immigration laws from taking a job for a year, stayed with the baby while Catherine found a job as a maid at a nearby farm for a meager salary and fresh milk. Father McCabe helped by paying Catherine to clean St. Clare's church, and she later found a job dipping chocolates in a candy factory.

Why Boris lost his job after such a short time remains a mystery. The economy had fallen into a deep recession, but a family member claimed Boris didn't find the job "congenial." Catherine later explained that Boris was sick, and while he did suffer frequent respiratory infections, it appears as if his compulsion for other women also resurfaced. Catherine tried to ignore the infidelities as she had in Russia, but in a later journal, she listed women from the Russian community, some married, some single, with whom Boris had affairs.

In November 1921, after months of unemployment, Boris

finally took a job as an engineer with the Toronto Carpet company. The founder of the company, F. Barry Hayes, invited Catherine and Boris to social events at his home, and through him, Catherine met Dr. Walter H. McKeown, a surgeon on the staff at St. Michael's Hospital, who had powerful connections in Ottawa. McKeown helped Catherine cut through the bureaucracy of Canadian immigration, and in the summer of 1922, her 17-year-old brother, Serge, arrived in Toronto on a student visa. He expected to find Catherine and Boris living in luxury, but wrote home that they were "very poor and lived on tomatoes from the garden."

Serge was only in Canada ten months when a telegram brought news that Theodore had collapsed from a heart attack and died in Emma's arms. Serge returned to Finland at once. Catherine urged him to bring Emma and André back to Canada, but Emma decided to move to Belgium where one of Theodore's former business associates promised to help her settle Theodore's estate. The unscrupulous business agent cheated Emma out of commissions Theodore earned, and left her in such a tenuous financial situation that she had to rely on aid programs for Russian refugees to pay for André's schooling. Catherine, who had taken a higher paying job in the mail order department at Eaton's department store, started sending money to her mother.

During these years, Catherine also helped Russian artists and intellectuals who arrived in Canada without language or job skills. Although she was only 26 years old, she became known as "the mother of Toronto's Russian Aristocratic colony" because she met the émigrés at the train station and took them into her home until they could find jobs and a place to live. Beyond the refugees' physical needs, Catherine also worried about their spiritual needs. Her hopes of leading Russians into the Catholic Church had repeatedly ended in failure. Even her brother, Serge, had shown an aversion to the Catholic Church, and Catherine concluded that Russians needed to worship in their native language. St. Josaphat the Martyr Church on Franklin Avenue had the trappings of Orthodoxy with icons and gold altars, but priests celebrated the Divine Liturgy in Greek. Catholics had Latin Masses, and Protestants worshipped in English, leaving homesick Russians with no place where they felt spiritually connected.

Catherine wanted to start a Russian Orthodox church, an idea inconceivable to Roman Catholics. Yet the far-sighted Archbishop McNeil not only gave Catherine permission, he presented her with a chalice for the Russians to use. With the help of Mrs. McPhedran and some Protestant society women, Catherine sought donations from prominent businessmen. When they raised enough for a down-payment on a wood frame house at the corner of Clarence Square and Spadina, Catherine begged for donations of coal to heat the house and building materials to convert the downstairs into a sanctuary. The upstairs bedrooms served as temporary lodgings for new refugees, and the third floor became living quarters for the Russian Orthodox priest.

On March 9, 1924, more than two hundred Russians stood through a two-hour dedication ceremony celebrated by the Russian Orthodox Archbishop Theophile of Chicago. One reporter noted the "eagerness with which these émigrés drank in every word uttered by the primate." Outside, Bolshevik sympathizers protested "this revival of the old order of things."

As news of Catherine's involvement with the Russian Church spread, criticism by Catholics mounted. "I hear they are flagellating you," Archbishop McNeil noted. Even Harry Baldwin, the godfather of Catherine's son, asked if Catherine had become "fed-up with the vulgarities of the Roman Catholics of Toronto" and returned to her mother church.

Catherine dispelled Baldwin's fears, and he apologized profusely, admitting that Toronto was "the most bigoted city in the world (and) I include Toronto Catholics, who head the list of complacent intolerants."

In the weeks that followed, Catherine organized a Russian bazaar in the home of Mrs. John Baird Laidlaw to raise money for a Russian community center with a health clinic and a library. During the festivities, Catherine appeared in Russian costume with several other émigrés, who sang folk songs, served tea from samovars, and sold embroidery. Newspapers called the bazaar a smashing success, and photos of a smiling Catherine provide no hint that she had recently discovered Boris had been carrying on a secret love affair with a Russian émigré Catherine had befriended.

Claudia Kartzoff Kolenova, a former dancer with the Imperial Corps de Ballet in St. Petersburg, had fled Russia after the revolution and roamed through Europe until she obtained immigration papers for Canada. When Catherine first met Claudia at Toronto's Union Station in November 1923, she realized that this graceful young woman, who spoke only Russian and French, would have difficulty adjusting. Catherine brought Claudia home to help Dunia care for little George, never suspecting that Claudia and Boris would betray her under her own roof.

Claudia was the same age as Catherine, but in temperament and appearance they were opposites. Petite, with dark auburn hair, violet eyes and porcelain features, Claudia became known as "the fairest of the exiles." She dreamed of returning to the stage. "I long for the footlights," she told a reporter. "Never a night but I dance in my room."

Rumors about Boris and Claudia oozed through the Russian community, and into Toronto society. Catherine felt so humiliated that she would leave the house at night after putting little George to bed, and spend hours weeping in the darkness of St. Clare's church. One night she fell asleep, and when she woke she felt as if God spoke "telling me He loved me, to be patient, that He would settle things in His own way."

The tragedy intensified when Boris lost his job, and they had to live on the $12 salary Catherine earned at Eaton's department store. Boris caused Catherine even more humiliation when he spent $75 raised through the sale of embroidery at the Russian bazaar, and Catherine had no way of repaying the money.

When Father McCabe, the pastor of St. Clare's, learned about Catherine's plight, he offered to pay her train fare to New York City, with the hope that she might find a better job there and move with Boris and George away from the scandals in Toronto. Sometime in the late spring of 1924, Catherine left three-year-old George with Dunia and boarded a train for New York.

Chapter Notes

"*Dear Serge...*": Boris de Hueck to Serge Kolychkine, Mar. 28, 1921, MHA.

"*Every newspaper man was around...*": "The Lady They Call the B," *World Religions*, produced by Mike McManus, TVOntario, Dec. 7, 1973.

"*As far as I am concerned...*": CD to G de H, Dec. 16, 1965, MHA.

"*I don't understand your explanations...*": Walter de Hueck to Boris and Catherine, Feb. 25, 1925, MHA.

"*place of meeting*": Karl Baedeker, *The Dominion of Canada, Handbook for Travelers*, p. 209.

"*They called it the Belfast of Canada...*": Interview, Olga LaPlante Charlton.

"*ten thousand Russians...*": "Revolution in Toronto's Russian Colony," *Toronto Star Weekly*, Dec. 3, 1921.

"*A Russian Baron with lively recollections...*": "Says Russian Trade Pact is Only Political Dodge...," *Toronto Globe*, Apr. 4, 1921.

"*To reject means not to accept...*": *Doubts*, p. 71.

"*a friend of the friendless*": "Mrs. H. M'Phedran is Widely Mourned," *Toronto Mail*, Mar. 6, 1934.

"*When I first came to Canada...*": "Mrs. Harris M'Phedran Dies," *Toronto Star*, Mar. 6, 1934.

a private meeting with Archbishop Neil McNeil: Archdiocese of Toronto Chancery Office to C de H, Apr. 9, 1924, MHA.

"*the best Presbyterian in Toronto*": George Boyle, *Pioneer in Purple*, Montreal: Palm Publishers, 1951, p. 207.

"*The price was $2,500...*": *Fragments*, p. 69.

"*The godfather was...*" and f.: Archdiocese of Toronto Chancery Office, Certificate of Baptism, June 12, 1980, MHA.

"*congenial*": Interview, Joan Kolychkine.

"*she made a list of women...*": Diary #9, Sept. 10, 1935, MHA.

"*very poor...*": Interview, Joan Kolychkine.

"*the mother of Toronto's Russian Aristocratic colony*": "One-Time Aristocrats of Monarchist Russia Now Toil Daily Here," *Toronto Star Daily*, Mar. 22, 1924.

"*I hear they are flagellating you*": Interview, CD by Sister Elizabeth Louise Sharum.

"*fed-up with the vulgarities...*": Harry Baldwin to C de H, Mar. 6, 1924, MHA.

"*the most bigoted city...*": Harry Baldwin to C de H, Mar. 22, 1924, MHA.

"*the fairest of the exiles*": "One-Time Aristocrats of Monarchist Russia Now Toil Daily Here," *Toronto Star Daily*, Mar. 22, 1924.

"*I long for the footlights...*": *Ibid.*

"*telling me He loved me...*": JC, "Confidential Notebook," Apr. 19, 1953, MHA.

12

New York City

1924

Catherine stood on the sidewalk outside Grand Central Station, and looked up at the Manhattan skyline. "You do not frighten me," she exclaimed. "I'll conquer you."

"Atta girl!" a passerby laughed.

Catherine did not conquer New York. She became one of the thousands of eager young women who discover the ugly side of America that hates immigrants and exploits lower class women. "Oh, you're a Polack," prospective employers scowled. "Can you speak English?"

Catherine finally found a job in a laundry on 14th Street. "I was put on ironing sheets, double sheets, single sheets, and the damn, constant heat that emanated from them made me feel dizzy." She slept at Ma Murphy's on Charles Street, where working girls shared third floor bedrooms. The rent was $1 a week and the girls slept three to a bed, six to a room. Catherine remembered "just about enough space between those beds for a wash stand, an old-fashioned basin and a pitcher, and a couple of chairs, an old-fashioned dresser, and nails on the wall to hang our clothes on."

"This was a strange period in my life," she later wrote.

> Every time we finished work we walked into a strange loneliness, a terrible loneliness. There is no greater loneliness than being in a crowd of people you don't know. The laundry girls and I lived in a profound, collective poverty.

From this poverty grew camaraderie among the women. They walked to work and bought breakfast from a street vendor who sold bagels and coffee. On their way home, they stopped at a cheap diner. The long hours combined with starchy meals left them constantly hungry, and Catherine admitted that one of the greatest temptations the girls faced was giving in to the sailors and longshoremen, who waited on the sidewalk promising money and a good meal "just to have a lay with you."

Catherine didn't last long at the laundry or at Ma Murphy's where "the ghost of starvation" haunted her.

> That ghost of starvation lived somewhere in me. I don't know exactly where it lived, but whenever I was hungry, it rose to the surface. It rose up and seemed to laugh. The ghost of starvation laughing! Hunger laughing! But that's how I felt sometimes.

She found a job as a waitress where she had unlimited access to food, but discovered a different kind of sexual exploitation by customers: "One of them started pawing me all over my bosom and back. For this I received $10. I quietly went into the bathroom, took off my waitress uniform, put on my own clothes, and walked away."

At another restaurant, the owner threatened to hold Catherine's wages if she refused to go to Coney Island with him. She left without the money.

"One night during this period, I found myself on the Brooklyn Bridge," she confessed, "and I experienced a powerful temptation to end my life."

From the bridge she saw giant skyscrapers on Wall Street where property sold for $600 per square foot. She also saw the East Side tenements that lined dark, narrow streets. An old mission near the waterfront had the words "JESUS SAVES" painted on the walls in large block-letters. Catherine felt like a failure, and the water seemed to offer an escape. "The call of the water was very powerful," she later wrote.

I found a space between the wires where I could slip through. I looked down and prepared to jump. Do you know what I saw? I saw Christ mirrored in the water! In a panic I stopped, turned and ran. I ran down the bridge so fast that a policeman yelled, "Hey, lady, slow down! You're shoving people around!" I was running away from the vision, which probably was no vision at all. But at that moment it was very real to me, and it saved my life.

Catherine stayed in New York a very short time — probably less than four weeks — and her memories mix together in a disjointed string of stories with no clear sense of time or place. Each incident reverberates with isolation and emotional pain.

"I stood in the midst of New York, friendless, shelterless, hungry," she wrote four years later, and she admitted that the experience stole her faith in humanity. She told how a Catholic nun peered at her through a crack in the convent door and said, "Go to Catholic Charities." When Catherine replied that she did not know where Catholic Charities was, the nun said, "Well, I cannot help you," and shut the door.

She spent a night in a Bowery mission, where a stern Christian woman assumed she was a prostitute and treated her in a harsh, judgmental way. She stood penniless in front of a restaurant when a Jewish cab driver stopped and asked if she were hungry. After Catherine poured out her story, he took her home to his wife, who fed her and helped her find jobs as a cleaning lady in wealthy Long Island households.

"In those days you got fifty cents for a whole day's work," Catherine recalled.

That was very little money. And yet the lady who hired me wanted to see my purse before I left. She said to me, "Catherine, do you object to opening your purse? I'm not a very trustful person." I said, "No Madam, I don't object." I opened my purse and the only thing in it was a handkerchief. I added the fifty cents she had given me.

> She said, "You have nothing in your purse." I said, "No
> Madam, I have nothing in the purse except the fifty cents
> you gave me for ten hours of work."

Catherine later admitted that she had seen poverty in Russia,
but had not really understood until she experienced it herself as
Katie the Polack. This kind of poverty possessed so much power
that it gripped her in its dehumanizing force and almost destroyed her. She survived, but just barely, and when she returned
to Toronto in humiliating defeat, she had to face Boris, who
blamed her for breaking the family tie by going to New York.
Weighed down by feelings of failure and frustration, she returned
to her job at Eaton's and contacted Marietta LaDell, Canada's
popular elocutionist and impersonator.

A few weeks before Catherine left for New York, Miss LaDell
had asked her to give an impromptu talk at an afternoon tea in her
apartment. Catherine agreed, and a few days later, Marietta
LaDell offered her a contract for a fall lecture tour with the
Community Chautauqua of Canada, a touring company that sent
entertainment, cultural events, and lecturers into small towns in
rural Canada. It was modeled after the highly acclaimed
Chautauqua Institution in upstate New York. By 1924, over 100
traveling Chautauqua companies performed in towns and villages throughout North America. Most operated only in the
summer, but a few, like the one Marietta LaDell represented,
extended programs into fall and winter seasons.

"I have great faith in your ability and message." Miss LaDell
told Catherine.

> You have that and all of the God given gifts that make it
> possible to "hitch your wagon to a Star." Chautauqua
> will certainly be a stepping stone lined with gold. This
> is a prophecy that I expect to come true. Of course it's
> hard work, but you are young — good to look at, of rare
> intelligence and have "food for thought" and while the
> Chautauqua movement is naturally for communities

remote from the hum of the city, it is an "Outdoor University" bringing instructive entertainment, music, lectures, etc., etc., to the small towns.

Miss LaDell promised Catherine a weekly salary of $75-$100 for a 12-week tour, but Catherine refused the offer because she did not want to leave home for three months. Instead, she went to New York City in a futile attempt to find a permanent job and save her marriage. When that dream shattered, the Chautauqua became Catherine's only hope of solving the financial problems she and Boris faced. Catherine signed the contract.

Her opening date was set for Monday, September 29 in Sudbury, Ontario. It marked the start of another journey that would lead Catherine from a life of obscurity toward a glittering world of fame, a world she was not prepared to enter.

Chapter Notes

"You do not frighten me...": *Fragments*, p. 73.

"Atta girl!": *Ibid.*

"Oh, you're a Polack...": *Gospel of a Poor Woman*, p. 42.

"I was put on ironing sheets...": *Ibid.*, p. 14.

"just about enough space...": *Little Mandate*, MHA.

"This was a strange period...": *Fragments*, p. 74.

"just to have a lay with you.": *Gospel of a Poor Woman*, p. 9.

"That ghost of starvation lived...": *Fragments*, pp. 74-75.

"One of them started pawing me...": *Ibid.*, p. 79.

"One night during this period...": *Ibid.*, p. 76.

"The call of the water...": *Ibid.*, p. 77.

"I stood in the midst of New York...": C de H to Mrs. A.M. Hadden, Apr. 19, 1928, MHA.

"Go to Catholic Charities" and f.: *IN ONE EAR*, p. 118-119.

"In those days you got fifty cents...": *Gospel of a Poor Woman*, p. 66.

"breaking the family tie...": Diary #4, Jan. 3, 1930, MHA.

"I have great faith in your ability...": Marietta LaDell to C de H, Apr. 8, 1924, MHA.

13

The Chautauqua Circuit
1924

Catherine trembled during her opening speech in Sudbury. Dressed in a black silk gown with a jeweled headband across her forehead, she talked about Russia, its vast land area, diverse climates, and rich natural resources. She spoke of her childhood on the family estate in Tambov, and her harrowing adventures in the war and revolution. She told how she and Boris had nearly starved to death at the hands of Finnish Communists.

> Half way through my story I began to cry. I was talking of my father at the time, but I wasn't weeping because of his death. I was weeping through sheer nervousness and a sleepless night and the thought that nobody here in Canada could possibly be interested in what had happened to a girl in distant Russia so many years before. I couldn't stop crying. And, strange to say, hundreds of people started crying with me.

From Sudbury, Catherine traveled to Killarney, Manitoba, where she began a grueling run of over 50 small towns. She gave the same lecture in each town, and afterward, she rated herself: "Very good. . . O horrors. . . So So. . . not bad. . . wonderful. . . nothing special. . . O Lord!"

Newspaper clips show, however, that her lectures grew in power and polish. Her magnetic stage presence created an emotional bond that Catherine called *"podusham,"* a Russian word meaning soul-to-soul with self-revealing intimacy./"Baroness gained the sympathy of her audience by her charming, unassuming manner," one reporter noted. Another wrote of her youthful appearance, "with the fair hair, deep blue eyes, and clear complexion characteristic of her country. She is of strong, graceful build and boasts vigorous health."

Catherine's performance was part of a three-day program that took place in a Protestant church or high school auditorium. She appeared at 3:30 p.m. on the afternoon of the third day following an all-female string ensemble with a coloratura soprano. On the evening of the third day, Marietta LaDell performed comedy skits and character impersonations. Throughout the 12-week tour, the third day talent traveled together in an eight-passenger Packard supplied by the Chautauqua company. If they arrived early in the next town, they gave free talks at a Kiwanis Club luncheon or high school assembly to boost ticket sales. At dawn, they packed their bags and drove to the next stop.

"No matter how hard conditions were we would manage to get through without a nervous breakdown if we had congenial traveling companions," recalled a Chautauqua veteran.

"The custom of humoring yourself, of indulging in small, unimportant acts that you believed essential to your happiness and well-being. You got rid of those," another performer confessed. "You forgot all your funny inhibitions about what you could and could not eat. . . You ate pretty much what was set before you. Ate it or went hungry."

Chautauqua troopers joked about washed out roads, flat tires, and lost luggage. The Chautauqua companies had very stringent standards — no drinking, no smoking, no dancing, no dating — and local townsfolk watched the performers scrupulously. "Rarely did we sleep at the hotels (which were terribly inadequate anyhow, especially on the prairies)," Catherine noted.

Staying with local families gave Catherine a deeper understanding of how towns depended on farmers, and farmers depended on decent crops. An entire region could drop to poverty levels in a single season of drought. She also saw the goodness of the people, who hungered for knowledge and self-improvement. She listened to their problems, and tried to help.

"Yes, it is truly an angel who led you to my home, I'm sure, dear Baroness," wrote a woman from Webb, Saskatchewan, after Catherine sent letters on the woman's behalf to wealthy Toronto Catholics, telling them about the struggle the community faced in trying to maintain their tiny Catholic church. Within days, townspeople received $100 in donations.

While Catherine was quick to help others, she never spoke of her own heartaches. She hid letters from a Toronto woman telling her what a charming impression Claudia Kolenova made when Boris brought her to dinner parties, and she presented a distorted image of Boris as a loving husband too ill to work. The only person on the tour, who knew the truth about Boris, was Marietta LaDell, who later revealed how Catherine sent Boris between $75 and $85 every week, depriving herself of enough to meet her own expenses, yet Boris sent weekly telegrams asking for more. "I withheld these demands until after her lectures, as her worry was so great that I felt it would mar her work," Miss LaDell confessed.

In December, Catherine returned to Toronto where she faced bills from Boris' extravagant spending and the loss of the house on Nairn. In humiliation, they moved to an apartment at 2204 Queen Street East on the opposite side of the city, and Boris found a room for Claudia within walking distance. He claimed to be self-employed as an architect and engineer, but Catherine kept them afloat financially. She signed as an independent lecturer with a talent agent named Erle George, who booked her into small towns throughout Ontario, with the agreement that they would split lecture fees ranging from $40 to $75. "I note with pleasure that her female tongue is earning more than Boris' professional brain!" chided Walter de Hueck.

During that long winter of 1925, Catherine appeared in more than 50 towns and villages. "I am using the idea very strongly that your work is a direct run against the Communists and all that Communism or Red Menace stand for," Erle George told her.

News clips show that Catherine began peppering her talks

with anecdotes and examples, some highly exaggerated and some blatantly untrue, such as claims that Bolsheviks executed her brother and his wife lost her mind, or that her father died from Communist persecution, her mother died from starvation, and over 20 relatives perished during the Red terror. Sometimes Catherine attributed experiences of other Russian exiles to herself or family members. When a relative asked why she did this, Catherine insisted that she was a storyteller with a strong message. Her intentions were not deceitful, she said, but an embellishment of the truth to add interest to the story.

While small town audiences accepted her without question, people in cities remained skeptical. In scathing letters to the editor, Marxist sympathizers attacked Catherine's criticism of the Bolsheviks, pointing out that while Catherine "was spending her summer in a villa," peasants and workers struggled on starvation wages, and young intellectuals rotted in Siberian prisons. Catherine saved the clips, and in speeches, she began to acknowledge Russia's class distinctions, the privileges of the upper classes, and the hardships of peasants and workers, but she never softened her criticism of the Bolsheviks.

What Catherine called "the biggest sacrifice," during this time was her long separation from four-year-old George. Father John Milway Filion, SJ, a 46-year-old priest, who came to Toronto in 1924 as Provincial of the newly established Jesuit community, sensed the first time he met Catherine that she carried a terrible emotional burden.

"Have you a spiritual director?" he asked.

"No, Father," Catherine replied.

"Come," he said, "I want to talk to you."

Catherine opened her soul to Father Filion. "I feel that there is a spiritual courage upholding you in the midst of your trials and moral sufferings," he told her. "As I get to know more about the situation I understand more and more what your heartaches must be at times, but I believe also that it is God's way of bringing you nearer to him and preparing you for the great work he has in store for you."

In June 1925, Catherine left Toronto again, this time, for a 12-week tour of the mid-western United States with the White and Brown Chautauqua Company of Kansas City, Missouri at a salary of $125 per week. She opened in Blanchardville, Wisconsin on June 12, the fourth afternoon of a six-day program. Each day's talent still rushed from town to town, but instead of lecturing in a church or school, they performed in a brown canvas tent on the outskirts of town. "The big tent is filled with row on row of folding wooden chairs," one reporter noted. "They face in one direction toward a miniature stage at the other end, all complete with a sylvan backdrop, electric footlights, two chairs, a table, a pitcher of ice-water and a glass."

The air smelled of musty canvas, mowed grass, perfume, and perspiration. Flies and mosquitoes buzzed. "When you lecture in a large tent you are competing with a great deal of noise," Catherine recalled. "There are cows mooing in the pastures, and trains passing by. Cars were being cranked up, and babies were crying. That's how I developed my voice — by competing with all those noises!"

After two weeks on the afternoon schedule, the program manager promoted Catherine to the evening performance on the fifth night, which she found much more pleasant with cool breezes and less noise. Marietta LaDell wrote at once to congratulate her on the promotion. She had disapproved of Catherine's lecture tour the previous winter with Erle George, and warned that speaking as an independent in small towns cheapened her work. She encouraged Catherine to go to New York City and sign with one of the large lecture bureaus for the winter season.

Father George Daly, CSSR, the priest Catherine had met on the pier in New Brunswick when she and Boris first arrived in Canada, now lived in Toronto, and he also worked behind the scenes with Archbishop McNeil to find Catherine a job in New York. They wanted her to sign with the Catholic Union, a society dedicated to the reunion of the Orthodox and Roman Catholics. "I am sure this work would appeal to you more than Chautauqua work," Fr. Daly urged, "for I know your heart and soul are in this great movement that would bring the Church in your dear country back to the fold which she left centuries ago."

Catherine felt torn: How could she go to New York when her personal life remained unsettled? Boris was still unemployed, and the young Danish girl named Carla, whom Catherine hired to help Dunia care for George, wrote weekly letters that ravaged Catherine's heart. "The Baron and Mrs. Kolenova took Georgie for a drive this afternoon," Carla wrote.

> I am so sorry to see your child near that woman. She is nothing to us. Georgie is number one in this house and not her. Dunia and I do what we can to keep Georgie away from her, but when his Pappa does not help, it is pretty hard to do.

In another letter, Carla described how little George held Catherine's picture and announced: "Carla, I don't like Mrs. Kolenova any more. I like Mamma." On George's fourth birthday, Carla wrote in excruciating detail how Claudia came to celebrate. "You were there too, dear Baroness," Carla added. "Your picture was on the table that Georgie had to think of Mamma. Georgie kissed you several times and told that he loved you so much."

Father Filion tried to comfort Catherine by reminding her that God sometimes allows pain in people's lives for a purpose revealed only in the course of time. He encouraged Catherine not to judge Claudia. "God's mercy is infinite and there seems to me to be in her an inability to reason. Therefore, she may not be very responsible before God, but keep on praying for her, still more for your husband and your dear child." He also encouraged Catherine to adhere to what he called a rule of life, which was a daily schedule including prayer, work, and relaxation that gave her days a sense of order and purpose, and allowed her to move from one activity to another without getting bogged down in indecision or despair that frequently accompanies life's painful moments.

By August, the situation worsened. Carla claimed Boris undermined George's religious upbringing by taking him to Mrs. Kolenova's on Sunday morning instead of to church. Boris accused Carla of filling George with negative attitudes toward Claudia. George wanted his mother to come home. "Indeed," Carla observed. "I don't want you to be away from him any more. That is not good for him at all — his Mamma must stay with him. Both of us pray that you may be allowed to stay at home when you come back. . . ."

By the time Catherine returned to Toronto in mid-September, she had lost weight and looked like a flapper with drop waist dresses, short skirts, long beads, and high heeled shoes. If she changed her appearance as a ploy to win Boris back, it had no effect. Catherine destroyed the bulk of her journals and correspondence from this time, but Father Filion noted that the days after her return to Toronto "were amongst the most trying of your life," and Lady Bertram Windle confessed that Catherine was "the most tired looking woman I ever beheld."

Sometime that fall, Catherine and Boris moved from the Queen Street apartment to an apartment on St. Joseph Street, across from St. Michael's College. Still unemployed, Boris had squandered the money Catherine had earned. With over $2,000 in unpaid bills, including the $75 Catherine still owed from the Russian bazaar, the situation reached a breaking point in early January 1926, and Catherine moved to New York City. Archbishop McNeil and Father Daly arranged for the Catholic Union to hire her at a salary of $50 per week. She left little George in Toronto with Dunia, promising that she would bring him to New York as soon as she got settled.

Father Filion approved of the move. He referred Catherine to Father Martin Scott, SJ, for spiritual direction, and encouraged her to stop sending Boris money because it enabled him to avoid responsibility and continue his scandalous lifestyle. "I will do as you say regarding Father Scott," Catherine replied. "Perhaps he will be able to help me and solve this strange situation. I am going to try for a few months more and then I will follow your advice regarding the cutting off of the payments. Pray for me, dear Father, for you know I need it badly."

Chapter Notes

"Halfway through my story...": *Tumbleweed*, pp. 128-129.

"Very Good... O horrors... So so...": "Schedule," Fall 1924, MHA.

"...Baroness gained the sympathy of her audience": Unidentified news clip, *Times Herald*, Oct. 14, 1924, Moose Jaw, Sask., MHA.

"with the fair hair...": "Chautauqua Notes," *Prairie Times*, Oct. 9, 1924, Dodsland, Sask., MHA.

"No matter how hard conditions were...": Gay MacLaren, *Morally We Roll Along*, p. 229.

"The custom of humoring yourself...": Marian Scott, *Chautauqua Caravan*, p. 33.

"Rarely did we sleep...": *Fragments*, p. 83.

"Yes it is truly an angel...": Mrs. Turcotte to C de H, Dec. 7, 1924, MHA.

a charming impression Claudia Kolenova made...: Grace Hardy to C de H, Oct. 9, 1924 and Oct. 26, 1924, MHA.

"I withheld these demands...": Marietta LaDell to Whom it May Concern, Apr. 21, 1930, MHA.

"I note with pleasure...": Walter de Hueck to Catherine and Boris, Jan. 9, 1925, MHA.

"I am using the idea...": Erle George to C de H, n.d., MHA.

"was spending her summer in a villa...": "Replies to the Baroness," *St. Catherine's Ont. Standard*, Mar. 17, 1925, MHA.

"the biggest sacrifice...": NM correspondence, MHA.

"Have you a spiritual director?": JC, "Confidential Notebook," Apr. 19, 1953, MHA.

"I feel that there is a spiritual courage...": JMF to C de H, June 16, 1925, MHA.

"The big tent is filled...": Bruce Bliven, "Mother, Home, and Heaven," *The New Republic*, Jan. 9, 1924.

"When you lecture in a large tent...": *Fragments*, p. 85.

"I am sure this work...": Fr. George T. Daly, C.S.S.R. to C de H, June 19, 1925, MHA.

"The Baron and Mrs. Kolenova took Georgie...": Carla to C de H, June 20, 1925, MHA.

"Carla, I don't like Mrs. Kolenova...": Carla to C de H, July 9, 1925, MHA.

"You were there too...": Carla to C de H, July 20, 1925, MHA.

"God's mercy is infinite...": JMF to C de H, July 16, 1925, MHA.

"Indeed," Carla observed...: Carla to C de H, Aug. 1, 1925, MHA.

"amongst the most trying...": JMF to C de H, Feb. 15, 1926, MHA.

"the most tired looking woman...": Lady Bertram Windle to C de H, Jan. 30, 1926, MHA.

"I will do as you say...": C de H to JMF, Jan. 8, 1926, MHA.

14

New York City
1926

Catherine found an apartment with a struggling actress on Morton Street in Greenwich Village, a healthy walking distance from the Catholic Union offices at 50 Union Square. Within two weeks, Count Augustine von Galen, OSB, the Benedictine monk who founded the Catholic Union, wrote a glowing letter to Archbishop McNeil: "Already she has secured 16 appointments for lectures in different places in New York."

Catherine loved the work, and she wrote often to little George promising that when she earned enough for an apartment of her own she would bring him and Dunia to New York. Catherine's success startled Boris. Fearing that he might lose control of her, he promised to give up Claudia if Catherine brought him to New York. Catherine latched onto his promise, and asked influential New Yorkers to expedite paperwork with U.S. Immigration. When the applications remained deadlocked, she started sending Boris money again as a show of faith. Seeing it as a sign that she would still support him, Boris moved Claudia into the apartment with him on St. Joseph Street. When Catherine found out, all the hurt and humiliation of the past returned with so much fury that she directed her outrage at other men: "From all I suffered with Boris. I wanted all men to pay for that."

She fell into a pattern of leading men on and dropping them. The famous Russian tenor, Feodor Challiapin, sang love songs to her in a crowded cabaret, and she teamed up with a handsome Russian artist to dance the tango in Greenwich Village speakeasies. She frequented the Cotton Club in Harlem, where white couples flocked to hear Black jazz musicians. While attention from other men fed her bruised ego and made her feel desirable after Boris' constant rejection, another part of her recoiled at becoming a sex object. "I didn't want to give my body because I feared it wouldn't be mine anymore." Catherine became known as "The Eternal Anticipation."

In the late spring of 1926, she left New York for a grueling six weeks on the White and Brown Chautauqua at $150 per week. Afterward she took five-year-old George on a holiday at the farm of some friends. George begged to come back to New York with her, and Catherine promised that she would find some way to bring him there, but her hopes vanished when she returned to Manhattan in late July and learned her job was in jeopardy. A personal vendetta between Catherine's old friend from London, the French Jesuit Michel d'Herbigny, and her boss at the Catholic Union, Count Augustine von Galen, had reached a climax.

D'Herbigny, who served as an advisor to Pope Pius XI, had succeeded in formulating as official Church policy a plan to convert Orthodox émigrés to Roman Catholicism through pros- elytizing and "spiritual conquest." Galen and the Catholic Union promoted a more ecumenical approach. Infuriated at Galen's tactics, d'Herbigny persuaded Pius XI to order the merger of the Catholic Union in the United States with another group called the Catholic Near East Welfare Association. At d'Herbigny's sugges- tion, the Pope appointed Father Edmund Walsh, a prominent Jesuit and friend of d'Herbigny, as President of the new organiza- tion. Galen tried to stop the merger, but failed, and a few weeks later, Father Walsh fired the entire Catholic Union staff, including Catherine. Stunned, she wrote a heart-wrenching letter to Galen:

> Life has been pretty hard for me, as you know, and after having refused as you remember I am sure, three en- gagements for this coming winter just to stay with the Catholic Union. . . . Honestly, dear Father, just now I am keeping my spirit together by sheer will power. Every-

thing looks so dark — it couldn't be darker. Yet I
remember that such must be the will of God, and therefore I submit.

During the next six weeks, Catherine tried to book herself as
an independent lecturer. Knowing that people considered women
over thirty as old and unappealing, she shaved two years off her
age, but rejection letters poured in anyway. Desperate, she took a
job as a salad girl in a sandwich shop at the subway station on
Broad and Wall Street, but quit when the manager hung a sign in
the window that read: *Salads served by a Russian Baroness.*

Behind the scenes, her spiritual director, Father Martin Scott,
SJ, kept trying to persuade Father Walsh to rehire Catherine. In
early October, Walsh reluctantly put Catherine on the payroll of
the Catholic Near East Welfare Association as a lecturer at $50 per
week. "Learn from my example to be selfish in the sense of
insisting on your rights and your price," a former Catholic Union
employee cautioned. "Otherwise you will only be taken advan-
tage of."

Catherine took precautions. She arranged for the Leigh-
Emmerich Lecture Bureau to book speaking engagements for her
before civic and social groups in the same cities where she appeared before Catholic audiences for the Near East Welfare Association. During November and December, she lectured in New
York, Pennsylvania, and Maryland. Before Catholic audiences,
she promoted the Catholic Near East Welfare Association. Before
other groups, she simply told her story. With both, she called
communism the enemy of religion, home, and government, and
stood adamantly opposed to the United States recognizing the
Bolshevik government. "Don't think it is not near you," she
warned. "The Bolsheviki are pouring money into this country in
behalf of their program."

Alex Kalpaschnikoff, a White Russian businessman, recognized that Catherine's lectures were "sufficiently strong to be
disliked and even feared by some of the Communist organizations in this country," and he noted that "one of these organiza-

tions actually is keeping a man following her the whole time, writing her threatening letters, and trying everything he can to put her out of commission." Kalpaschnikoff hired a body guard for Catherine, but she hated being followed. "Get this agent off my back," she insisted.

Knowing that Catherine sent part of her salary to support George and part to her mother, leaving little for herself to live on, the Bolsheviks made her a lucrative offer to lecture for them. She refused.

By December, the tension pushed Catherine toward a nervous breakdown.

Seeing her plight, a vice president on the board of the Catholic Near East Welfare Association, Father Paul James Francis Wattson, SA, invited her to spend some time at Graymoor, a Franciscan friary he had founded on a mountain overlooking the Hudson River 50 miles north of New York City. "He was immediately interested in my Orthodox heritage," Catherine recalled.

Father Paul was also a convert to Catholicism. Ordained an Episcopalian priest, he joined with an Episcopalian nun named Lurana White in 1898 to form a religious congregation of men and women called the Society of the Atonement. When the Episcopalians banned him from preaching because he advocated the reunion of Protestant churches with Rome, the brown-robed friar took the train to Manhattan and delivered his message of Christian unity to stockbrokers, civil servants and street workers from the steps of City Hall. In the fall of 1909, with pressure from the Episcopal Church mounting, Father Paul, Mother Lurana, and the 15 members of their congregation converted to Catholicism.

Father Paul's devotion to St. Francis of Assisi reminded Catherine of how much she had admired that saint during her school days in Egypt, and in a quiet Graymoor chapel, Catherine knelt before the altar as Father Paul received her into the Third Order of St. Francis, which meant she would try to live the Franciscan spirit as a lay person. She started keeping a spiritual journal in which she wrote a daily examination of conscience, and before long, she saw the same character faults surfacing again and again: "Untruth, pleasure of being paid attention to and made much of. Lord, when will I be able at least to start and overcome my vanity, self glory and pride! Jesus mercy! Heated argument, exaggerated impatience, showing off." Catherine selected a daily virtue to practice, such as humility, patience, or kindness, and she made daily resolutions: "Try to be humble for one day only. . ." "Speak the truth in small things. . ." "Be more recollected, use your gentle voice, quietness. . ." "Be at peace one day at a time. . ." "Fight outbursts of temper."

In January 1927, after a year of waiting, Boris finally received a visa for the United States. Mother Lurana sent Catherine money to pay the train fare for Boris and George. Father Paul offered the use of an old farmhouse at Graymoor, and in February 1927, the family reunited after a 14-month separation. It was a difficult adjustment for Catherine, who took on all the household responsibilities because Dunia stayed in Canada to join a convent. Catherine also remained the sole financial support of the family. She had just completed a five-week lecture tour for which she earned $375 for herself, and $920 for the Catholic Near East Welfare Association. Her position with the organization remained precarious, however, and it became even more so after she told Father Walsh that the staff did not meet the needs of Russians. Only through personal contact, she insisted, would Russians give up prejudices toward Catholicism. "I advocated the establishment of a mixed American-Russian Committee, which would not only assist the Catholic Near East Welfare Association in its money raising campaign, but likewise bring to the attention of this organization, the various needs of the Russians, residing in and outside of the United States."

Walsh ignored Catherine's suggestions. He had already launched a membership drive with the goal of one million members at $1 per person, and the ease at which money flowed in from Catholic parishes throughout the United States must have made Catherine's contributions from lectures seem minuscule. It is unclear whether Catherine quit or whether Walsh fired her, but in late February she began to pray for "our mutual employment, Boris and I."

She eventually landed a job selling stocks and bonds with the John Nickerson Company at 61 Broadway. After a chance meeting with Long Island real estate developers, Catherine sold one piece of property. The deal was a scam, and as soon as Catherine discovered the land was too swampy to pour a foundation, she reported the developers to the police, and promised to repay her client with her own money. The situation thrust her into another financial crisis, and Father Paul of Graymoor helped by lending her money. He also insisted that Catherine, who was exhausted from the ordeal, spend the summer at Graymoor with Boris and George.

That fall, Dunia left the convent in Toronto and came to live with Catherine, Boris, and six-year-old George. They rented a duplex on Goodrich Street in Astoria, and Catherine took a job with the Leigh-Emmerich Lecture Bureau, where she worked as a lecturer and booking agent for $75 per week. Stuart, James, and Cooke, an engineering firm located across from Battery Park in lower Manhattan, hired Boris. During this time, Catherine drifted away from her intense involvement with Catholicism. The last entry in her spiritual diary was on August 10, 1927, when she wrote: "Sometimes I seem to have fallen away from all good practices, but am praying hard for love of God. A time of dryness and indifference. God have mercy on me." She later admitted that she "decided to make the break and become an average, ordinary Catholic. . . the other kind paid too high a price."

After this point, Catherine's diaries contain no examinations of conscience, no virtues, no resolutions. Instead of fasting, she embarked on a serious weight reduction program that included daily workouts in a gym and a vigorous morning walk to her office on West 42nd Street in Manhattan. Leigh-Emmerich promoted her to sales manager, and she had business dealings with celebrities like actress Eva LeGallienne — "people say she is a lesbian maybe," and publisher/physical fitness guru Bernarr MacFadden — "another shattered illusion. He is terribly old." She booked $1,000 lectures for politicians, philosophers, writers and poets. She hosted publicity lunches for reporters and entertained clients over champagne and oysters in expensive speakeasies. She kept her own limited lecture schedule, which took her to major cities in the East and Mid-west, and she planned a European business trip to book celebrities for American lecture tours.

On January 1, 1928, Catherine did not return to Graymoor as planned to make her permanent profession as a member in the Third Order of St. Francis. She explained to Mother Lurana that George had tonsil surgery and Dunia had appendicitis. Boris, who had gone to Canada to negotiate a deal for Stuart, James, and Cooke, had landed a $500,000 contract, and the firm asked him to open a branch office in Montreal. Financially secure at last, Catherine promised to repay her debt to Graymoor by March. "Boris is a reborn man," she noted in her diary. They decided that Boris would leave in February to set up the office in Montreal, while Catherine and George would stay in New York until June, when she would leave for her business trip to Europe. Sometime in August, Boris would meet Catherine and George in Belgium for a family vacation. In September, they would return to Montreal to live as a family for the next two years while Catherine worked as a freelance lecturer and booking agent. "It is strange but little by little the pain is going from my soul and the love returns for Boris," Catherine confessed. She admitted that she had grown weary of the business world, and she began to pray that she and Boris would have another child, a little girl. A short time later, however, Catherine recorded in her journal a nightmare in which Claudia Kolenova washed Boris in the bath. It was a strange dream, which became painfully real when Catherine learned that Claudia had moved to Montreal. By May, Catherine's trust in Boris had dissolved, and she saw no hope of reconciling the marriage.

During this time, several strange mystical experiences left Catherine even more unsettled and apprehensive. One night, she dreamed about Ma Murphy's boarding house and the laundresses. The images seemed so real that Catherine felt as if she had moved back in time. Too shaken to sleep, she made herself a cup of tea, and as she sat in the quiet kitchen, thoughts of Kiskile crashed into her consciousness. She remembered her promise to God on the brink of starvation that if her life were saved, she would offer herself to him.

> And then, a sentence came to me. I thought it came from somewhere outside of me... "Has God saved me from death in Russia so that I should return to bourgeois society..." The only difference in this sentence, since everybody is maybe interested in wording, is that I have to be truthful and say that it seemed to begin in this way: "Why have I saved you?" It seemed as if God said "I"... From that day, a certain uneasiness entered my life. Now don't get any big ideas about it. I was going around having quite a few dates, dancing, in fact.

Arthur Van Rensselaer Thompson, whose grandfather founded Thompsonville, Connecticut, pursued her so passionately that Franz Emmerich jokingly referred to him as Catherine's "48th Street boyfriend." George remembered flowers, candy, and boxes of grapefruit arriving at their apartment, and Catherine later admitted that Thompson wanted to divorce his wife and marry her. "I was doing no wrong," she insisted, yet one night, while dancing with Thompson, Catherine thought she heard a strange, gentle laughter. "I heard what I thought was the voice of God laughing and saying, 'You can't escape me, Catherine, you can't.'"

Catherine tried to escape. She closed her Astoria apartment, stored her furniture, and told Emmerich that after her European buying trip, she would return to New York with George. She looked into the possibility of a divorce, which she could obtain in New York State on grounds of adultery, and in *Who's Who in New York*, she listed her religion as Greek Orthodox instead of Roman

Catholic, which raises the question as to whether she considered a return to the Orthodox Church, which allows divorce and remarriage.

On the evening of June 3, Catherine took the night train to Montreal. The next morning, Boris would be waiting at the station. "Wonder about Kolenova," she wrote in her diary.

Chapter Notes

"Already she has secured...": Count Augustine von Galen (hereafter Galen) to Archbishop Neil McNeil, (hereafter McNeil), Jan. 26, 1926, ARCAT.

"From all I suffered with Boris": NM correspondence, MHA.

"I didn't want to give my body...": *Ibid.*

"The Eternal Anticipation": *Ibid.*

A personal vendetta...: See *Bishop Michel d'Herbigny.*

"Life has been pretty hard...": C de H to Galen, Aug. 16, 1926, MHA.

shaved two years off her age: In 1928, Catherine shaved off two additional years, claiming her year of birth was 1900, a date she adhered to for the rest of her life.

"Learn from my example...": Louis Wetmore to C de H, Nov. 2, 1926, MHA.

"Don't think it is not near...": "Red Terror Told Again," unidentified newspaper clip, n.d., MHA.

"sufficiently strong...": A. Kalpaschnikoff to H.A. Jung, Aug. 27, 1926, MHA.

"Get this agent off my back...": *Fragments*, p.88.

"nervous breakdown...": C de H, "1936 Autobiographical Statement," MHA.

Father Paul James Francis Wattson...: See David Gannon, *Father Paul of Graymoor*, New York: The Macmillan Company, 1951.

"He was immediately interested...": IN ONE EAR, pp. 27-28.

"Untruth, pleasure of being payed attention...": Diary #3, Feb. 13, 1927, MHA.

"Try to be humble..." and f.: Diary #3, Feb. 1; Feb. 18; Feb. 28; Mar. 7, MHA.

"our mutual employment, Boris and I.": Diary #3, Feb. 16, 1927, MHA.

"I advocated the establishment of...": C de H to Msgr. William Quinn, Nov. 1, 1927, MHA.

Walsh ignored Catherine's suggestions: See *Bishop Michel d'Herbigny.*

"Sometimes seem to have fallen away...": Diary #3, Aug. 10, 1927, MHA.

"decided to make the break...": Diary #17, Jan. 18, 1938, MHA.

her diaries contain...: See Diary #2, MHA.

"people say she is a lesbian maybe": Diary #2, Jan. 9, 1928, MHA.

"another shattered illusion": Diary #2, Mar. 1, 1928, MHA.

On January 1, 1928...: C de H to Mother Lurana White (hereafter Mother Lurana), Jan. 15, 1928, FAA.

"Boris is a reborn man": Diary #2, Jan. 5, 1928, MHA.

"It is strange but little by little...": Diary #2, Mar. 29, 1928, MHA.

"And then a sentence came to me...": *Little Mandate*, MHA.

"I was doing no wrong..." and f.: *Fragments*, p. 92.

"Wonder about Kolenova": Diary #2, June 3, 1928, MHA.

15

Europe
1928

C atherine spent two miserable days in Montreal before
sailing for Europe with six-year-old George. Boris made
no attempt to hide the fact that Claudia Kolenova lived
with him, and the situation left Catherine anxious and depressed.
When she arrived in Brussels on June 15, letters from Emmerich
awaited with news that the lecture bureau faced financial problems. With no salary, no expense money, no basis for negotiating
contracts with lecturers, Catherine felt suspended. Even her hopes
of spending a lovely summer with her mother and brothers
resulted in tension and misunderstanding. Emma had little money,
and lived in a small apartment on Rue Marie-Henriette with
André, a strapping teenager. Serge had joined an underground
group that plotted to overthrow the Bolsheviks and restore the
Russian monarchy. "On the whole I am sorry I went to Europe,"
Catherine admitted. "Mother and my brothers? I wonder how
much I mean to them now. Strange how one becomes a separate
part from those one loves most. And Boris is a ? mark more than
ever."

Catherine's thoughts turned to Nicholas Makletzoff, the
handsome officer she met during the war. Through the years, she
made several unsuccessful attempts to locate Nicholas through
the Red Cross. She decided to try once more, and this time, she
found his brother, Alexandre, who sent her Nicholas' address in
Sofia, Bulgaria. Catherine wrote, and Nicholas replied. He had
escaped from Russia after the revolution and nearly died from

typhus. He settled in Sofia where he earned a meager living. He had not married and had no romantic attachments. He warned Catherine that he had become cynical, but Catherine wanted only one thing: "Be tender with me. I am at the end of my forces. My life with Boris is very tragic — like a nightmare."

Over the next weeks, Catherine wrote long letters to Nicholas detailing everything that had happened over the past ten years. This sudden obsession with Nicholas alienated Catherine even more from her mother and brothers. "Nicholas is the one who loves you," Emma admitted, but she warned that if Catherine pursued this relationship she would suffer. Catherine insisted that finding Nicholas was an answer to her prayers.

On Friday, August 8, Boris arrived in Europe. They celebrated Catherine's birthday on August 15 in Brussels, and two days later, Catherine, Boris, and George left for Helsinki to visit Guido de Hueck. From Helsinki, they took a train to Kiskile, and stayed in the *dacha* where Catherine and Boris had nearly starved to death. Local peasants had maintained the property, and Catherine felt as if she had lapsed into a different lifetime. One afternoon, they hiked to the Russian border. Boris leaped the fence and walked on Russian soil for the last time, but Catherine, who sobbed uncontrollably, refused to join him. The deep emotion made a profound impression on George, who felt at last as if they were a family. George was too young, however, to interpret the tensions between his parents or to recognize the blatant flirtation Boris had with another woman during the visit. When they returned to Brussels, problems intensified. Catherine's brother described Boris as "a man, who lived only for himself, a man with no depth, a mushroom." On September 1, Boris took George back to Montreal, while Catherine stayed in Europe to finish her work for Emmerich, who had finally given her permission to book lecturers. Emma did not approve. "Oh, my poor little one," she told Catherine. "What a terribly sad life you have."

Catherine left for London, where she set up a temporary office in the Whitehall Hotel, and had started contacting publishing houses and literary agents. She became known as *"Draga,"* a

Russian word meaning "dear one," and rumors spread that she offered a lucrative lecture contract to Hilaire Belloc, but rejected Arnold Bennett because he stuttered. She set up appointments with G.K. Chesterton, Bernard Shaw, Sir Arthur Conan Doyle, A.A. Milne, Winston Churchill, and the Belgian Prime Minister, Van der Velde, who was visiting London. "Things are just pepping up," she noted.

When her reports to Emmerich went unanswered, she dismissed it with the observation: "Doing business with Emmerich requires the patience of an angel. . ." Catherine became so caught up in the glamour of her life that she could not see the market for lecturers in the United States steadily eroding as radio brought speakers into people's homes for free. While larger lecture bureaus would continue to operate, the financially troubled Leigh-Emmerich agency had little hope of survival. Still, Catherine kept negotiating contracts.

Several writers tried to woo her. Irish novelist Liam O'Flaherty gave her a copy of his novel, *The Tent* with the torrid inscription:

> To Draga, whose eyes are the most wonderful I have seen because they can compare in beauty with the Blue Pool at *Au Bhinn Bridhe* when the sun is streaming in upon it at noon. . . .

Catherine was unmoved by their attentions. In October, she flew to Darmstadt, where she continued her round of celebrity gatherings. She told Count Hermann Keyserling, an eccentric philosopher, about a luncheon date she had with British publisher Jonathan Cape, who bragged about having the most comprehensive sex library in the world. "And he loved to know women—did I like to be hurt? I said I did not know. Did I smoke opium? I would not say yes, for I did not." Keyserling speculated that men took liberties with Catherine because she was oversexed on the outside and pure on the inside. He suggested that Catherine ran from sexual contacts because she was afraid.

"I shall have to ponder that over," she mused.

On October 10, Catherine returned to London, where she met with feminist author, Nina Boyle, at the all-female Power Club. Catherine was not impressed: "This is the most uncozy club in London," she noted. "My idea of the feminist movement is to remain feminine but make men see our worth as beings/ One should not wear ugly skirts to be a feminist. Men do not wear baggy trousers!"

With Radclyffe Hall, the lesbian author of the controversial new book, *The Well of Loneliness,* Catherine felt more compassion. They met at a dinner party. "I hear," Miss Hall said to Catherine, "that you believe in God. . . ."

Catherine replied that she did.

"You know," Miss Hall continued, "so do I in a strange fashion. You remember the last line of my book when I cry out to God 'Why am I What I Am!' Factually, it is the cry of the psalmist, 'Out of the depths I cry to Thee, O Lord.'"

When Radclyffe Hall spoke of the depths of loneliness, Catherine admitted that "an absolute wave of compassionate understanding flooded me." She wanted to bring Miss Hall to America as a lecturer, but her grandiose plans had already started to crumble. A letter from Emmerich in late October left no doubt that the lecture bureau was "on the rocks." He wanted to bring Catherine back to the States but had no money to send for even minimum fare. He insisted that she stop booking lectures because

> . . . it is preposterous for me to be spending time working out contracts and offers for you when none of my staff have any money and I have not got any myself, and absolutely no place to go for it for tomorrow's meals. . . .
>
> I have no money to cable you — not even a dollar to spend on a cable. . . I am not going to answer any more of your letters with others or talk celebrities to you until November 1st at the earliest unless we get money. I do not give a damn at present if we never see a European celebrity over here and I absolutely refuse to consider any more offers, and I forbid you to enter into any offers yourself.

With an almost perverse optimism ("Smile, Draga, smile. There is a silver lining to every cloud. . ."), Catherine ignored Emmerich's orders and met with Hilaire Belloc to discuss a series of debates with Chesterton. She also met with Bertrand Russell, who was writing a new book that advocated sexual freedom. Intrigued with Catherine's marriage at age 15, Russell asked whether Boris had "possessed" her at once. "No," she replied sarcastically. "He took eight months to do it in." Catherine did not like Bertrand Russell, whose relentless questions culminated with a direct query as to why Catherine refused to sleep with him. "Have you looked in the mirror lately?" she replied.

Bertrand Russell was Catherine's last celebrity interview. By the end of October, truth had eaten away all illusions. Emmerich owed her over $1,000 in salary and expenses, but she had received only $314 from him. "Hell on earth," she wrote in her diary.

A few days later, she boarded a train for Bulgaria to find Nicholas Makletzoff. Their first meeting was marred, however, when Nicholas showed obvious disappointment in Catherine's appearance. He remembered a lively 20-year-old — strong, passionate and beautiful — but before him stood a 32-year-old matron, whose eyes reflected 12 years of pain, rejection, loneliness, failure, and fatigue. If Catherine had been less desperate, she might have seen that Nicholas was not the man of her dreams. It never occurred to her that the stage of life had turned and she was rescuing the man she had hoped would rescue her.

On November 14, Catherine and Nicholas went to the British Consulate in Sofia where Catherine signed an affidavit saying she had known him for 15 years and would guarantee his employment in Canada. She succeeded in getting Nicholas out of Bulgaria, and found him a job in Brussels, where he would stay until he received immigration papers for Canada. They planned to marry in the Russian Orthodox Church as soon as Catherine divorced Boris.

In late December, Catherine boarded a steam ship in Liverpool and sailed for Montreal. Deep feelings of apprehension weighed on her. With the lecture bureau headed toward bankruptcy, she feared that she would become financially dependent on Boris. She knew that both Boris and Emmerich would confront her about her trip to Bulgaria, but she didn't want to tell them about Nicholas until she had finalized arrangements. It was a difficult crossing. Winter storms in the north Atlantic rocked the ship, and Catherine suffered constant nausea that left her weak and severely dehydrated. Yet the worst, as she knew so well, was still to come.

Chapter Notes

"On the whole I am sorry...": Diary #2, June 30, 1928, MHA.

"Be tender...": NM correspondence, MHA.

"Nicholas is the one who loves you...": *Ibid.*

"a man, who lived only for himself...": Interview, André Kolychkine.

"Oh, my poor little one...": NM correspondence, MHA.

"Things are just pepping up...": Diary #4, Sept. 14, 1928, MHA.

"Doing business with Emmerich...": Diary #4, Sept. 20, 1928, MHA.

"To Draga...": To Draga from Liam O'Flaherty, Handwritten inscription in *The Tent*, MHA.

"And he loved to know women..." and f.: Diary #4, Oct. 6, 1928, MHA.

"This is the most uncozy club in London...": Diary #4, Oct. 12, 1928, MHA.

"'I hear,'" Miss Hall said to Catherine..." and f.: *IN ONE EAR*, p. 135.

"on the rocks...": Diary #4, Oct. 16, 1928, MHA.

"it is preposterous...": Emmerich to C de H, October 10, 1928, MHA.

"Smile, Draga, smile...": Diary #4, Oct. 17, 1928, MHA.

"He took eight months to do it in.": Diary #4, Oct. 19, 1928, MHA.

"Have you looked in the mirror lately?": Interview, Fr. Emile Briere.

"Hell on earth...": Diary #4, Oct. 19 to Nov. 9, 1928, MHA.

Catherine signed an affidavit: AH Papers, AUND.

16

Montreal

1929

Boris met Catherine at the station and told her in excruciating detail how Emmerich overdrew lecture bureau accounts, and had a string of lawsuits awaiting court dates. Catherine's fear of financial dependence on Boris suddenly became very real. He insisted that she live in his apartment on Bayle Street, yet having to find another apartment for Claudia left him "tormented like a soul in hell."

"My return forced Claudia out as lady of the house," Catherine admitted. "Their freedom is destroyed and she resents it. Both are unhappy."

Only seven-year-old George, who detested Claudia, was "crazy with joy" to see Catherine, but he looked "skinny and pale," and Catherine decided that only with Nicholas Makletzoff could she give her son a normal life. She contacted Canadian Immigration, informing them that Nicholas was a relative. "It will be impossible for us to marry now," she wrote to Nicholas, "but in five years, you will be a Canadian and the doors will open."

In the midst of Catherine's frenzied attention to the details of Nicholas' coming, a strange restlessness gripped her. The promise she made in Kiskile to give her life to God if he saved her from starvation echoed like background music, barely heard, and yet never ceasing. She tried to pray, to read the Bible, to meditate, but the restlessness remained. One day her eyes fell on the Scripture passage, "Arise, go. . . sell all you possess. . . take up your cross and follow me," and after that, each time she picked up a Bible, it opened to the same passage. "No matter whose Bible I took (and

I even went to the public library once and opened a Bible there),
it always opened at the same sentence. I confess, I got frightened,
really frightened. There is such a thing as fear of the Lord and this
repetitious kind of stuff made me think that He really meant
business but what kind of business?"

Catherine dreamed about Ma Murphy, the laundresses, the
waitresses she had met over the years. "I am scared," she wrote to
Nicholas.

> What am I good for? Do I have value for anything? Oh,
> God, my God. I lower my head in shame... Kolya, please
> help me. Take my hand and let's walk toward what is
> shiny and good. I have to go away from the vanity of this
> world, find a place of tranquillity, live in peace, and do
> only good actions. I came here on this earth to serve and
> I should serve every human being for the glory of the
> Lord. Please, God, help me find a way. You have to go
> with me because grace brought you into my life. God
> wanted it. Why? His wants are secret. But you came into
> my life and you have to go with me to find out. My soul
> is embraced by a new flame — very clear — and it was
> never gone, this flame of goodness and charity was
> burning many years. Who can say what made the flame
> come back after all these years? One has to live for
> others, give them happiness and joy. Oh, God, please
> help me and show me the way.

Nicholas saw a spiritual force in Catherine's anguish. Identifying it as a call to saintliness, he offered to stay in Europe, but
Catherine dismissed his concerns. "What you said about sainthood in others," she replied, "your love makes you see me like
that. I'm not as good as you think. I simply love Christ and I want
to imitate him, but I am not able. My small attempts to be good
look like perfection because no one else around me is trying."

Catherine's "small attempts" centered on works of charity.
She told herself that "part of the dedication of one's life to God is
to share one's goods with others," and she did this by giving

money to the poor and raising funds for the Russian Church, but nothing calmed her churning soul. On a streetcar one day, as she thought about giving everything to the poor, the word "directly," and then the word, "personally" came to her: ". . . give it directly, personally to the poor." Catherine recalled her mother's stories of working in peasant villages, and she remembered Theodore's notebook entitled, "My Debt To God," in which he recorded money he gave to people in need. She sensed that God pursued her for some purpose, but what, she wondered, did God want?

The words — "pick up *my* cross" came to mind, but when she checked, the Scripture passage read *"thy* cross." In the midst of her confusion, the words, "their cross" came: ". . . take up my cross, their cross, and follow me." Later, the words "going to the poor — being poor" haunted her. One day in a train station, she heard, "Be one with them, one with Me."

Catherine wrote the phrases on scraps of paper, and they eventually formed what she called her "Little Mandate" from God. At this early point, however, she did not understand why these phrases came to her in such bizarre fashion, and the experience left her feeling badgered, broken, and confused.

> . . . there is no way I can relate to you this agony, this search, this pilgrimage, this restlessness, almost a terror. How can I put that into words. . . it could happen any place, any time, in the midst of a group. . . suddenly a little light, a little addition of a word or something that seemed to be part and yet not part of the Scriptures. . . just came to me. . . and all this was coming at me, so to speak, from God at the time when I was in my own little hell, shall we put it.

The Russian community in Montreal rejected her for being bossy, unsociable and opinionated. They recognized Claudia as Boris' mistress, and gave tacit approval to his affairs with other women. "He was a well-known womanizer and everybody liked him. He loved a good time. He loved to party."

Boris spent most nights with Claudia. "It's better like this," Catherine admitted, "because he disturbs me." On one occasion, he accused Catherine of stealing some things Claudia had left in the apartment. "I will go and not take any money from him," Catherine promised herself.

On April 1, 1930, Nicholas Makletzoff arrived in St. John, New Brunswick and boarded a train for Montreal. Catherine rented a room for Nicholas and coaxed Boris into giving him a job as an architect, but before long, her dream of Nicholas rescuing her crumbled, and she began to see that "he can't get along in life by himself." People pegged them as lovers, but Catherine denied it. She desperately wished she could escape from Boris, from Nicholas, from everything in her life that held no promise or meaning. She wrote to Father Filion, and he replied that she would be "quite justified" in getting a legal separation, but Boris used George as a pawn to keep her in the marriage.

In late September 1929, Catherine and Boris moved to a new apartment on Hope Avenue. Boris had just negotiated a deal with Stuart, James and Cooke to buy out their interests in the Montreal office, and he had construction contracts pending with Curtiss Reid Aircraft and Dominion Rubber. Catherine's plans to start a literary agency and lecture bureau remained stymied, and without money or a job, she felt trapped.

During this painful period Catherine noticed a gray house on St. Lawrence that was "so humble and yet had such a distinctive face all its own." Curious, she rang the bell, and a nun answered. The house belonged to the Franciscan Missionaries of Mary, a religious order that trained young women to work with lepers. "Before me rose picture-shows that left me weary of life, with a bitter taste in my mouth," Catherine confessed. "Books that would have better been left unread. . . parties with their expenditure on accessories that would have better been left unattended . . . all came back to my mind and with them came the dollars so foolishly wasted. . ."

A few weeks later, on Tuesday, October 29, the New York

Stock Exchange crashed. By mid-November, Canada's economy crumbled. Construction ground to a halt and Boris' clients defaulted. A five dollar check Catherine wrote bounced for lack of funds.

Catherine sought out another Jesuit, Father Arthème Tétrault, for spiritual direction, and poured out the story of her disastrous marriage to Boris, her dashed hopes of marrying Nicholas, and her failure as a mother to George. Father Tétrault warned against despair: "I do not want you to consider even for a single moment that *little thing* which worldly people see when they have reached the end of their rope, when they have seen and tasted the emptiness of pleasure. . . SUICIDE. No! No! Faith is stronger than all that. You shall win the victory. It is not suffering that you must fear but discouragement and sin."

Catherine drew up a new rule of life with time for prayer and volunteer work with the Franciscan nuns. On December 14, she looked back on the year and called it "a nightmare I do not want to live over again." Three days later, she poured out an agonizing prayer:

> Strange how the pain of things goes deep. How far from all the virtues, from the Gospel, I am is astonishing. Of course, I know I am a sinner. I knew it all along. But it seemed to me that I at least dreamt and strove. But lately I have come to realize my nothingness — utter and infinite. Life is just a joke as far as I'm concerned. And my whole soul longs for death. Yet, today, for the first time I was a little afraid of death. For what have I to bring to Christ! Empty hands — empty heart — I look back on my life and have to cry. A little good strewn here and there and everywhere, lost, submerged in the pride of heart, the lack of real charity, of love for my neighbor.
>
> And so I have to forget what has gone before and start anew as if life just started today. And, Jesus, I do not want to make resolutions and promises. This time I will start out just in sitting at Your feet — a child, I will pray

incessantly for a child's spirit. Make me humble, humble, humble. Oh how I beg this of You, my God. In all the rest, Your will be done, not mine.

As Catherine tried to move closer to God, however, she became more despondent. She struggled with the Christian concept of unconditional love, which she interpreted as passive acceptance of whatever Boris said or did, no matter how cruel, no matter how unjust, no matter how immoral. One day Boris asked her to lie to one of his mistresses so he could go to another, and in her confusion, Catherine did what he asked. "Why do I have to go through all this humiliation of being a looker on, a sort of helper on," she prayed. "Lord, you see how Boris, little by little, is killing my life."

Catherine kept trying to imitate a model of Jesus that was meek, humble, and silent in the face of suffering, but after Father Tétrault suggested that she read the Passion in the Gospel of St. John, Catherine saw a different side of Jesus, who testified to the truth and challenged someone who struck him unjustly. Gradually, she began asking herself the right questions: "I often wonder why do words possess such power?" she wrote after describing an incident in which Boris verbally assaulted her. She questioned his spending over $100 per month on his mistresses while she and George barely made ends meet on a monthly budget of $25. She recoiled at gossip "which is so terrible to my rights as a wife that I return from them completely humiliated." She asked herself why Boris treated her so harshly and why she seemed to lose her own clarity of vision when he was around: "My heart goes so slowly, my pulse stops, I get so weary, everything seems a burden, because unconsciously to himself he is antagonistic to me and cruel."

Catherine wept for days, and in her pain she began to see that she had to get away from Boris. Thoughts of suicide, and fantasies about going to Europe with George or fleeing to a convent plagued her. Father Tétrault jarred her back to reality with the suggestion that her marriage to Boris might not be valid in the Catholic Church, and he urged her to apply for an annulment.

In April 1930, Catherine wrote to Archbishop McNeil asking for formal permission to separate from her husband. She took a job at Eaton's department store for $18 a week to support herself and George. Boris, who had moved into Claudia's apartment, agreed to pay $20 a month in child support, but he rarely gave Catherine the money. She also discovered that physical separation from Boris did not mean emotional detachment. The powerful bond between them didn't break until that summer, when Boris wanted to reconcile and Catherine agreed to try. They spent the weekend at the cottage they had purchased several years before on Lac Castor near Ste. Marguerite. Catherine later recalled how Boris reverted to his abusive ways, and "goaded me beyond all endurance." She ran from the cottage and rowed to the middle of the lake. Despair crept over her, and the water beckoned as it had the night she stood on the Brooklyn Bridge. "Yes, as I gazed into the water I realized that I had been tired for a long, long time.

> I had been tired since I left home at the age of 15 or 16. Then I closed my eyes and thought about what the waters offered me: home. . . birches. . . sparkling sunshine. . . Russia . . . mother and father. I began to hear my mother playing Debussy on the piano by the soft light of the three-branched candelabra. All the while the water lapped gently around the boat, and the oars made funny little noises as they floated with the current: and the fog was coming closer.
>
> Then a most strange thing happened. It's very hard to explain. It wasn't the sun, because the sun was going down. It was more like a shimmering curtain. It moved in folds, as curtains do. Suddenly, it stood between me and the fog.
>
> I woke from my dreaming and realized that I was standing on the last bench of the boat. I hadn't noticed that I was standing there, and that somehow I had gone

from one end of the boat to the other. But I "woke up" from my dream. Above all, I woke up from despair, and from the gray-black fog which vanished at the coming of the shimmering curtain. With great energy I rowed back to the house.

In recognizing the value of her life, Catherine smashed whatever power Boris held over her. He would remain a source of pain and frustration, but she could forgive him because she saw that he was driven by his own compulsive inner agony, which she had not caused, but for which he had unjustly blamed her. On October 15, 1930, Catherine renewed the promise she had made to God in Kiskile with a commitment to live a life of service, and she celebrated this day every year as the anniversary of what she called her apostolate. At first, she seemed unclear as to what form this apostolate would take. She discussed with Archbishop McNeil the possibility of lecturing or doing social work, but with the deepening economic depression, jobs became impossible to find. She thought about entering a convent, but Fr. Daly reminded her that she still had the responsibility of George. She finally decided on nursing. "I will be able to work at the thing I like best," she told McNeil, "the poor and the sick."

Since Catholic nursing schools would not accept married women, Catherine applied to Montreal General Hospital. She arranged for 10-year-old George to enter a Catholic boarding school, and in September 1931, Catherine, at the age of 35, became a nursing student with a rotating schedule of classes and floor duty. Her supervisor noted that "she did not seem to fit into the scheme of things here, and though I have nothing to complain of as to her general behavior, there seemed to be a perpetual misunderstanding between herself and my staff nurses."

Father Tétrault urged Catherine to persevere: "I am sure that you are doing good around you. Go to the heart, to the soul, by healing bodies. Your apostolate is very beautiful."

Catherine finished her first year, but as new scandals involving Boris and his mistresses raged through Montreal, she wrote a

desperate letter to Mother Lurana in September 1932, begging for
an invitation to live at Graymoor with George. The letter got lost
on Mother Lurana's desk, and as weeks passed with no reply,
Catherine panicked. On October 18, 1932, she quit school. When
Madeline Sheridan, her only real friend in Montreal, tried to
phone a few days later, someone gave her a Toronto address
where Catherine could be reached. Stunned, Miss Sheridan wrote
at once:

> I hate the thought that you're hurt again in the same way
> by 'circumstance', but out of the confusion of my mind
> about you at the moment, you somehow emerge always
> the same valiant figure, the Catherine I love with the
> beautiful face and the brave bearing. . . you always look
> like a bright spot because you have all the signs of
> ultimate victory about you— when this dreadful dying
> period of history will be ended, you'll come into your
> own. I know I'm to rejoice in your visible success some-
> day, just as I rejoice now in your presence on this planet.
> I just wish it were in Montreal.

Chapter Notes

"tormented like a soul in hell": NM correspondence, MHA.

"My return forced Claudia out...": *Ibid.*

"crazy with joy... skinny and pale...": *Ibid.*

"It will be impossible for us to marry...": *Ibid.*

"no matter whose Bible I took...": *Little Mandate*, MHA.

"I am scared...": NM correspondence, MHA.

"What you said about sainthood...": *Ibid.*

"part of the dedication of one's life..." and f.: *Little Mandate*, MHA.

"there is no way I can relate to you this agony...": *Ibid.*

"He was a well-known womanizer...": Interview, Nina Youmatoff Doull.

"It's better like this...": NM correspondence, MHA.

"I will go and not take any money...": *Ibid.*

"he can't get along...": Hmelevsky to C de H, Feb. 28, 1929, MHA.

"quite justified...": JMF to C de H, May 14, 1929, MHA.

"so humble..." and f.: C de H, "The Little Gray House," *Franciscan Review*, n.d., MHA.

"I do not want you to consider...": Arthème Tétrault, S.J. to C de H, n.d., MHA.

"a nightmare I do not want to live...": Diary #4, Dec. 14, 1929, MHA.

"Strange how the pain...": Diary #4, Dec. 17, 1929, MHA.

"Why do I go through all this...": Diary #4, Jan. 13, 1930.

"I often wonder why do words possess such power?": Diary #4, Jan. 14, 1930, MHA.

"which is so terrible to my rights...": Diary #4, Feb. 3, 1930, MHA.

"My heart goes so slowly...": Diary #4, Feb. 17, 1930, MHA.

asking for formal permission...: For terms and procedures under which the Catholic Church would allow marital separations because of adultery see Rev. Marion Leo Gibbons, *Domicile of Wife Unlawfully Separated from Her Husband, A Historical Synopsis and Canonical Commentary*, pp. 47-57.

"goaded me beyond all endurance": Diary #51, Mar. 4, 1970, MHA.

"Yes, as I gazed into the water...": *Fragments*, pp. 89-90.

"I will be able to work...": C de H to McNeil, July 23, 1931, ARCAT.

"Catholic nursing schools...": *Ibid.*

"she did not seem to fit...": M.K. Holt to Sister M. Jeanne, Oct. 25, 1932, Archives of St. Michael's Hospital, Toronto.

"I will be able to work...": C de H to McNeil, July 23, 1931, ARCAT.

"I am sure that you are doing good...": Arthème Tétrault, S.J. to C de H, Dec. 28, 1931, MHA.

"I hate the thought...": Madeline Sheridan to C de H, n.d., MHA.

17

Toronto

1932

Like a child awakening from a nightmare, Catherine ran to Archbishop McNeil and poured out her feelings of failure. McNeil persuaded Catherine to return to nursing and arranged for her transfer to St. Michael's Hospital School of Nursing in Toronto where she could finish training at his expense. From the first day, Catherine's take-charge approach and the suspicion that she received special privileges because of McNeil led to misunderstandings and resentment among instructors and students. After 51 days, she quit. School records claim Catherine "found the discipline too hard," but she told McNeil that she quit because the Council of Social Hygiene on Bond Street had offered her a job, and she needed the money to bring George to Toronto at the end of the school year. McNeil suggested that she work for the Archdiocese instead, and hired Catherine at a salary of $15 per week to investigate the spread of communism among Catholic immigrants. Within weeks, Catherine reported to McNeil that Communists lured immigrants, who lacked food, clothing, and medical care, to labor halls and reading rooms.

> There he finds a warm welcome, a good free entertainment, and mischievous propaganda sapping slowly but surely his spiritual strength. Yet, when he turns to his own, they know him not. There are no parish halls open to welcome him any time of the day or evening. There are no recreational activities to cheer him up; no intellectual endeavors are made to explain the bewildering

situation of our days. . . . There are no study hours to
strengthen his faith against a new kind of unknown-to-
him, seemingly logical reasoning.

The best way to combat communism, Catherine insisted,
was to do what the Communists did, but from a Christian perspec-
tive. McNeil encouraged her to test some of her ideas. With flair
and a little fast talking, she found jobs for the unemployed and
apartments for evicted families. She acted as a court advocate and
begged local merchants for food, clothes, toys, and medicine for
the poor. When one woman said she liked to cook, Catherine
suggested that the woman and her husband start a Russian
restaurant.
"How?" the stunned couple asked.
"We are going to beg for it," Catherine explained.
Catherine rallied the support of Toronto society women, and
within four weeks, they transformed an old house on Hayden
Street into a Russian cafe that employed seven people and a
balalaika trio. Patrons sang and danced, Catherine appeared in
costume as a fortune teller reading tea leaves, and newspapers
hailed the restaurant for having "a continental charm only too rare
in the staid city." It became the cornerstone on which Catherine
built a Russian business colony with a beauty salon, bakery,
dressmaker's shop, art gallery, dance studio, bookbinder, interior
decorators, batik artist, and other businesses that utilized immigrant skills and removed families from relief rolls.
"I am afraid you are going to over-work," Mother Lurana
told her.
Mother Lurana did not realize, however, that Catherine had
discovered her true vocation, and the work exhilarated her.
"During our visit," one reporter wrote, "her eyes sparkled with
delight because of a generous and unexpected gift of clothing for
her poor."
Catherine lived in a Catholic women's boarding house on
Bloor Street, but she felt a strange desire to move into the slums.
McNeil told her the idea was 50 years ahead of its time. He

suggested that she wait one year, and if the desire still remained, he would give his permission and his blessing.

Catherine plunged back to her work with renewed zeal. She lectured to Catholic and Protestant church groups, private schools, women's clubs, and businessmen's associations. Calling herself "the voice of those who are voiceless," she was the first woman to speak before the Toronto Rotary; the second to appear before the Board of Trade. "We are to blame who allow conditions to exist which develop a down-trodden class!" she thundered.

Audiences squirmed as she exposed their pettiness toward the poor: "We say they must not have a radio, they must not go to the movies, if they are on relief. . . We give them prohibitions — you must not do this — you must not do that. But we do not provide them with the things they can do!" She asked why churches refused to open their doors to help people, and answered her own question: "We don't live up to our religion!" Her graphic accounts of Communists helping immigrants, stealing their belief in God, and twisting the minds of children, who would mature into militant atheists of the future, made audiences tremble. Then she softened her tone and suggested that groups and individuals could sponsor an immigrant family, providing not only food, clothing and coal, but money for a family outing, or new curtains, or a fresh coat of house paint. "In a word, play the fairy godmother to one family, making it at least feel that Canadians are really not at all as distant and unapproachable as our foreign arrivals seem to think."

The idea ignited people's imaginations. A women's social club sponsored three families, a Protestant youth group organized a picnic for 25 girls, and businessmen offered paint, lumber, plumbing supplies, household furnishings, and coal. "I am sorry to say," she told McNeil, "that it is very hard to organize the above amongst our Catholic laity; somehow they do not seem to realize the importance of it all."

Most Catholics of that era believed social work belonged in the exclusive domain of nuns and priests, and Catherine's methods made them even more wary. She fraternized with Protestants and spoke before groups like the YMCA, which Pope Benedict XV had censured for "professing absolute freedom of thought in religious matters." Flashy, impetuous, and strong-willed with a penchant for cigarettes and salty language, Catherine did not fit their image of Catholic womanhood. People wondered why she lived apart from her husband and child, and the way she used the Russian restaurant on Hayden Street as her headquarters seemed shocking. Catherine insisted that she made important contacts with wealthy businessmen at the restaurant. In one six-week period, she told Archbishop McNeil, she found full or part time work for 37 people and tuition assistance for three through contacts with restaurant patrons.

While most Catholics remained aloof, Bernard Harrison, a publisher of law books, found the talk she gave at a communion breakfast in St. Peter's Catholic church in May 1933 so compelling that he invited her to his home for Sunday dinner. Bernard and Patricia Harrison were not typical Torontonians. Their social circle included a German professor who advocated mud baths; a Black physician and his wife from the West Indies; a Hungarian dentist; Father Thomas Keating, a highly intellectual, yet witty Irish Jesuit; Mrs. Beatrice Field, a recent convert to Catholicism, who was raising two daughters in Toronto while her husband, Jack, worked as a mining engineer in northern Ontario; and Grace Flewwelling, an eccentric but lovable spinster, known to everyone as Flewy. Mrs. Field called the group "that little clique," and they offered Catherine new ideas, talents, and information.

Flewy was an artist, and in addition to drawing posters and signs for Catherine, she became one of her most loyal friends. From Mrs. Field, who had set up a library at St. Peter's parish, Catherine learned where to find Catholic books at discount prices, and she opened a reading room in the Catholic settlement house on McCaul Street to offset a nearby Communist reading room. From Bernard Harrison and Father Keating, Catherine learned about the social encyclicals of Pope Pius XI, who condemned the rise in nationalism, the deepening economic depression, and the unequal distribution of wealth. Father Keating had already started a study group called "The White Front," for business and professional men, who wanted to discuss these encyclicals. That fall, Catherine would start study groups of her own, but in the meantime, she spent the summer arranging for 12-year-old George to live with her.

During the previous year, George had lived with the Sherman family in Montreal, an arrangement he negotiated after a disastrous attempt to live with Boris and Claudia ended in Boris threatening to send him back to boarding school. Mr. Sherman worked as a tailor, while his wife cared for their two daughters. George loved the customs, the food, and the rituals of this Jewish family, but most of all, he loved the stability of a home. Boris feared, however, that George's future would suffer if it became known that he lived with Jews, and he was about to remove George from the Sherman home when Catherine intervened, promising that she would bring George to Toronto at the end of the school year. George never knew any of this, and in the summer of 1933, when Boris informed him that he had to live with his mother in Toronto, George blamed Catherine for ending what he considered "the happiest days of my life." He arrived with a deep-seated anger that Catherine had not anticipated and did not know how to handle.

"I think she tried to do her best," recalled a friend of George's. "I don't think anybody could say anything against that."

Archbishop McNeil loaned Catherine $100 to move her furniture out of storage in Montreal, and she rented the downstairs of an elegant old house at 141 Isabella Street. In September 1934, she enrolled George as a day student at St. Michael's College, but George hated the school and felt alienated from the other boys, who had what he considered normal families. As hard as Catherine tried to make a home for him, it never measured up in George's estimation to what the Shermans or his schoolmates had. His parents' separation and his mother working at a time when working mothers were frowned upon made George different. He heard rumors that Catherine was a Communist, and some of the priests at school criticized her openly. George's resentment festered. "He thought his mother was crazy for what she was doing," Mrs. Field recalled.

Even more humiliating for George was the way Catherine took in boarders to make ends meet. Nicholas Makletzoff, who followed Catherine to Toronto and rented a room nearby, came every day for meals. "She was helping Nicholas quite a bit," one Russian recalled, "finding him jobs, a position, promotions. He was a very nice person, but he was always dependent on the Baroness."

Catherine also attracted a constant stream of strangers, who heard her lectures and came to ask questions about spiritual matters. Catherine felt uncomfortable advising people, but McNeil insisted that God orchestrated it. "I have accepted this angle of my work only because of your desire," she told him, "as frankly I do not feel competent in all humility to deal with complicated situations."

While Catherine seemed oblivious to the spiritual presence that emanated from her, Olga LaPlante, a 21-year-old Canadian girl, noticed it the first time she came to Catherine's study club. "You didn't just see it," Olga insisted, "you felt it."

> I remember after the meeting, she talked and the kids talked, and then Catherine served tea, as usual with her samovar. . . Well, I had never heard God spoken with such reverence and with such familiarity as a friend/I just couldn't believe it. You felt her reverence. You felt that she was very close. . . and he was alive. . . and he was a vibrant person to her.

Catherine's diaries from this time show a deepening relationship with God, a relationship so intimate that it seemed as if God instilled in her an understanding of her own human nature and his divine nature. She became acutely aware of her faults: "I speak too much. I boast too much. I lie too much." Yet, she understood that in her humanness she would always be "falling, falling only to get up and fall again!" She knew that God would forgive her in the same way a parent forgives a child, and in the quiet stillness of a church one day the words, "Little — be always little. . . simple — poor — childlike," came to her. For Catherine, "childlike" meant relying on God to guide and instruct her: "Teach me to live by the day! Teach me to be kind in word, thought and deeds. Teach me to be poor, to serve Thee well by serving well Thy poor." As her trust in God grew, she experienced a sweet spiritual tenderness that surrounded and penetrated her: "As I knelt before the Blessed Sacrament it was as if music of inexplicable charm filled my ears. My heart was full to overflowing with the love of Him who is forever so gentle with me, so forbearing! So patient!"

Catherine never shared the intimacies of her spiritual life, and yet, everything she did reflected it. "It was like a star she was following," Olga explained. "And when she spoke of the Gospel and she spoke of God, she spoke in a way that your heart started on fire."

There were six members of Catherine's study club — a young man named Charlie Rogers, Catherine, Olga, Mrs. Field, Flewy, and a young woman named Kay Kenny. "I really and truly think we were all peculiar people," Olga admitted.

They met on Thursday evenings in Catherine's living room to read Scripture and discuss social encyclicals. "Oh, it's all so simple," Catherine insisted. "It all amounts fundamentally to preaching the Gospel with your life — not so much your work — but your life." The group interpreted this as a call to follow Catherine's dream of helping the poor.

"Never in my wildest dreams had I visualized anyone joining me," Catherine told McNeil. She saw her vocation as something personal between herself and God, but McNeil shook his head no. A short time later Olga moved into the house on Isabella, and only then did Olga realize that Catherine lived in voluntary poverty. "When you walked in you had the impression of comfort, pleasantness," Olga explained, "but after you were in a while you could see all the furniture was very worn, because I believe Catherine got most of it second hand. She used to buy all these discarded things. She had a whole wall of glass cupboards with all this china. It was very impressive until you started to use it, and then you saw that there were nicks and flaws. But I think she valued it for what it had been. It was simply that to her it originally had been very lovely and still had some loveliness."

Every morning Catherine gave Olga a dollar to buy milk, bread and a few eggs or a can of salmon for supper. In the late afternoon, Catherine came home with over-ripe fruit and wilted vegetables from the farmer's market. Relying on her own domestic training as a girl, Catherine showed Olga how to pare away bruises and sift grain mites from flour. Once she brought home fermenting strawberries and taught Olga how to make jam.

During the day, Olga, Mrs. Field and Flewy worked in the slums, nursing sick mothers, caring for children, scrubbing floors, washing clothes. In the first three months of 1934, they visited over 150 families, while Catherine gave 49 lectures, wrote 4 articles, and found jobs for 36 people. They also stood outside factories and at Communist rallies distributing *The Catholic Worker*, a newspaper published in New York City by Dorothy Day, a former Communist who had converted to Catholicism, and Peter Maurin, a radical Catholic visionary who insisted that the Gospel proclaimed concern for the poor and justice for the worker. Catherine sent Dorothy a description of her plans for a House of Friendship to fight communism in the slums of Toronto. Dorothy encouraged her to open the house at once, but Catherine would not act without the permission of McNeil, who still insisted that she wait out the year.

Instead, Catherine opened a Catholic lending library in her living room on Isabella, and organized a youth group with guest speakers. Three new study groups formed that spring: one for domestic workers, one for new converts, a third for working girls. As study group members expressed interest in Catherine's work, they decided to form an organization of men and women, who would help the poor under Catherine's leadership. Catherine called it the Guild of Our Lady of Atonement, partly because of her association with Graymoor, but mostly because she believed that atonement was the duty of every Catholic. Father William Muckle, rector of St. Michael's Cathedral, agreed to serve as chaplain, and they planned to launch the Guild at a special ceremony in June.

The frenzy of new activity left Catherine dazed, and she later admitted that one night as she prayed for guidance, she felt as if God told her: "Listen to the Spirit, He will lead you." Over time, other inspirations came: "Do little things exceedingly well for love of Me/. . Love — love — love, never counting the cost. . . . Go into the market place and stay with ME. . . pray. . . fast. . . pray always . . . fast."

For Catherine, going into the market place meant moving into the slums, and when her year of waiting ended, she begged McNeil for permission to open a House of Friendship. Her plan was simple: "Convert an empty house into a reading room, meeting room for social activities. Make friends with those who need Friendship above all."

With the deepening depression and the increased unemployment among Catholics, the Archdiocese faced growing financial problems. McNeil tried to raise money to cover the start up costs of Catherine's Friendship House, but was unsuccessful. Catherine assured him that Guild members would staff the house and beg for their needs, but McNeil hesitated. A few weeks later, when Canon H.P. Plumptre of St. James Anglican Cathedral offered Catherine his parish hall for her House of Friendship, she drafted a detailed proposal for McNeil on how an interdenominational Friendship House might operate. Yet Catherine, herself, felt apprehensive about the plan.

> Look at it, O Lord! Is it Thy wish? This mixture of Catholic and Protestant — is it Thy wish that I should take this on me? Think of all it is going to bring me in jealousies, misunderstandings, etc. Please, dear Lord, I am afraid but not my will but Thine. If this is Thy commission really, I'll do it if it crushes me. I love Thee, for Thee I'll do anything, everything.

McNeil told Catherine to decline the Anglican offer, and look for a place where she could operate a Friendship House as a

Catholic center. She found a storefront on Bathurst Street, but the deal fell through. Her second choice was an old meat market on Portland, a side street in an area where Communists were active, but before she could consult McNeil, he was hospitalized with a kidney infection that led to pneumonia.

Catherine was on retreat at the Loretto Abbey on the morning of May 26 when she received word that McNeil died the night before. Panic-stricken at the uncertainty of her position, she promised herself that she would continue the work of Friendship House and the Guild if it were God's will. "There is worldly fear," she prayed, "there is uncertainty of vocation. I have received so little light, but perhaps you wished it so. Peace has come and a little stronger will. But give me the grace of really meaning [it] when I say, 'Your will be done!' Tomorrow, I will have to face the world with all its trials, maybe with a loss of job. O Jesus, stand by me, help me. Somehow I think I am right — your blessing is on my work."

Two days later, Catherine rented the storefront on Portland.

Chapter Notes

"found the discipline too hard": "Student History Card," Archives of St. Michael's Hospital, Toronto.

she told McNeil...: C de H to McNeil, Jan. 3, 1933, ARCAT.

investigate the spread of communism: This was not the first time McNeil hired someone to do investigative work. In the 1920's, he hired Mrs. S.F. (Antonia) Duplantier to investigate the impact of Protestant evangelization on Catholic immigrants. See McNeil papers, ARCAT.

"There he finds...": "Report on Communistic Activities in Toronto, Canada in Relation to the Catholic Church," ARCAT.

The best way to combat this kind...: "Report," March 1 - April, 1933, ARCAT/MHA.

start a Russian restaurant... and f.: Frederick Griffin, "Imperial Refugees," *Toronto Star Weekly*, Dec. 9, 1933.

"a continental charm...": Frank Chamberlain, "Are You Listening," *Toronto Star*, n.d., MHA.

"I am afraid you are going to over-work...": Mother Lurana White to C de H, Feb. 21, 1933, MHA.

"During our visit...": "Social Service Work in Russian Colony In Hayden Street," *Commercial Traveler*, n.d. MHA.

"the voice of those who are voiceless...": "Almsgiving Good, But True Charity Also Needed," unidentified newspaper clip, n.d., MHA.

"We are to blame..." and f.: "Unemployed Cannot Live By Bread Alone..." unidentified newspaper clip, n.d., MHA.

"play the fairy godmother...": "Report of Activities from April 9th to June 1st, 1933," ARCAT/MHA.

"I am sorry to say...": Ibid.

"professing absolute freedom of thought...": "Pope's Censure of Y.M.C.A.," *The Times*, London, Dec. 24, 1920.

"that little clique": Interview, Beatrice Field by Fr. Ric Starks, MHA.

social encyclicals of Pope Pius XI: Divini Illius Magistri (Christian Education, 1929); *Casti Connubii* (Christian Marriage, 1930); *Quadragesimo Anno* (On Restructuring the Social Order, 1931); *Nova Impendet* (Threating News, 1931); *Caritate Christi* (The Sacred Heart and World Distress, 1932).

"the happiest days of my life": Interview, George de Hueck.

"I think she tried...": Interview, Joyce Field.

"He thought his mother was crazy...": Interview, Beatrice Field by Sister Louise Sharum, MHA.

"She was helping Nicholas...": Interview, Anatole Avtzine.

"I have accepted this angle...": "Report of Activities From 1st November 1933 to 1st January 1934," ARCAT/MHA.

"You didn't just see it...": Interview, Olga LaPlante Charlton.

"I speak too much...": Diary #5, July 2, 1933, MHA.

"falling, falling only to get up and fall again!": Diary #5, June 10, 1933, MHA.

"Little - be always little...": *Little Mandate*, MHA.

"Innocence, love, simplicity...": Diary #5, July 13, 1933, MHA.

"Teach me to live by the day!": Diary #5, July 7, 1933, MHA.

"As I knelt before the Blessed Sacrament...": Diary #5, Nov. 13, 1933, MHA.

"It was like a star she was following...": Interview, Olga LaPlante Charlton by Fr. Ric Starks, MHA.

"I really and truly think...": Interview, Olga LaPlante Charlton by Sister Louise Sharum, MHA.

"Oh, it's all so simple...": *Little Mandate*, MHA.

"Never in my wildest dreams...": CD, *The History of the Apostolate*, unpublished manuscript, p. 36, MHA. (Hereafter *History of the Apostolate*).

"When you walked in...": Interview, Olga LaPlante Charlton.

"Listen to the Spirit..." and f.: *Little Mandate*, MHA.

"Convert an empty house...": "Further Confidential Report," March, 1934, ARCAT/MHA.

With the deepening depression: "Contrasting Approaches to Social Action: Henry Somerville, the Educator, and Catherine de Hueck, the Activist," by Jeanne R. Beck, *Catholics At The Gathering Place: Historical Essays on the Archdiocese of Toronto, 1841-1991*, p. 219.

"Look at it, O Lord...": Diary #5, Apr. 10, 1934, MHA.

"There is worldly fear...": Diary #4, May 28, 1934, MHA.

Two days later...: "Report from May 1 - July 1, 1934," ARCAT/MHA.

18

Toronto

1934

Thousands lined the sidewalks on the morning of May 30 as Archbishop McNeil's funeral procession inched its way through Toronto streets. Twice during the following week Catherine called the Chancery to ask if she should continue her work. Nearly three weeks later, she received permission to proceed under the direction of Msgr. Francis Carroll, who had been appointed diocesan administrator until the Vatican appointed a new Archbishop.

On June 23, Father Muckle officiated as 16 charter members of Catherine's Guild of Our Lady of the Atonement promised "active service and loyal obedience to the pastor of any parish where they were called to labor." The next day Guild members started renovating the dilapidated meat market on Portland with the lumber, yellow paint and linoleum that "the begging Baroness" collected.

When Catherine saw neighborhood children peeking through the big front windows, she invited them in, sat them down on the floor because someone was painting the chairs, and told them fantastical stories, which she illustrated with pictures from an old catalog. The next day, the children brought friends for more stories, and the Friendship House children's program unofficially started. Catherine postponed the "official opening" of Friendship House until September because she had already committed herself to attend a six-week summer workshop in Connecticut. If God wants Friendship House to exist, she told the volunteers, it would happen without her. She put the ever-dependable Flewy in charge.

Kay Kenny worked with 40 neighborhood kids, who came each day for stories and games. Mrs. McMahon, who had been referred by Archbishop McNeil before he died, visited the homes of the immigrants. Mrs. Field helped Father Muckle launch a summer day camp for 200 underprivileged kids. Olga ran the apartment on Isabella and looked after George.

By the time Catherine returned to Toronto at the end of August, Friendship House had hundreds of books lining the walls, and unemployed men dropped by daily to read foreign editions of Catholic magazines and newspapers. Father Muckle rented the upstairs flat for the children's program, and young mothers with toddlers clinging to their skirts sat in the kitchen pouring out their troubles over a cup of tea with Flewy. Catherine generated more excitement by telling of her meeting in Connecticut with Dorothy Day and Peter Maurin, who encouraged her to start a Canadian newspaper like *The Catholic Worker*. Msgr. Carroll immediately squelched the idea: "During the vacancy of the See new things are forbidden," he insisted, "as they prejudice the rights of the new Archbishop."

Accustomed to getting results through begging, Catherine assumed Msgr. Carroll would change his mind, and she told a newspaper reporter about plans for a Catholic paper. Carroll was livid, and Catherine later admitted that she had not yet mastered "ecclesiastical etiquette."

Another serious breach of "etiquette" involved Father Campbell W. James, pastor of historic St. Mary's church, within whose boundaries Friendship House had opened. Catherine never contacted Father James when she leased the storefront on Portland, and it wasn't until much later that she learned that the oversight infuriated him. Father James grew more outraged when he did not receive an invitation for the official opening of Friendship House on September 14, and he started keeping track of every mistake Catherine made.

At first, it seemed that nothing at Friendship House could go wrong. The little storefront, named in honor of St. Francis of Assisi, offered English classes for immigrants, sewing lessons, first aid training, meals for homeless men, and free clothing. Study clubs met and guest lecturers challenged listeners with new ideas about God and social justice. The after school program for children swelled to 100, and when the house next door became vacant, Catherine asked Father Muckle: "Would you take another house on nothing but trust in God?"

"I would take a whole block and trust in God!" he laughed.

Within four days of signing the new lease, they received a Quebec heater, four tons of coal, furniture, supplies, and pledges to pay the rent. Within ten days, the children's program moved to the new house, and they opened a dormitory upstairs with 10 beds for transient men. "Early Friendship House was a place where Christ was," Mrs. Field insisted. "He definitely was there. He was living. He was with you. You were with him. He was there blessing the work. He was working with us."

When a businessman refused to donate a load of coal, Catherine prayed, and the next day, a coal truck delivered a donation from a women's group. Catherine and Flewy carried overdue bills and overdraft notices to church so God could see for himself how much they needed. Money — sometimes to the exact penny — seemed to fall out of the sky. Once, after Catherine offered temporary shelter to a group of prostitutes, a van pulled up with an unexpected donation of blankets salvaged from a fire.

"We got so used to things like this happening," recalled Mrs. Field. "It was more than mere coincidence. It was so obviously an answer to prayer."

Even Msgr. Carroll seemed impressed: "It is a wonder that you are able to do so much on such little means."

Window posters announced daily activities and the large yellow sign on the front of the storefront read: FRIENDSHIP HOUSE — ALL WELCOME. Country parishes sent bags of produce and dairy products. Hotels and restaurants donated food. Society women hosted card parties and teas to raise money. People sent canned goods and used clothes. Students and blue collar laborers worked side by side with businessmen, professors, lawyers, and doctors. "That's why she called it Friendship House,"

Olga explained. "Every type of society that mixed in came to know others and you forgot the differences. You didn't see that they were French or Slavic or any other race. They were people. It broke down prejudices and people became sympathetic and understanding."

As Friendship House grew, Communist efforts also intensified. Catherine told stories about children spitting on a crucifix during the Communist Sunday School, and about a young man who joined a Communist cell at the university "because I cannot reconcile my father's church going and his treatment of his factory hands, because I cannot reconcile my mother's church going and her treatment of her maid." Bolshevism thrived, Catherine insisted, because lukewarm Christians did not live the Gospel message. She called communism a movement against God, fueled by hate, which could only be countered with Christian love. "Follow the teaching of Christ, 'Thou shalt love thy neighbor as thy self,' and there will be no Bolshevism," she pleaded.

In February 1935, Catherine invited Dorothy Day to lecture in Toronto, and Dorothy echoed Catherine's warning about the Communist intrusion of a materialistic and atheistic philosophy on society. Inspired by Dorothy's stories about the Catholic Worker's House of Hospitality in New York, Father Muckle suggested to Catherine that they open a Catholic Worker house in the Cathedral parish. While Friendship House focused on immigrants, Father Muckle wanted the Catholic Worker to serve unemployed Canadians with a library, a reading room, and a lecture series on Catholic social issues. Catherine rented a storefront at 82 Church Street, and the house opened the following April.

While Catherine's work appeared to prosper, tensions and gossip grew among Guild members. Mrs. McMahon felt slighted because Catherine had not introduced her to Dorothy Day. Joe O'Connor returned from a visit to Montreal with disturbing rumors about Catherine's past. Kay Kenny became increasingly moody. Three male staff members threatened to quit. Olga questioned inconsistencies in what Catherine said and did. Even Mrs. Field complained about personality conflicts.

Catherine listed her own irritations: "eternal interruptions, no privacy, a coming and going through my room, having to listen to all the foolish ideas of everybody, straightening unstraightenable things, lack of money." At the same time, she agonized over whether her shortcomings, ("Lazy, proud, full of self-satisfaction, irritable, talkative, foolish, untruthful"), drove people away.

Catherine had the ability to both attract and repel people with an intensity few others possessed. People felt drawn by her spontaneous generosity and self-sacrifice, her empathy for others, and the love that radiated from her inner being, but she could also be abrupt, domineering, argumentative, and downright mulish, with idiosyncrasies and strange Russian habits that some described as coarse and rude. "She would chew away at biscuits and dip them in her tea cup like they did in Russia, and they criticized her," Mrs. Field recalled. "What kind of a Baroness could she be if she had such bad manners in a place where manners meant everything?"

Catherine seemed to fit Dostoevsky's description of Russians as "half-saint, half-savage." She loomed larger than life with both faults and virtues magnified to an extraordinary degree. She was a paradox. Highly efficient and organized, she held little regard for details, dates, or rules. She could express strong opinions one minute, and contradict herself the next. She could walk into a room and unconsciously claim everyone's attention, but if someone tried to put her in the spotlight, she would react as if they had insulted her. For North Americans, who lived with a rigidly defined sense of right and wrong, she seemed illogical and unpredictable. "These Anglo-Saxons are unappreciative of imagination and sometimes judge one unkindly when facts do not jibe perfectly," a priest warned. "You can work splendidly with them, for a while. But if you are forced to spend 24 hours a day with them they will get on your nerves and you on theirs."

Olga walked out one night in frustration, and when she returned three days later, Catherine exclaimed: "Well, have you got your feet on the ground? Do you see that I am just an ordinary woman?"

Catherine agonized in the confessional about her difficulty with people, and the priest told her there was no way she could live up to everyone's standards. He said she had to meet God's expectations, and he told her to select one fault a month and work hard to fight it. Despite her efforts, friction among Guild members grew to such intensity that Father Muckle advised her to ask one of the more difficult men to leave. Another resigned publicly, which caused Catherine extreme embarrassment. She posted signs in Friendship House that read: WE DO NOT DISCUSS PEOPLE IN THIS HOUSE — ONLY POLICIES. PLEASE REFRAIN FROM GOSSIP.

Gossip continued, however, and it centered not just on Catherine, but on 13-year-old George, who had become sullen and withdrawn. His language toward Catherine had grown increasingly abusive. He skipped school and lied about where he had gone. He refused to go to church. He always had spending money, but would not say where he got it. When someone stole a purse at Friendship House, suspicion centered on George. "She used to cry to me about him," recalled Mrs. Field. "I'd tell her she was just wasting her tears."

What Catherine and Mrs. Field did not know is that a priest at school was sexually abusing George, and George's whole being revolted in anger against God, school, the Catholic Church, and his mother. As George's behavior spiraled downward, Catherine prayed with greater intensity, pouring out fears that she had failed him as a mother. She agonized over whether she should give up Friendship House and try to create a more normal home life for him. She begged for guidance and understanding, but concrete answers never came, and in her confusion, she waffled in the way she treated George — too strict on unimportant things and too lenient when she should have remained firm.

Boris complicated matters. He came frequently to visit George, often bringing Claudia with him, and they would stay at the house on Isabella for as long as a week or two. Olga recalled the way Boris raged at the dinner table, while Catherine sat in silence allowing his angry accusations to wash over her. "He was

Emma Kolyschkine holding
Catherine. "You are born," Emma
told her daughter, "under the
shadow of the cross".

Theodore Kolyschkine (left) and the Russian
Ambassador to Egypt pose in Egyptian dress.

Catherine as a young girl.

The Kolyschkine summer estate in Antrea, Finland was 105 miles by train from St. Petersburg.

Catherine's half brother, Vsevolod Kolyschkine. "I actually venerated Vsevolod," she recalled.

Dunia Vassova, a young Russian woman from Murmansk, worked for Catherine and Boris as a maid in London. Dunia later emigrated with them to Canada.

While stationed in Murmansk during the Russian Civil War, Catherine wore on the jacket of her uniform the St. George Cross, Russia's highest military honor, which she received for bravery during World War I.

Boris, George, and Catherine in Toronto, 1922.

Claudia Kolenova, known in Toronto as "the fairest of the exiles," was a former ballerina with the Imperial Corps de Ballet in St. Petersburg, Russia.

Leaving four-year-old George was Catherine's "biggest sacrifice" during her years as a lecturer.

Catherine dressed in Russian costume during her lecture tour on the Chautauqua circuit.

Nicholas Makletzoff, the man Catherine hoped would rescue her from a tragic life with Boris, arrived in Canada in 1930.

Dorothy Day (left), founder of the Catholic Worker, encouraged Catherine (right) to open a Friendship House in Toronto.

Grace Flewwelling (top) and Olga LaPlante (bottom) were among the first Friendship House staff workers.

Mrs. Beatrice Field was one of Catherine's first friends and supporters in Toronto.

Catherine opened the first Friendship House in 1934 on Portland Street in the slums of Toronto.

Boris de Hueck with 14-year-old George outside Catherine's apartment on Isabella Street in Toronto.

Ellen Tarry, a black reporter for the *Amsterdam News*, came "under the spell of the Baroness" the first time they met.

Grace Flewwelling, known to everyone as Flewy, came to Harlem to help Catherine. Flewy later followed Catherine to Combermere.

In 1938, Catherine opened Friendship House in Harlem where she became a forerunner of the Civil Rights Movement.

A 1940 portrait of Catherine.

Eddie Doherty, "the highest paid reporter in America," came to Friendship House in 1940 to write a story about Harlem for *Liberty Magazine*.

In February 1943, Catherine disappeared into the slums of Chicago where she worked as "Katie Hook," an immigrant waitress.

On the evening of June 25, 1943, the Doherty clan gathered at the family homestead to celebrate Eddie's secret marriage to Catherine. From left: Bishop Bernard J. Sheil, Eddie Doherty, Catherine, and Eddie's mother, surrounded by Doherty family members.

Catherine and Eddie in Combermere.

Eddie, Catherine, and Father John Callahan at dinner in the Madonna House dining room.

Catherine lecturing during summer school on the back porch at Madonna House.

Louis Stoeckle, Kathleen O'Herin, and Mamie Legris leaving Combermere in a truck named "Mickey" for their trek across Canada to open the first field house in the Yukon Territory.

Father Emile Briere arrived in Combermere for a one-year sabbatical in 1956. By the following year, Catherine and Fr. Callahan had drawn him into a leadership position at Madonna House.

Joe Walker and Ronnie MacDonnell clear rocks from the fields on a farm purchased by the de Vinck family of New Jersey, who allowed Madonna House to use the land for growing produce and raising pigs and chickens.

In 1957, Father Callahan (left) gave Melkite Rite priest, Father Joseph Raya (right), a Pax Caritas cross, making him the first Madonna House Associate priest.

Catherine outside the first Poustinia in Combermere, 1961.

Catherine and Father Callahan (center) gather with staff members in the yard to say farewell to the newest Madonna House priest, Father Bob Pelton (right), who was leaving to study in Rome during the Second Vatican Council, 1964.

On May 17, 1972 Catherine's dream of a Russian chapel came true when Bishop Joseph Windle of Pembroke consecrated Our Lady of the Woods chapel in a clearing surrounded by tall pines on the Madonna House property.

Archbishop Joseph Raya (right) ordained Eddie Doherty (left) a Melkite Rite priest on August 15, 1969.

Credit: John Evans.

In April 1976, Jules Leger, the Governor General of Canada, presented Catherine with Canada's highest civilian award, the Order of Canada, for her dedication to helping the poor.

Credit: Arturo Mari, Servizio Fotografico, L'Osservatore Romano.

Catherine and Father Briere with Pope John Paul II during a trip to Rome in 1981.

Catherine and Father Briere leaving the Madonna House chapel in 1979. As Catherine grew older, Father Briere became a constant source of help and consolation.

a highly intelligent man. He had all the charm of the cultured person. But you felt that anger was in him, and she was certainly the object of it."

Catherine's diary entries during these visits often contained only two words: "Boris — misery."

The situation infuriated Mrs. Field: "I could not stand the man; I detested him. He was a typical aristocrat of the dirtiest, the meanest kind. And he was horrible to her."

To Catherine only one thing seemed clear: That she had received a call from God to which she had to be faithful. She placed George and Boris in God's hands and continued with her work: "I have begun the Guild at the request of His Grace Archbishop Neil McNeil. I have begun it for the glory of God. I will stop only at the request of the next Bishop."

Catherine intended this journal entry as a steely commitment to continue in spite of all obstacles. It proved to be an eerie premonition.

Chapter Notes

"active service and loyal obedience...": "Guild of Our Lady of Atonement," *The Catholic Register*, June 28, 1934.

"the begging Baroness...": During this time, Friendship House volunteers started referring to Catherine as "the B," a shortened form of the Baroness. Years later, in Harlem, some children nicknamed her "The Bee who brings us honey," and joked that she was always "as busy as a bee."

"During the vacancy of the See...": Msgr. Francis P. Carroll to C de H, Sept. 12, 1934, MHA.

"ecclesiastical etiquette...": *History of the Apostolate*, p. 119.

"Would you take another house..." and f.: *Friendship House*, p. 14.

"Early Friendship House was a place...": Interview, Beatrice Field by Sr. Louise Sharum, MHA

"We got so used to things...": *Ibid.*

"It is a wonder...": Msgr. Francis P. Carroll to C de H, Dec. 12, 1934, MHA.

"That's why she called it Friendship House...": Interview, Olga LaPlante Charlton.

"because I cannot reconcile...": "'We Spit on Christ Yesterday...'" unidentified newspaper clip, n.d., MHA.

"Follow the teaching of Christ...": *Ibid.*

"eternal interruptions, no privacy..." and f.: Diary #4, Feb. 12, 1935, MHA.

"She would chew away...": Interview, Beatrice Field by Sr. Louise Sharum, MHA.

"These Anglo-Saxons...": Fr. T. Smith Sullivan (Hereafter Sullivan) to C de H, Sept. 22, n.d., MHA.

"Well, have you got...": Interview, Olga LaPlante Charlton.

the priest told her...: Diary #11, Feb. 9, 1935, MHA.

"WE DO NOT DISCUSS PEOPLE...": *Ibid.*, Mar. 22, 1935, MHA.

"She used to cry to me...": Interview, Beatrice Field by Sr. Louise Sharum, MHA.

What Catherine and Mrs. Field did not know...: Interview, George de Hueck.

"He was a highly intelligent man...": Interview, Olga LaPlante Charlton.

"I could not stand the man...": Interview, Beatrice Field by Sr. Louise Sharum, MHA.

"I have begun the Guild...": Diary #10, Mar. 15, 1935, MHA.

19

Toronto

1935

On March 20, 1935, the new Archbishop of Toronto, James Charles McGuigan, arrived at Union Station with all the pageantry of a crowned prince. A procession of cars, marching bands, and uniformed Knights of Columbus escorted him to the Bishop's palace on Wellesley Place. That evening at St. Michael's Cathedral, the Papal Delegate installed 40-year-old McGuigan as spiritual shepherd of the archdiocese. "My heart will go out in particular to the poor, the unfortunate, the unemployed, the sick in body, and soul — according to the pattern of the Master," McGuigan promised.

Encouraged by his words, Catherine sent him a detailed report on Friendship House, and asked for an appointment. McGuigan's secretary denied her request, and informed her that Father Hugh Gallagher, director of Catholic Charities, would oversee her work. A quiet, unassuming man, Father Gallagher assured Catherine of his full support, but Catherine insisted on sending monthly reports to the Archbishop's office anyway. The response from McGuigan's secretary remained the same: The Archbishop is busy with other matters.

As it became obvious that McGuigan did not favor Catherine as McNeil had, her relations with Toronto clergy deteriorated. Questions arose about her background, her son, her estranged husband, and her work in the slums. At this difficult point, when Catherine desperately needed someone whose opinions she could trust, Father Henry Carr, the highly respected Superior General of the Basilian Fathers in Toronto, offered to help. "There is one side of the work, and it is a very important one, in which I think I could be of some assistance to you," he wrote. "It is in helping to win the cooperation of priests."

Father James, the pastor of St. Mary's, still loomed at the forefront of Catherine's growing list of ecclesiastical enemies. Only four years older than Catherine, he was authoritarian with a high-strung temperament. St. Mary's prided itself on being one of the oldest and largest Irish parishes in the city with activities ranging from guest preachers, novenas, and special Masses to sodality meetings, a boy's bugle band, several choirs, and men's and women's bowling leagues. Parishioners ignored the influx of Slavic immigrants and Communists in nearby neighborhoods. It was the kind of parish Catherine accused in speeches of being inbred and self-serving with no concern for the poor. Her speeches did not endear her to Father James. Their first encounter occurred when she brought an immigrant to the rectory for convert instructions. Father James turned her away claiming no one ever informed him of her official standing in the diocese. Their next encounter was at St. Mary's parish bazaar. "What is your business here?" he scowled. "No one asked you to come!"

In April 1935, when the president of St. Mary's Mother's Club invited Catherine to the grand opening of the pre-natal health clinic the women had started in the parish hall, Catherine noted that Father James' behavior left her feeling "insecure and miserable."

Problems also surfaced between Catherine and Father Muckle, who had been one of her staunchest supporters. A series of disagreements about the operation of the newly opened Catholic Worker house resulted in Father Muckle banning all women — including Catherine — from the premises. A few weeks later, he resigned as spiritual director of Friendship House, ending his monthly $30 donation, and making it clear to diocesan authorities that he had no affiliation with Catherine.

Differences of opinion between Catherine and Father Keating, who had been acting as her spiritual director, culminated in his telling her she was imprudent and made overstatements. "He also warned me that I was losing all my friends, and would soon be friendless here as I antagonized so many people."

Stunned at the extent to which people had turned against her, Catherine decided to present the situation to McGuigan, and offer to resign. The Archbishop denied her request for an appointment. Fr. Paul of Graymoor, who had supported Friendship House financially since its inception, tried to intercede: "The late Archbishop took the greatest interest in her work, and she misses him sadly," he wrote to McGuigan, but McGuigan replied that he had no time for the Baroness because he was "absolutely overcrowded with strictly essential business."

When Catherine reached what she thought was her lowest point, Boris stormed into Toronto demanding a divorce. She refused on the basis that the annulment was still in progress. Infuriated, Boris threatened to start a scandal, and hired a private detective to follow her. "I think he just wanted to tear her down," Olga recalled. "You see, she had abandoned the type of life he understood, and he didn't understand the type of life she was aiming for. If he could destroy her image that would all be a wash. I don't think that he hoped to gain anything in his own personal life because he had what he wanted. He had a mistress. He had a good job. He had a good home and money. But what he couldn't have he wanted to smash."

It seems almost miraculous that in the midst of this turmoil, Friendship House prospered. That spring, Catherine leased a third house near Portland Street and transformed it into a boy's club with a carpentry shop, an art studio, and a game room. Father Carr served as the spiritual director for Friendship House, and on June 23, in a ceremony at St. Basil's, he officiated as nine members of the Guild of Our Lady of Atonement renewed their promises and a new woman joined. There were six fewer members than the year before, but Catherine did not seem worried: "I was just walking on air — one year!!!"

As summer wore on, however, the work expanded rapidly, and Catherine accepted volunteers without bothering to check backgrounds. New problems erupted: The retired army cook, who promised he could stay sober, disappeared on all-night binges. A woman volunteer suffered a nervous breakdown. A male staff member had an affair with a married woman in the neighborhood. Another male staff worker ended up in jail after exposing himself to a group of boys at the beach. To outside observers it appeared as if even Mrs. Field deserted Friendship House when she moved to the country to work as a nurse in a "back to the land" farm community started by a local priest.

Two spiritual truths saved Catherine that summer: The first was the understanding that she had to live by the minute, not worrying about the past or the future, but trusting God moment by moment. The second was the idea that in each moment God would reveal to her his will, and she coined the phrase: "The duty of the moment is the will of God."

The final words of her Little Mandate also took hold: "Be hidden, be a light to your neighbor's feet. Go without fears into the depths of men's hearts. . . I shall be with you. Pray always. I will be your rest." She told Fr. Carr in confession that she had a strong desire for a hidden life with God and that sometimes an over-whelming sensation seemed to sweep her off her feet. At times, she told him, God's presence seemed sweet, but at other times, it terrified her. Father Carr told Catherine that these experiences of God were a great gift. He explained that there is a kind of knowledge, divinely inspired, which comes not through study, but through prayer and through grace. He encouraged Catherine to remain open to inspirations of the Spirit, abandoning herself to God's will, and accepting suffering as it comes because it may have a purpose beyond her understanding. He warned that her work must always be secondary to the goal of personal holiness, and he tried to temper her dealings with other people without suppressing her spirit.

That September, the attitudes of the Toronto clergy changed abruptly. Toronto radio priest, Father Charles Lamphier, asked if he could broadcast a special program about Friendship House. Father James proposed a truce, and gave Catherine names of five

Irish families in St. Mary's parish that might benefit from her help. Rumors ceased and several priests stopped to visit. The sudden reversal in attitude became understandable when McGuigan's secretary called to say the Archbishop decided to visit Friendship House in October.

At three o'clock on the afternoon of October 2, McGuigan arrived with Father James and Father Gallagher. "His Grace saw all things," Catherine noted, "went thru all the rooms, stayed a long time in our upstairs offices where the atheistic literature is located and showed a great interest in all its phases, asked me innumerable questions — How many children? Boys? Girls? Did we reach the teenagers? Why not? Figures on communism, etc. About myself, again Communists and how they worked? Where came the money for their activities? So forth and so on. He blessed the children and in going away said, 'It is a good work and I will pray God to bless it.'"

When McGuigan allocated $100 a month from Catholic Charities to assist Friendship House, Catherine was elated. A few days later, Lamphier gave Friendship House a glowing report in his radio broadcast. Catherine followed up with a note to the chancery, asking for an appointment with McGuigan and a letter of approbation to solidify her relations with the clergy. The letter never came and Catherine's request for an appointment was denied.

That fall, 14-year-old George received a summons to appear in Juvenile Court on delinquency charges. The court was, in the words of Judge Hawley S. Mott, "not a place of shame, but a clinic to discover and treat adolescent misbehavior in the same way a hospital would treat the body." Yet not even the court psychologists could get to the root of George's pain, and the judge decided George should go to boarding school as a disciplinary measure. Catherine made arrangements at Assumption College, a Basilian school in Windsor, Ontario, where one of the priests George knew from St. Michael's had recently transferred. She hoped the priest's presence would ease George's transition. She had no idea this was the priest who had abused George. On November 9, 1935, George boarded a bus for Windsor, and Catherine wept inconsolably.

Three days later Dorothy Day came to Toronto for a visit. "It is the devil at work," Dorothy insisted, and she told Catherine that constant trials simply proved her work was all right in the eyes of God/Catherine wanted more concrete assurances. She wanted the stability that she believed could only come from the approval of someone in authority/and she asked Father Paul of Graymoor about affiliating Friendship House and its staff under his direction. He arrived in Toronto that December to discuss the matter with McGuigan. Catherine accompanied him to the meeting, but McGuigan's secretary asked her to wait outside. "They seem all to take this attitude of barely tolerating and barely allowing me to do good! Jesus, what have I done to antagonize them so?"

Later that evening Father Paul told her that McGuigan approved plans for affiliation with Graymoor. Thrilled at these new developments, Catherine decided Christmas at Friendship House would be a celebration beyond compare. Her joy withered and died on December 21, however, when George staggered off the train from Windsor with a strep throat and a 103 degree temperature. "O Mother of God," she prayed, "what have they done to my baby in six weeks!" Within days, George's throat abscessed and pneumonia set in. He remained hospitalized until late January, and had not fully recovered when trouble erupted again over a money order that detectives said George forged with the signature of a man who lived in the upstairs apartment on Isabella. "Jesus, Jesus mercy," Catherine prayed. "How can this be!!!" Judge Mott ordered that George could no longer live in that house, so Catherine put him on a train to Montreal where he would live with Boris and Claudia.

"I do not try to understand why my life must be a series of increasing suffering," Catherine prayed. "Boris, George's life, even my work — are a cross exquisitely painful. I cannot see, my eyes are blinded with tears, my heart is torn, my soul crucified but if it is your will so it will be."

At Friendship House, staff workers bickered among themselves, and as new people came, others left. Father James stirred up more trouble by insisting the Friendship House boys and girls' clubs overlapped with the work of his parish youth groups. "For pity's sake," Catherine observed, "five years I work in this neighborhood and his 50 boys club of "chosen" boys functions without affecting the ones who need it most — the poor boys — foreign ones. So in sheer desperation I went to Fr. Puchniak and asked him to take us over. After all, we started to work for the foreigners, why not do it wholeheartedly and we must work with a parish priest, not against him, as we are doing with Fr. James."

Father Stanley Puchniak, 35 years old, had recently been named pastor of St. Stanislaus, a small Polish parish within the boundaries of St. Mary's. St. Stanislaus church had opened 20 years before when Polish immigrants began arriving in Toronto. At first, Father Puchniak seemed excited about the idea of transferring Friendship House to his jurisdiction, but as new rumors about Catherine circulated, he became wary and started asking questions about where Friendship House fit in Canon Law.

"Everything weighs so heavily," Catherine prayed, "so big loom all my little problems."

It was the worst possible time for Catherine to even think about expansion, but a study group had already formed under her direction in Hamilton with the hope of eventually opening a Friendship House there. In February 1936, she gave a series of lectures in Ottawa, and the Diocesan Council for Catholic Action voted unanimously to open a Friendship House. Catherine promised that she would return to Ottawa later in the spring to help them get started, but as spring approached, doubts plagued her: "It seems so difficult to see what to do and Ottawa again looks like a nightmare to me."

In March, Catherine found a 10-room house on Cameron Place, a slum street three blocks from Friendship House where she could live with Olga, Flewy, and several other women staff workers. Father Paul of Graymoor liked the idea of Catherine living with the staff and promised to send $40 monthly to cover the rent. The house was large enough for Catherine to make a home for George, who hated living with Boris and Claudia in Montreal. Mrs. Field also wanted to move into the house with her two daughters, and offered to look after George while Catherine went to Ottawa. Olga agreed to move Catherine's furniture and belongings from Isabella Street. Michael Gray assured Catherine that he would oversee the daily operation of Friendship House with Flewy handling finances. Catherine still felt apprehensive about going to Ottawa, but she could find no reason to renege on her promise to open a Friendship House there. On the evening of April 2, 1936, she boarded a train for Canada's capital.

Chapter Notes

"My heart will go out...": Claude Laing Fischer, *James Cardinal McGuigan, Archbishop of Toronto*, p. 28.

a quiet, unassuming man...: Interview, Fr. Joseph O'Neill.

"There is one side...": Fr. Henry Carr, CSB (hereafter Carr) to C de H, Apr. 11, 1935, MHA. [For information on Fr. Carr see Edmund J. McCorkell, *Henry Carr - Revolutionary*, Toronto: Griffin House, 1969.]

authoritarian with a high-strung temperament: Interview, Fr. Joseph O'Neill.

"What is your business here?": *History of the Apostolate*, p. 121.

"insecure and miserable": Diary #10, Apr. 25, 1935, MHA.

"He also warned me...": Diary #10, May 11, 1935, MHA.

"The late Archbishop...": Fr. Paul James Francis Wattson (hereafter Fr. Paul of Graymoor) to Archbishop James Charles McGuigan (hereafter McGuigan), June 5, 1935, FAA.

"absolutely overcrowded...": McGuigan to Fr. Paul of Graymoor, June 13, 1935, FAA.

"I think he just wanted...": Interview, Olga LaPlante Charlton.

"I was just walking on air...": Diary #11, June 23, 1935, MHA.

Two spiritual truths: During this time, Catherine was reading *Abandonment to Divine Providence*, by Jean Pierre de Caussade, SJ, which espouses both of these ideas.

"Be hidden...": Little Mandate, MHA.

She told Fr. Carr...: Diary #9, Sept. 9, 1935, MHA.

"His Grace saw all things...": Diary #7, Oct. 2, 1935, MHA.

"not as a place of shame...": *The Catholic Register*, Mar. 3, 1934.

She had no idea this was the priest: Interview, George de Hueck.

"It is the devil at work...": Diary #9, Nov. 13, 1935, MHA.

"They seem all to take this attitude...": Diary #7, Dec. 4, 1935, MHA.

"O Mother of God...": Diary #8, Dec. 21, 1935, MHA.

"How can this be!!!": Ibid., Jan. 27, 1936, MHA.

"I do not try to understand...": Diary #14, Mar. 27, 1936, MHA.

"For pity's sake...": Diary #8, Feb. 6, 1936, MHA.

"Everything weighs so heavily...": Diary #14, Feb. 14, 1936, MHA.

"It seems so difficult...": Diary #14, Mar. 11, 1936, MHA.

20

Ottawa

1936

As Catherine's train steamed into Ottawa, a welcoming committee headed by Mrs. Martha French, a middle-aged matron interested in Catholic Action, and Father Thomas Smith Sullivan, a handsome young Oblate working on his doctoral degree, waited for her on the platform. Their enthusiasm did not calm Catherine's churning stomach. "I am sorry I am such a coward," she prayed, "but it is frightening."

Within a few days Catherine met an angry woman, who criticized the work of Friendship House. Several people told her they knew Boris, and someone warned about a rift between Mrs. French's Catholic Action group and the Catholic Women's League. Animosity also brewed between French-speaking Catholics and English-speaking Catholics. "Watch your step," a sympathetic priest warned.

Refusing to allow her fear to show, Catherine plunged into the work with a zest that fascinated Father Sullivan. "You, of course, are a fox," he told her, "and I like you all the more for it." An American, Thomas Smith Sullivan had a sharp mind, a quick wit, and keen understanding of people and Church politics. He saw Catherine as a superb lecturer and a master organizer: "I never once thought you to be a saint!" They met on her first trip to Ottawa, and Catherine encouraged him to start a Catholic newspaper. The following month, Father Sullivan and members of a Catholic Action group published the first issue of the *Social Forum*. Both Catherine and Father Sullivan envisioned the paper as an extension of Friendship House, and one week after her arrival, Catherine, Father Sullivan, and Mrs. French leased an old hotel at 279 Rochester Street that would become the site of Friendship House and editorial offices for the *Social Forum*.

On June 3, Friendship House officially opened with Archbishop Guillaume Forbes presiding: "I welcome to this city this house where Christian charity will be practiced, where both the body and mind will be fed." Within one month, over 400 homeless men sat down every day to free meals. Study clubs formed, a clothing room opened, and an open forum with guest speakers started. "Madame la Baronne is the talk of the town," Father Sullivan noted.

Like thunder clouds in the west, however, news from Toronto cast shadows over Catherine's success. Letters detailed quarrels among staff. The City of Toronto condemned the house where the boys club met. Flewy reported several hundred dollars in unpaid bills and a $70 checking account overdraft. Mild mannered Father Gallagher exploded when a hardware store sent a letter telling McGuigan that the Friendship House account was past due. Catherine diverted excess money from Ottawa to bail them out. "Many are my worries now," she prayed, "deep and profound they are about Toronto. Help me go through this trial."

No relief came. Instead, George arrived to spend the summer. Boris and Claudia followed a few days later to visit George. "It is like wave after wave of misery coming either from one side or another," Catherine wrote.

On June 19, less than three weeks after the Ottawa Friendship House opened, the chaplain, Father Henri St. Denis, told Catherine that rumors about Ottawa money sent to Toronto had reached Archbishop Forbes. Catherine spent a sleepless night worrying: "They crucified Him," she wrote in her journal. "Be ready to be crucified."

In mid-July, Forbes sent Father St. Denis on a fact-finding mission to Toronto to uncover the truth about the Baroness. St. Denis met privately with McGuigan, and a few days later, McGuigan announced that a commission of Toronto priests would investigate Friendship House. Named to the commission were Father James; Father Puchniak; Father Gallagher; Father J.M. Clare, the diocesan Chancellor; and Father George Daly, CSSR, Catherine's long-time friend and supporter. "Father Puchniak as well as the priest in charge of the Ottawa Friendship House are not satisfied with the solidity of the Baroness' work," McGuigan confided in a letter to Father Paul of Graymoor.

> Ottawa really wants to quietly take the whole matter under local direction and to have the Baroness retired from that centre. It would seem that she wants to be a free lance, wants undue publicity and is too vague in her endeavors. Father Puchniak and others seem to feel that while her intentions are excellent, her field is too vague and the results of the work doubtful.

Father Paul of Graymoor responded with a strong defense:

> It seems to me that God has given her a real apostolate to the Communists. She possesses a grasp and understanding of the red propaganda quite beyond that of the ordinary student of Bolshevism. Ever since she came to America she has been a public lecturer on the subject as well as a public writer, but whether she "wants undue publicity" I personally question. If she has been heretofore "a free lance," nevertheless she has shown a disposition to be under direction and ecclesiastic control. . . Has she not, both in Toronto and Ottawa, sought to do all things under the approval and direction of the Archbishop? Some have called her proud, but in reality, I regard her as a very humble woman, not hesitating to scrub the floors and to do the most menial tasks in ministering to the poor, to spend and be spent in the service of humanity. As to the vagueness of her field, it seems to me that during the two years of her work in Toronto she accomplished much that was very practical, particularly in reaching so large a number of boys and girls, youths and young women, drawing many of

them away from communistic influence and bringing them back into touch with Our Lord in the Sacraments of Holy Church. That she has done all this, not for vainglory and self-aggrandizement, but out of pure love for the Sacred Heart and the souls that He redeemed by His Precious Blood, I have no doubt.

Catherine knew nothing about these developments. Exhausted physically and emotionally, she spent the last two weeks of August at the cottage in Ste. Marguerite. When she returned to Ottawa, she learned that Archbishop Forbes planned to turn Friendship House over to an order of French-speaking brothers. Mrs. French was fighting to keep Friendship House under the control of English-speaking lay people. Father Sullivan was out of town and Father St. Denis remained aloof. "I was glad to get out of my connections with her," St. Denis later admitted. "There was always something mysterious and shady in her dealing."

Father Paul of Graymoor advised Catherine to return to Toronto: "There is undoubtedly a whole lot of prejudice existing among the clergy relative to yourself and I dare say some of it exists in the commission appointed by the Archbishop of Toronto."

Catherine arrived in Toronto on September 13. Father James looked away when he saw her at Mass that Sunday. "I will be glad when all this is over," she thought. The study group from Hamilton still wanted to open a Friendship House, and she had inquiries about opening houses in Windsor and Quebec, but she decided to wait until the commission finished its investigation before making any commitments. "The whole trouble is that gossip credits me with 100 things I never did," she told Father Paul.

However, as I said before it really does not matter if God knows the truth, as he does in this case. The fact is that I have done what I have done for God alone — He knows that no laurels or vanity or glory have come to me through it. I have just refused a contract for Chautauqua work — $100 per week in 12 weeks — so it is certain I am not in the work for the money. I have none. Instead of glory, I got nothing out of it, but reviling, suspicion, calumnies, and persecution.

In late September, the commission met and secretly recommended to McGuigan that Friendship House close. When Catherine confronted Father Daly about the meeting, he confided to her that Father James had insisted that her work was a duplication of what his parish already did, and that St. Mary's could make better use of the diocesan funds Friendship House received.

McGuigan did not act on the commission's recommendation. Instead he invited Father Paul of Graymoor to discuss the matter with the commission members during a closed meeting on October 15. After the meeting, Father Paul told Catherine several committee members described her as domineering and uncontrollable. They accused Friendship House of financial mismanagement and not doing the work it claimed. Outraged, Catherine denied every accusation. No one came to see Friendship House except Fr. Daly. No one looked at the books. No one asked her to explain or defend herself. "All censure was informal, closed and personal!"

Four days after Father Paul's departure, the commission met again. Fr. James insisted he could not tolerate Friendship House in his parish.

"Would we be losing something even if ever so small?" Father Gallagher asked.

"I'm certain that Friendship House is not doing much against communism," Father James countered.

Father Daly defended Catherine, but Father James remained adamant, and in a four to one vote, with Father Daly the only dissenting member, the commission recommended that Friendship House close.

Torn over whether Catherine was "a saint or an adventuress," McGuigan appealed one last time to Father Puchniak, promising that if he allowed Friendship House to operate in his parish the diocese would pay all expenses. Puchniak saw it as "a raw deal." He was wary of the Friendship House staff ("They struck me in general as disturbed people, helpless people. . . they had no training."), and he wanted Polish-speaking nuns for his parish. "Sometimes," he later reflected, "spiritual visionaries seem impractical to the general run of us." Saying no, he admitted, "was one of the most painful things I've ever had to do."

In mid-November Catherine wrote to McGuigan begging for answers. "The suspense is very hard to bear, not only for me, but for my associates and is intensely detrimental to the work." She added a heart wrenching personal note, insisting that whatever mistakes she made were not malicious or intentional: "Your Grace," she begged, "please give me a chance to see you and explain the matter."

An appointment was arranged with Father Gallagher, who told her that Friendship House had to close by year's end.

"The Archbishop has spoken and Friendship House is no more," Catherine wrote Father Carr. "There is nothing one can do except to accept humbly the verdict without trying to think about it — just in imitation of the obedience of Christ. . . The truth can never be told by me because if I do so it will be detrimental to my Archbishop and, little as I understand his actions, no one will ever hear from me anything detrimental to the Archdiocese."

True to her word, Catherine never spoke a negative word in public about the closing of Friendship House. When she went to Hamilton, she said only that the parishes had absorbed the work of Friendship House. She could not bear to go to Ottawa, and sent Olga, while she remained in Toronto to dismiss staff and dispose of furniture.

With no official reason given for the closing, rumors ran wild. A nun at the Loretto Abbey told her class Catherine was unmasked as a Communist and had fled to Moscow. Another nun claimed Catherine took $3,000 in Friendship House money and escaped to Paris. Both nuns apologized, but gossip persisted.

"I spend so much time on the phone refuting the charges they bring against you," Mrs. French admitted.

"I never knew a person who had so many enemies in one town," Father Gallagher confessed.

Early in December, McGuigan asked Catherine to stay on the payroll of the Archdiocese, writing articles about communism, giving lectures, and surveying parishes for Communist infiltration. A great tiredness flooded over her. Two years before everything seemed so clear, but now she wondered if God had really called her to this work. A few weeks later, George, who had gone to live with Boris in Montreal, ran away. Police found him, and Boris insisted that George live with Catherine in Toronto. "Is life going to beat me?" she wondered. "Are all the values I live by false?"

She saw an indifferent, corrupt hierarchy keeping the letter of the law, yet removed from the spirit of truth. She saw Catholic lay people steeped in materialism. She saw atheism gaining, and she reeled from intense inner pain. She couldn't sleep or eat. She spent her day in a tiny office assigned to her at the Chancery where she wrote articles and submitted them to Catholic magazines. No one asked her opinion or her help. Only Flewy, Mrs. Field, and Olga stood by her. Thoughts of suicide taunted her, and she sank deeper into despair until she finally realized she had to get away from Toronto for a while.

Father Paul of Graymoor sent money, and Catherine went to New York City to visit Dorothy Day, which was "like a breath of fresh air all around." She met with Father John LaFarge, editor of *America*, who told her about possibilities for Catholic Action in the States — especially in the black community. Father Theophane McGuire, editor of *Sign Magazine*, who had published a number of her articles, offered her an assignment in Europe to report on Catholic Action. A few days later, Catherine went to Washington to meet Father Paul Hanly Furfey, author of the controversial new book, *Fire on the Earth*, which called for radical change in society according to Gospel values. Furfey asked Catherine to speak to the Sociology Department at Catholic University, and when he acknowledged her as "the Dorothy Day of Canada," her broken spirit started to heal.

On her way back to Toronto, Catherine stopped at Graymoor, and in the quiet of the Franciscan friary, she decided to accept the

Sign Magazine offer to go to Europe. In the weeks that followed, she lined up a few more magazine assignments to provide her with extra spending money. Archbishop McGuigan insisted on upgrading her passage to first class. A few days later, Father Gallagher informed her that her job would be cut from the diocesan payroll as of July 1. Catherine took all of this as a sign God wanted to her to go to Europe, but she changed her mind within days of her departure when George ran away again. Her first instinct was to cancel her trip, but Flewy and Mrs. Field talked her out of it. "Experience is the only way to teach youth," Flewy insisted, "and I believe all will be for his ultimate good. How could it be otherwise since God has called you to give him entirely into His care and go to do big work for Him abroad."

Mrs. Field pointed out that George was clever and could outwit anybody: "Don't worry about him. He'll play cards and win money hand over fist and get enough that way."

On June 4, Catherine sailed for Europe, and looking back at the Canadian shoreline she felt pain beyond description: "For long ago and far away I realized I really had no home ever since I left Russia. I was always a homeless person, and evidently I will not have deep roots anywhere."

Gradually, as the distance between Catherine and Canada grew, she felt "as if slowly the walls that seem to wall in one's life, move aside on quiet hinges and open further and further an ever-wider horizon." When the Canadian shoreline slipped out of view, peace entered her soul, and she turned toward Europe. In Russia, Stalin waged a reign of terror and the long tentacles of communism inched their way throughout the continent. Militant fascism shrouded Germany and Italy with hatred and extreme nationalism. In Spain, a savage civil war turned the country into a sadistic hellhole.

"What is going to happen to me?" Catherine wondered as the ship passed Plymouth and entered the English Channel, but the future remained well beyond anything she could imagine.

Chapter Notes

"I am sorry I am such a coward...": Diary #8, Apr. 3, 1936, MHA.

"Watch your step...": Diary #8, Apr. 9, 1936, MHA.

"You, of course, are a fox...": Sullivan to C de H, July 19, 1936, MHA.

"I never once thought...": Sullivan to C de H, n.d., MHA.

"I welcome to this city...": "Archbishop Forbes Officially Opens Friendship House," unidentified news clip, n.d., MHA.

"Madame la Baronne...": Sullivan to Olga LaPlante, June 2, 1936, MHA.

"Many are my worries...": Diary #14, June 5, 1936, MHA.

"It is like a wave...": Diary #14, June 10, 1936, MHA.

"They crucified Him...": Diary #14, June 20, 1936, MHA.

"Father Puchniak as well as...": McGuigan to Fr. Paul of Graymoor, Aug. 11, 1936, FAA/MHA.

"It seems to me...": Fr. Paul of Graymoor to McGuigan, Aug. 26, 1936, FAA/ARCAT/MHA.

"I was glad to get out...": Interview, Fr. Henri St. Denis by Sr. Louise Sharum, MHA.

"There is undoubtedly...": Fr. Paul of Graymoor to C de H, Sept. 14, 1936, MHA/FAA.

"I will be glad...": C de H to Fr. Paul of Graymoor, Sept. 18, 1936, FAA/MHA.

"The whole trouble is...": Ibid.

Father Paul told Catherine... and f.: Diary #16, Oct. 15, 1936, MHA.

"All censure was informal...": Ibid.

"Would we be losing something...": Handwritten Minutes from Commission meeting, Oct. 19, 1936, ARCAT.

"I'm certain...": Ibid.

"a saint or an adventuress...": Interview, Fr. Stanley Puchniak by Sister Louise Sharum, MHA.

"a raw deal..." and f.: Ibid.

"The suspense is very hard...": C de H to McGuigan, Nov. 13, 1936, ARCAT.

"Please give me a chance...": C de H to McGuigan, Nov. 12, 1936, ARCAT.

"The Archbishop has spoken...": C de H to Carr, Nov. 25, 1936, MHA.

"I spend so much time...": Mrs. Martha French to C de H, Nov. 1, 1936, MHA.

"I never knew a person...": Diary #15, Jan. 4, 1937, MHA.

"Is life going to beat me?": Ibid.

"like a breath of fresh air...": Diary #16, Mar. 12, 1937, MHA.

"Experience is the only way...": Grace Flewwelling (hereafter Flewy) to C de H, May 30, 1937, MHA.

"Don't worry about him...": Interview, Beatrice Field by Sr. Louise Sharum, MHA.

"For long ago and far away...": Diary #17, June 5, 1937, MHA.

"as if slowly the walls...": Ibid.

"What is going to happen to me?": Diary #17, June 13, 1937, MHA.

21

Europe

1937

When Catherine arrived in London on the morning of June 14, the hotel clerk handed her a note from Flewy saying George had written and that "God will make everything work out okay." What Flewy did not tell Catherine is that George was hopping freight trains throughout the United States, and had no intention of coming home. He found jobs hoeing cotton in the deep south, picking peas in California, and pushing wheelchairs on the boardwalk in Atlantic City. He spent a few days in a South Carolina jail on vagrancy charges, but a kind woman bailed him out, and he skipped town.

Trusting that George was safe, Catherine began her investigation of Catholic Action in England. She visited the editor of a Catholic newspaper, the staff at the Catholic Worker house, and the illustrious Frank Sheed of the Catholic Evidence Guild, who had started a Catholic publishing company with his wife, Maisie Ward. Everyone agreed that the world was on the brink of crisis, but no one knew what to do. "While we are waiting for geniuses to produce this system," Catherine noted, "we all have to go gather straws in the wind."

After three days, she crossed the Channel and boarded a train for Brussels. Nine years had passed since Catherine last saw her mother and brothers. The shock of finding them in a second story flat by the railroad tracks with no bathroom and only a small coal stove for heat devastated her. "I came home to my mother, and cried all night," she wrote to Father Paul. "She is so poor that the people on relief are better off at home than she is, and they would not tell me for fear of bothering me."

Father Paul cabled Catherine $100 to help Emma. After settling family matters, Catherine continued her investigation. Belgian Catholics had a Catholic political party, Catholic trade unions, an Association of Catholic Employers, networks of Catholic peasants and farmers, and a Catholic school of social service that left Catherine "breathless, and oh so envious." Even more exciting were the Young Christian Workers. Started 20 years before by Cardinal Joseph Cardijn, who believed that with spiritual and moral training, young people between the ages of 14 and 25 could identify and solve social problems, the Young Christian Workers had grown to over 300,000 members. The only thing Catherine found disturbing in Belgium was the pervasive lure of communism and socialism. "It is more and more evident that something far more drastic than Catholic Action must come forth to help to put us on top," she noted, but like the English Catholics, Catherine remained puzzled as to what that drastic action should be.

On July 3, she boarded a steamer bound for Portugal, where Maria da Luz, her old friend from the London days, waited to greet her. Maria had married a wealthy man, and lived in an elegant home sandwiched between the mountains and the sea. For the next three weeks, Maria and her sister, Visitation, took Catherine on day trips through tiny villages and bustling cities, stopping to visit famous churches and monasteries, the birthplace of St. Anthony, and the shrine at Fatima. They arranged for Catherine to meet Cardinal Emmanuel Gonçalves Cerejeira of Lisbon, and secured for her a private interview with António Salazar, the Premier of Portugal. Salazar told Catherine he had based his corporative state with a one party government on the Papal encyclical, *Quadragesimo Anno*, because he wanted to reform the country according to Christian principles. Before Catherine could delve into the intricacies of Salazar's unusual dictatorship, however, she was off on another adventure into war-torn Spain, where Maria da Luz had arranged for her to visit the headquarters of General Francisco Franco in Salamanca.

Like most Catholics of her day, Catherine saw the Spanish Civil War as a holy war between the forces of communism and Christianity. She read about the desecration of churches, the rape of nuns, the execution of priests, the seizure of land, and the harrowing slaughter of innocent women and children. This war reminded Catherine of all she had experienced in Russia, and it served as a terrible testimony to what she repeatedly warned would happen in an uprising of atheistic communism. "There cannot be on this issue a neutral position," she insisted. "It is a crusade — that of Christ against anti-Christ."

She regarded Franco as the great defender of Christianity and savior of the people. She dismissed as Communist propaganda reports of atrocities committed by Franco's army. She knew Stalin supported the Spanish Communists, but she did not see the significance behind Franco's German and Italian backing — not even after she met German soldiers, who told her Hitler would someday conquer the world. Catherine believed a victorious Franco would implement a corporative state similar to Salazar's, offsetting both communism and fascism, and nothing that she saw in the next few days altered her opinion.

On an excursion to Brunete, a small town captured by Franco's forces in a bloody series of battles that claimed over 35,000 lives, Catherine saw altars desecrated with feces. She saw a churchyard with corpses of monks and nuns arranged in positions of intercourse. In a hospital, she stood silently by the bed of a dying nun whose breasts and thighs had been slashed unmercifully after soldiers raped her. "It was a kind of surrealistic hell, and it remains etched forever in my mind," she later wrote.

Back in Salamanca, Catherine interviewed several priests and bishops who told her the leftist army brutalized wealthy parishes, convents, and monasteries, but spared poor parishes. The tragedy of Spain, they admitted, lay in the greed and selfishness of clergy and upper classes, who disregarded the teachings of Christ and the warnings of the Popes. Catherine identified with both the suffering and the sins of the Spanish people, and she came to a deeper understanding that in some strange way God suffered, too.

"Dear B, there were tears all through your letter so I know they were still in your soul," Flewy wrote. "You are one of His chosen ones. There is no doubt about that. I believe you are very close to the Sacred Heart or you would never be called upon to go through all you have to."

Catherine left for Paris during the first week in August. At the border, guards forced her to strip and undergo a body search. "I never felt so humiliated, so depersonalized," she admitted. The next few weeks in Paris gave Catherine a resurgence of hope, however, as she began to see that forces of good still prospered. In addition to the Young Christian Workers, which had spread from Belgium with great success, France had an innovative youth group called the Companions of St. Francis, who acted out slice-of-life dramas with a strong Christian message on the streets. She witnessed one of these skits while sitting at an outdoor cafe one afternoon. A young man waiting impatiently for his girlfriend caught the attention of other bystanders. Moments later, a young woman arrived with another couple, and the foursome carried on an animated conversation about communism and Christianity that drew bystanders into the debate. When the skit ended, the actors introduced themselves. People applauded and passed a hat.

While in Paris, Catherine also frequented a Russian Catholic church, and one of the priests introduced her to Helene Iswolsky, daughter of the former Russian Ambassador to France, and Nikolai Berdyaev, a Russian philosopher. At Berdyaev's home, Catherine met another noted philosopher, Jacques Maritain, who tried to apply the work of St. Thomas Aquinas to modern life. Maritain believed there were many ways to discover truth and that cooperation became possible when people worked toward a common good. "Will you tell me," he asked Catherine when he heard about her work in Toronto, "how is it that you practice so well what I

preach?" His words soothed her woundedness and a deep friendship developed between them.

Catherine found the intellectual atmosphere in Paris stimu-
lating, but she felt something lacking. She described Paris as a
place where "the brain alone functions. . . but the soul and heart
are dying and degenerating." On an impulse she applied for a
temporary working permit and took a job in a small food shop in
a slum, known as the "red belt" because of the Communist
infiltration. "One thing I have realized," she wrote to McGuigan,

> that the menace of communism is much greater than
> even I, who have spent 10 years telling Canadians about
> it, knew. Everywhere they are active, everywhere they
> wear various cunning masks, yet everywhere they are
> the same. And although poor Russia alone knows their
> true face, we should realize that we must not allow
> events to reach the place where we too will see that
> terrible face in all its nakedness. If only Catholics could
> be made to realize that tragic and terrible danger.

When Catherine returned to Brussels, a letter waited with
the horrifying news that a vagrant had brutally beaten George and
left him in a boxcar to die. When George regained consciousness,
he called Boris, and begged to come home. Boris insisted, however, that George's only option was boarding school in England,
and that he would have to work his way across the ocean on a
cattle boat. George agreed to Boris' terms. On August 28, Boris and
one of his mistresses sailed for Europe on a luxury liner to arrange
for George's schooling. Catherine met them when they arrived.
Her blood pressure was low, and she was exhausted from travel.
She asked herself again and again whether she had failed as a
mother, but Flewy insisted that Catherine had not failed, and that
George had finally come to his senses:

> He has the two examples in his parents. He cannot but
> see that the one who is striving to follow in the footsteps
> of the Divine Saviour is the one whom he can call upon

for help and forgiveness for things he feels he has done
that he may feel he shouldn't have. If he doesn't now he
will later, there is no doubt about that.

That fall, George entered Clayesmore, an independent boarding school in Dorset, England. Catherine's brother Serge, who had
married a young English woman, and André, whose wife was
Spanish, promised to bring George to Brussels during school
holidays. With everything settled, Catherine booked her own
passage back to Canada. During the previous weeks, she had
received several strange letters from Flewy, who suggested that
Catherine might not want to live in the house on Cameron Street
when she returned. Flewy called the house a barn with people
coming and going all the time, and noted that Mrs. Field feared
Catherine would freeze during the winter because of her low
blood pressure. "It seemed to me they were hiding something."
Catherine knew that the *Social Forum* staff had moved to
Toronto from Ottawa and used the house on Cameron as an office.
She did not know that her old enemy, Father James, had promised
the managing editor of the *Social Forum* that he would pay for and
distribute 500 copies of the paper each month on the condition that
Catherine not live in the house when she returned from Europe.
Olga, Flewy and Mrs. Field found a tiny attic apartment on St.
Mary's Street and moved some of Catherine's things into it. When
Catherine arrived in Toronto in late October, they told her what
happened. "The story was so fantastic I felt I had entered the
world of make believe! But unfortunately, grotesque and painful
as it was, the 'fairy tale' was true!"
It was also apparent from the hostile looks and comments of
nuns, priests, and people she met at church that she was no longer
wanted or needed in Toronto. "I still have the lectures which start
soon to fall back upon and my writing," she wrote to Father Paul,
"so given a little start of a few months I'll straighten out again but
the question is broader than that — What am I to do?"
She saw four options: She could stay in Toronto where she
could be what Father Carr called "the voice straightening the path

of the Lord." She could go to Harlem, where Father Paul of Graymoor was paving the way for her to open a Friendship House for black Catholics. She could live at Graymoor and start a Franciscan Tertiary movement similar to what she had tried to start with the Guild of Our Lady of Atonement. Or she could accept Dorothy Day's offer to use the Catholic Worker as a home base while she spent six months of the year in Europe and six months in America as a Catholic-at-large, supporting herself by writing and lecturing.

Father Paul suggested that she come to Graymoor and discern in the quiet of the friary what God wanted her to do.

"My soul is more at peace," she wrote on her third day there, "but evidently nothing is coming out of what I planned and the burning question, what I do next, is still at bay."

Catherine left Graymoor in early December and took the train to New York City, where she stayed with Dorothy Day. Still undecided over what to do, she returned to Toronto for Christmas, and alone in her apartment, she prayed for guidance: New York with its loneliness? Or Toronto with its pain? "I am sorely afraid. I tremble in every limb. I know that the road I am taking leads to Calvary. Jesus, be my guide. Stop my tears. I weep because I am afraid, but the fire in my soul will not let me be."

Sometime in late January, Catherine took the train to New York.

Chapter Notes

"God will make everything work out okay...": Flewy to C de H, June 9, 1937, MHA.

"While we are waiting...": Diary #17, June 16, 1937, MHA.

"I came home to my mother...": C de H to Fr. Paul of Graymoor, June 17, 1937, FAA.

"breathless, and oh so envious": C de H to Mrs. Field, June 28, 1937, MHA.

"It is more and more evident...": Diary #19, July 9, 1937, MHA.

"There cannot be on this issue...": C de H, "The Spirit of New Spain," *Sign Magazine*, October, 1937.

"It was a kind of surrealistic hell...": *Fragments*, p. 126.

"Dear B, there were tears...": Flewy to C de H, Aug. 15, 1937, MHA.

"I never felt so humiliated": Fragments, p. 127.

"Will you tell me...": Interview, Fr. Emile Briere.

"the brain alone functions...": C de H to Fr. Paul of Graymoor, Aug. 26, 1937, FAA.

"One thing I have realized...": C de H to McGuigan, Aug. 15, 1937, ARCAT.

"He has two examples...": Flewy to C de H, Sept. 20, 1937, MHA.

"It seemed to me...": History of the Apostolate, p. 158.

"The story was so fantastic...": Ibid., p. 160.

"I still have the lectures...": C de H to Fr. Paul of Graymoor, Oct. 22, 1937, FAA.

"the voice straightening the path...": Ibid.

"My soul is more at peace...": Diary #18, Nov 22, 1937, MHA.

"I am sorely afraid...": Diary #17, Jan. 24, 1938, MHA.

22

New York City

1938

Catherine stayed in a slum apartment near the Catholic Worker until mid-February, when she moved with just her suitcase, a typewriter, and a few dollars into a tenement building across the street from St. Mark the Evangelist church on West 138th Street in Harlem.

"No white folks live here, Lady," the janitor told her.

When Catherine replied that she was Russian, the janitor assumed she meant Communist, and knowing that Communists accepted blacks when no other white people would, he led Catherine to a tiny unfurnished apartment on the third floor. "There was a gas stove, standing against one wall, in plain sight, and near it a sink," Catherine recalled. "At the other wall stood the Frigidaire, all gleaming and white, as if to say to all and sundry: *'Well, here I am, in your bedroom and living room, and what are you going to do about it?'* The little hall hardly deserved the name — it was so tiny, but the bathroom looked clean and pleasant."

That night Catherine slept on a pile of newspapers with cockroaches scampering about. She missed Canada so much that she ached inside. "Spiritually, I am in darkness with only one glimmer of light — to do the will of God — that is all."

In the days that followed, Catherine had long talks with the pastor of St. Mark's, Father Michael Mulvoy, a tall, handsome Irishman with fiery red hair and freckles, who was so loved that people called him "the blackest white man in Harlem." Mulvoy felt apprehensive when Father Paul of Graymoor first told him

about the Baroness from Canada, but after a good word from
Father John LaFarge, the editor of *America*, who had known
Catherine since the 1920's, Father Mulvoy agreed to give her a
chance.

Father Mulvoy introduced Catherine to Harlem by taking
her into the streets where over 350,000 people of black ancestry
crammed into 40 city blocks. Black entertainers and professionals
lived in affluent areas known as Sugar Hill, Golden Edge, and
Striver's Row. Prostitutes congregated at "the Market" along
Seventh Avenue. St. Mark's parish nestled in a neighborhood
known as "the Valley" with monotonous rows of tenements,
"whose walls bulge, creak and groan under the ever-increasing
human burden." Slum landlords demanded rents 50% higher
than comparable apartments in white neighborhoods. On "Lung
Block" near 142nd Street the death toll from tuberculosis soared to
heights unheard of in any other part of Manhattan. Catherine and
Fr. Mulvoy passed pool rooms, pawn shops, saloons, churches of
every denomination, and kids of all ages with nothing to do. Run-
down school buildings with overcrowded classrooms had no
playgrounds. Except for barber shops and beauty parlors, whites
owned most small businesses and refused to hire blacks, who
were forced to find jobs in downtown Manhattan as domestics,
elevator operators, porters, and messengers. The unemployed
went on relief.

Father Mulvoy warned Catherine that after centuries of
persecution, black people did not trust whites, and she could
expect little cooperation until she won their respect. He talked
about his own struggles, and how he prayed to Blessed Martin de
Porres, a 17th Century mulatto from Peru, known for miraculous
intercessions. Catherine decided to name her apartment "Blessed
Martin de Porres Flat," and she claimed that the dark-skinned
saint immediately started sending people and things to help her.
Within days, curtains, a lamp, a small table, a desk, a chest of
drawers, a tattered rug, and a lumpy brown couch arrived. Cash
donations covered the phone bill and the rent. Ade Bethune, a
young artist whose work appeared in the *Catholic Worker*, sent a

picture of Blessed Martin which Catherine hung in a place of honor. "I cannot believe that in less than a week all this has happened!" she wrote.

Visitors also trudged up three flights of stairs to see her during that first week. Father Andre Rogosh, pastor of the Eastern Rite Russian church in lower Manhattan, blessed the apartment. Father George B. Ford, pastor of Corpus Christi church and director of the Newman Club at Columbia University, asked if Catherine could involve white college students in her work. Father James M. Gillis, CSP, editor of *The Catholic World*, interviewed her, and wrote a powerful article about Catherine's decision to live in voluntary poverty. He noted that Catherine could have helped the poor without giving up everything, in the same way Jesus Christ could have saved humanity without leaving heaven. "But the better way," Gillis insisted, "as it seemed to Our Lord and to those who imitate Him closely, is to 'come down' in more senses than one."

Between the Gillis article, which appeared in hundreds of newspapers, and Catherine's own articles in *Interracial Review* and *The Lamp*, a flood of letters, books, money, clothes, food, and requests for lectures poured in. Catherine, who was still trying to learn about Harlem, admitted that these were "hectic days." She spent hours at the public library studying history, politics, sociology and economics. As she learned about the horrors of slavery, the Civil War, carpetbaggers, and the Ku Klux Klan, "the terrifying and alien pattern of segregation became crystal clear to me." She saw Communists try to win over the black community with demands to integrate professional sports, end housing and employment discrimination, halt degrading image of blacks in Hollywood movies, and force New York City hospitals to accept black patients.

In mid-March, Fr. John LaFarge, who had worked for racial justice during the past ten years, invited Catherine to speak before a group of black Catholic intellectuals. When she described her work as an apostolate designed to fight Communist lies with the truth of Christianity, the audience response left her speechless.

"There was in those eyes, a sort of hope and it seemed for a moment as if Christ has smiled out of them on me." Afterward, on the bus ride back to Harlem with people from the meeting, Catherine ignored "all white eyes in the bus" staring in contempt as she carried on an animated conversation with young black men and women, who promised to help her start a Catholic library in her apartment. A few weeks later, while sorting books, one of the volunteers told her about his own experience with racial prejudice. "It must be ghastly to be faced with this," Catherine observed, "and so utterly inexplicable in the face of Catholic teachings."

As white college students from Fr. Ford's Newman Club started mixing with the black volunteers, Catherine formed an interracial study club, which met in her apartment every Monday night for tea, cookies, and rousing discussions. Ellen Tarry, an intelligent and beautiful black reporter for *The Amsterdam News*, recalled how the crowd squeezed into every available space with people sitting on the floor, on tables, and even on the kitchen sink. Latecomers overflowed into the stairway. "I would catch phrases like 'the Fatherhood of God, and the Brotherhood of man,' or 'the Negro and the Mystical Body' which indicated much more depth than I had attributed to these youngsters," Ellen admitted. "Then the Baroness talked about 'Christ in the Negro' and along with all the others in the room I came under the spell of Catherine de Hueck. I had entered the room a Doubting Thomas and left as an ardent disciple."

Catherine still had the magnetic spiritual quality Olga LaPlante recognized five years before. She spoke passionately about the Holy Spirit, whom she saw as a Spirit of Love, and she left her awe-struck listeners with a vision of the Spirit setting hearts on fire with passion for goodness and truth. One of the Newman Club members tried to capture the phenomenon in verse:

> The Baroness and the Holy Ghost are a Combine hard
>   to beat,

Who turn tea into ambrosia, and the floor —
    a palatial seat.
By their good works shall you know them;
    You'll meet them everywhere —
The Baroness and the Holy Ghost are a
    very lovable pair.

On May 17, the Catholic lending library officially opened in Catherine's apartment. *The Amsterdam News* ran free ads, four people borrowed books, and Dorothy Day came with Father Mulvoy to celebrate. In three months, Catherine's work had mushroomed. St. Mark's youth group, which attracted 40 teenagers at its first meeting, now neared 100, and earned the distinction of becoming the first minority Catholic Youth Organization in the country. Catherine started a study club for nurses and a weekly lecture series. On Thursdays, she distributed used clothes from her living room. Her lectures took her on day trips to Brooklyn, Flushing, New Jersey, Connecticut, and throughout Manhattan. On overnight jaunts she traveled to upstate New York, New England, Ohio, and Pennsylvania. She sent some of the money from lectures to her mother and George, but most went toward her work. As her apartment became more cramped with people and activities, she moved the clothing room into the basement of St. Mark's rectory, and started praying for rent money to open a storefront: "Blessed Martin, please! please! It is for your neglected black brothers!"

Ann Harrigan, a 28-year-old high school English teacher from Brooklyn, answered Catherine's prayer. She had heard Catherine lecture, and arrived at Catherine's apartment one afternoon with a donation of books and clothes. Tall, slim, smart, and sophisticated, with quick wit and an uncanny resemblance to Ingrid Bergman, Ann pledged $30 a month to cover the rent for a storefront. She told Catherine she wanted to do something special with her life — "to burn out, rather than rust out," and Catherine assured Ann that as a volunteer, she would battle Communists, inspire young people, feed and clothe the poor, confront racial prejudices, save souls, and work with an unusual combination of other volunteers. Ann volunteered to help on weekends.

Betty Schneider and Josephine Zehnle, impressionable third year students from a Catholic women's college in Minnesota, also volunteered that summer. Catherine arranged for them to stay with the Romero family in a large brownstone on West 120th Street, and for the next 8 weeks, the girls walked 18 blocks every morning to Catherine's apartment where visitors ranged from destitute mothers looking for food or clothes to curious society matrons. Reporters, businessmen, nuns, new volunteers, and old friends dropped by, along with famous priests and lay people, whom Betty and Jo had read about in Catholic magazines, but never expected to meet. Guests dined with the Baroness on tea, cabbage soup and day-old bread. "I still can't get over how we banter celebrities around and treat them to our simple but delicious bill of fare," Betty admitted.

As afternoon temperatures soared into the 90's, Catherine and her two young volunteers escaped the stifling heat of the apartment and sat on the rectory steps talking to the swarms of people passing by. Catherine called it a chit-chat apostolate, and after a few weeks, Betty realized in a shocking moment of candor: "I never notice if people are white or colored anymore."

In the evenings, the girls coached the CYO baseball team, and chaperoned hobby nights and social events that always ended in a jam session with one teenager playing the piano and another using folding chairs for drums. They planned bus excursions to nearby monasteries where they would have a picnic and play games on grassy lawns. Betty, who had grown up on her father's poultry farm, could not believe that some of these children had never seen grass growing. "The other day, a little kid was up, wanting to know if flowers actually came out of the ground when they grew," she wrote home in amazement.

Before long, the girls began to rely, as Catherine did, on the Holy Ghost and Blessed Martin. They appreciated the times Fr. Ford brought steaks for dinner or the sultry evenings when Fr. Mulvoy surprised them with ice cream and ginger ale. After seeing how voluntary poverty placed Catherine in the midst of the people, they understood why people in Harlem did not trust the young social worker from downtown, who dressed in stylish clothes with her hair, nails, and make-up done perfectly.

In September, Betty and Jo returned to Minnesota, and took with them two black girls, who attended St. Benedict's College with scholarship money Catherine raised. Catherine had not expected to miss their help and companionship as much as she did. A few weeks later, Flewy came from Toronto to fill the void.

"I have never known anyone who was as loyal to a friend as Flewy was to the Baroness," Ellen Tarry recalled.

That fall, Catherine finally found a storefront on West 135th Street near the Harlem YMCA, the public library, and the NAACP. Tom Keating, who started volunteering during the summer, built shelves and laid a new linoleum floor, while the women sewed curtains and set up the kitchen. Students at St. Mark's moved library books from Catherine's apartment.

On the evening of November 14, Friendship House officially opened. Father Mulvoy blessed the store, and everyone laughed as he splashed holy water into Catherine's face. Elated with her success, he told a newspaper reporter: "Life can be like a lot of children running up a mountain. Those who reach the summit first either sit down to admire the view or rush on to the next peak. One child in a million will run back to help the stragglers catch up. The Baroness is a big sister who saved some of her breath to do just that."

That winter, Catherine lectured throughout the eastern and mid-western states. Pacing across stages like a lioness, she roared: "Do you realize that it is inevitable that someday you are going to appear BEFORE THAT SAME CHRIST WHO SAID, 'I WAS HUNGRY. . .' AND WHO ALSO SAID, 'WHATSOEVER YOU DO UNTO THEM, YOU DID IT TO ME. . .' Look into your own soul — in the blinding light of the Holy Ghost — and see Christ saying to you: 'I was THAT NEGRO — there and there, whom you DISCRIMINATED AGAINST. . . . THEREFORE DEPART FROM ME.'"

A gasp — sometimes in shock, sometimes in hatred — would rise from the crowd. Then Catherine's voice softened to a purr as she begged her audiences to reject prejudice and give black people justice, dignity, and a chance to live as human beings.

Sometimes Catherine stayed overnight with a host family or in a convent, but more often she slept on the night train between cities. In April 1939, her confessor, Father Thomas Gately, recognized that she was on the verge of spiritual and physical exhaustion, and he insisted that she go on retreat. In the silence of a convent chapel Catherine prayed for 17-year-old George in England, her mother and brothers in Brussels, and for Boris, who had come to Harlem seeking Catherine's sympathy a few months before when one of his mistresses was pregnant again. He brought a half-empty bottle of whiskey and asked bluntly if Catherine would sleep with him. She told him to leave. Several months later, he sent a desperate note saying he owed $500 in debts and begged her to bail him out. Catherine refused, and he lashed out at her in a scathing letter, but she did not respond.

"I see quite a difference in you since those T(oronto) days," Flewy told her.

Perhaps the greatest change in Catherine was her apparent lack of concern when the Vatican appointed Francis J. Spellman, Auxiliary Bishop of Boston, to replace the late Cardinal Patrick Hayes as Archbishop of New York. She made no attempt to seek Spellman's approbation as she had with McGuigan. She felt confident enough about the progress of Friendship House to plan a trip to Europe that summer to visit George and her family. She planned to pay for the trip by writing a series of articles for Catholic magazines on how Catholics fared under the shadow of the Swastika.

Flewy felt uncomfortable about taking responsibility for Friendship House for such a long period of time, ("It staggers me to be left here to keep things going. . ."), but Ann Harrigan, who had 8 weeks of summer vacation, agreed to move into Catherine's apartment and take charge.

On the afternoon of July 21, 1939, Catherine sailed for Europe. Passions ran high among passengers, with some sympathetic toward Nazi Germany and some adamantly opposed. Anti-Semitism hung in the air like polluted smog, and Catherine knew with gnawing certainty that this was only a preview of what she would encounter in Europe. "It grips one," she admitted, "and makes one afraid for the future!"

Chapter Notes

"No white folks live here, Lady...": C de H, "St. Francis Comes to Harlem, *The Lamp*, June 1938.

"There was a gas stove...": *Ibid.*

"Spiritually, I am in darkness...": Diary #18, Feb. 25, 1938, MHA.

long talks with Father Mulvoy: See Diary #18, and "Harlem Diary," *RES*, Oct., 1963.

"the blackest white man...": Interview, Ellen Tarry.

"whose walls bulge, creak and groan...": C de H, "The Long, Long Journey," *Eikon*, April, 1953.

rents were 50% higher: Lou Gody, editor in chief, *The WPA Guide to New York City*, pp. 257-265.

"lung block": *Ibid.*

"I cannot believe...": Diary #19, Mar. 2, 1938, MHA.

"But the better way...": Rev. James M. Gillis, CSP, "Catholic Action on the Spot," unidentified news clip, March, 1938, MHA.

"hectic days": Diary #19, Mar. 5, 1938, MHA.

"the terrifying and alien pattern...": "Harlem Diary," *op. cit.*

"There was in those eyes...": Diary #19, Mar. 13, 1938, MHA.

"It must be ghastly...": Diary #19, Mar. 29, 1938, MHA.

"I would catch phrases...": Ellen Tarry, *The Third Door: Autobiography of an American Negro Woman*, p. 144.

"The Baroness and the Holy Ghost...": BS, "Three months in Harlem," unidentified news clip, n.d. 1938, MHA.

"Blessed Martin, please! please!": Diary #19, May 17, 1938, MHA.

"to burn out, rather than rust out": AH to C de H, June 27, 1938, MHA.

"I still can't get over...": BS, "Diary," June 23, 1938, MHA.

"I never notice if people are white or colored anymore": *Ibid.*, July 8, 1938, MHA.

"The other day, a little kid was up...": BS to Aunt Katie, July 4, 1938, MHA.

"I have never known anyone...": Interview, Ellen Tarry.

"Life can be like a lot of children running...": "Fights Marxism in Harlem," *New York Sun*, Nov. 19, 1938.

"Do you realize...": "The Dynamite of Christianity," text of a speech delivered by C de H at Notre Dame Academy, January, 1939, MHA.

"I see quite a difference...": Flewy to C de H, Jan. 18, 1939, MHA.

"It staggers me...": Flewy to C de H, Jan. 18, 1939, MHA.

"It grips one...": C de H to Fr. Paul of Graymoor, July 29, 1939, MHA.

23

Europe
1939

When Catherine's ship docked in England, she reeled at the sight of blimps, trenches, antiaircraft guns, and public notices about rationing and evacuations. "All these make you feel as if Europe was ready for momentary emergency," she noted. "The temper of the people is short. . . It is a sort of 'nerve war' that is in progress. All seem to live in expectation of news from Germany."

Anxiety stemmed from recent developments in Danzig, a former German seaport on the Baltic Sea. After World War I, Danzig became a "free city" under a League of Nations mandate. Poland received special shipping, customs, and railway privileges, but Danzig citizens remained predominantly German. Earlier in 1939, Hitler sent clear signals that Danzig would reunite with Germany. The Poles vowed to fight a German takeover, and the British promised to support Poland. In fact, Germany was using the Danzig issue as a pretext for a war with Poland. Although Britain had followed a policy of appeasement towards Germany for most of the 1930's, by this point it had become obvious that this policy had failed. Europe was on the eve of the Second World War.

Only 18-year-old George de Hueck, who had graduated from high school that spring and had started an apprenticeship in mechanical engineering, seemed unconcerned about world affairs. His headmaster assured Catherine that George had great intelligence and many talents. For the first time in more years than Catherine could recall, she felt relieved.

On August 4, she arrived in Brussels where her mother and brothers waited to greet her. Everyone, they told her, lived in fear of Nazi Germany. People hoarded food. Business lagged and efforts to spur the economy failed. Shocked at the radical change Europe had undergone in less than two years, Catherine boarded a train bound for Germany on August 15 with a mixture of curiosity and apprehension. The trip took ten hours, and she noticed an ominous sense of order among passengers, who replied politely when spoken to, but refused to engage in conversation. "People in the train are definitely afraid. They do not laugh — even children."

In Berlin, Catherine avoided tourist haunts, and searched instead for clues as to how the nearly 4 million people in this showcase capital of the Third Reich lived their lives. "Little by little things sort themselves out," she noted after a few days. "Poverty well hidden — butcher shops besieged by people who only get 75 oz. of meat a week — tired even faces — blooming sunburned youth with set mouths and a fanatic gleam in their eyes — No butter, no milk, no eggs for the population — a mighty effort on the side of the Third Reich to impress visitors."

Catherine hoped a visit to the parents of a priest she had met in New York might provide deeper insights, but fear kept the elderly couple from telling her anything. They referred her to Father Dlussky, an Eastern Rite Catholic priest, who confirmed Catherine's suspicion that beneath the facade of a prosperous and efficient society hid a ruthless government with no concern for God or man. The Nazis censored mail and suppressed books and newspapers. Informants turned in friends and relatives without hesitation. Laws prohibited listening to foreign broadcasts. People struggled with low wages, high rents, and food shortages. When Catherine expressed surprise at the sausages, butter, and pastries Father Dlussky offered at tea time, he admitted they were artificial substitutes, created by German chemists from codfish, which was cheap and plentiful.

The priest painted an even darker picture of Nazis persecuting the Catholic Church. They closed schools, eliminated social work, expelled religious orders, and flooded young people with Nazi propaganda. Father Dlussky admitted that ties to the Vatican put him in peril, and he watched helplessly as Russian exiles, outspoken German Catholics, and Jews disappeared in the night with no explanation. "Sorrow and worries fill the land," he told Catherine.

The next day, Father Dlussky arranged for Catherine to meet Count Konrad von Preysing, Bishop of Berlin, and she noted how the chancery echoed with eerie silence. "The Bishop was really afraid to speak, to say even yes or no — perhaps from him again as from his secretary I learned more from the silences and half-silences, the soft slow head movements, the tears that came to his eyes, than I did from the words he spoke, and yet the picture of the Church in Germany became tragically clear. Christ is not being killed with one mighty sweep, like Stalin did it in Russia; it is being scientifically, slowly strangled, and that not unto death — only unto half-death that is this strange twilight between the two!"

As Catherine walked back to her hotel, people on the streets carried on as if they did not see marching soldiers and large gray military convoys. She felt an overwhelming temptation to escape on the next train back to Brussels and forget she had ever seen the Third Reich, but a deeper conviction that she had to find the truth sustained her.

At 11:00 p.m., on the night of August 21, a special radio broadcast announced that Germany and Russia had negotiated a non-aggression pact. The following day, German newspapers claimed Poland had troops positioned on the border near Danzig. Catherine had heard enough. Later that afternoon, she boarded a small plane bound for Danzig where she hoped to see for herself what transpired in this beleaguered city.

From the air, Catherine fell in love with Danzig's red tile roofs and gabled houses with stone balconies. "The beauty of Danzig could make one dream and drink, but its modern inhabitants had lost their heads," she noted. "They had hidden the lovely archways of their old houses under long blood-red swastikas and as one went along pavements trodden by Knights of old, who worshipped God so completely, one's ear was continually assailed by the harsh, loud, "Heil Hitler" that seemed to come from all sides and finally became like a thunder from which I wanted to run."

At the British Embassy, an angry official wanted to know "what in hell are you doing in Danzig." American officials seemed friendlier and gave her directions to the Nazi rally scheduled that night in Zoppot, a seaside resort twenty miles outside the city. On the beach at Zoppot, floodlights beamed at a wooden platform with a huge picture of Hitler as the backdrop. Red and black swastikas hung everywhere. Catherine sat at the press table with a reporter from Belgium and his wife. They watched as hundreds of young people in German uniforms cheered Nazi speakers, who insisted that Danzig did not belong to Poland. "We belong to the Third Reich," the crowds chanted. The soft sound of waves lapping against the beach seemed incongruous with the threatening voices. "I shivered in the warm air, got up and went home by train, walking in the quiet night for a mile or more, wanting to cry, and not daring to."

On the morning of August 23, Catherine interviewed Carl Maria Splett, Bishop of Danzig. Splett was a German aristocrat, and after making Catherine promise not to quote him, he explained that Roman Catholics constituted 43% of the Danzig population. Some opposed the German takeover, but others, like himself, felt divided, wanting to return to the Reich, but as a Catholic, somewhat afraid. He detested the thought of domination by nationalistic Poles, who were, he insisted, Poles first and Catholics afterward. Catherine cringed.

The next day, an American reporter told her Germany lied when they said Poles had mobilized along the borders. The reporter had just returned from a tour of the frontier and saw only nine Polish soldiers. "I realized then," Catherine admitted, "how terrible the next war was going to be."

That night, the sound of tramping feet and loud voices jarred her awake. From her balcony Catherine saw German soldiers, trucks, and artillery in the streets. The next morning, officials requisitioned taxis and buses for war use. People had a terrified look in their eyes. "Only the ones in uniform have a fanatic gleam which seems worse even than fear, for it speaks of madness and evil," she wrote.

At the railway station, Catherine squeezed into a third class compartment on a train bound for Warsaw. The train steamed into the station at 2:00 a.m. on Friday, August 26 — ten hours behind schedule — and Catherine had to drag her luggage to the hotel because there were no taxis. She woke the next morning to the sounds of a frenzied city caught in last minute preparations for war. Long lines of people, hoping to get out of the country, waited at banks, travel agencies, and railroad stations. Hundreds of Jews begging for exit visas crowded the British Consulate. At make-shift booths on city streets, civil defense workers distributed gas masks with goggles and pig-like snouts. In parks, women and children dug trenches. Catherine helped dig for a while, and the patriotism of the people impressed her, but she also saw how terribly disorganized and ill-equipped they were, and she wondered how they could ever withstand the Germans.

After two stress-filled days, Catherine took a train to Lwow, a medieval city in Eastern Poland, where she arranged an interview with His Excellency Count Andrei Sheptycki, who headed the Ukrainian Eastern Rite Catholics. "The first thing I noticed were his eyes — incredibly young and alive they looked in his lined face," she recalled. "His whole face radiated charm, simplicity, and to me sanctity."

Count Sheptycki was acutely aware of <u>nationalistic interests</u> <u>among Poles and Ukrainians</u>, and he insisted that <u>nationalism</u> <u>posed the greatest barrier to peaceful cooperation among Roman</u> <u>Catholics, Orthodox, and Eastern Rite Christians.</u> Catherine told him she had learned in Warsaw that the Poles destroyed 50 Russian Orthodox churches in an attempt to wipe out all vestiges of the former Russian occupation. It was tragic, he agreed, and inexcusable for Christians. He seemed genuinely pleased that Catherine chose to investigate these issues, and he urged her to stay a few more days so they could continue their talks. Catherine agreed even though rumblings of war made her increasingly nervous. Newspapers reported that over 80,000 German troops had assembled along the Polish border, and on August 31, officials declared Lwow in a state of emergency. Soldiers marched every-where. Heavy trucks jammed the streets. Machine guns perched on roofs of buildings. People hurried about in a crazed state of confusion. The British Consul demanded that Catherine leave the city at once, but not wanting to miss her final interview with Sheptycki, she begged permission to stay one more day. "I am frankly, afraid," she wrote in her diary, "terribly, hopelessly afraid. Lord help me. I am neither worthy to live nor ready to die."

The next morning, just before dawn, Germany launched an air attack on Poland, hitting cities, towns, villages, railroads, and military arsenals. Catherine awakened to the roar of planes and the sound of shelling. "War is declared!! It has come. All that we feared — all that was hidden came up — and now we are face to face with the result of having left Christ out of the last peace," she scribbled in her journal.

At the railroad station, frenzied people pushed and shouted in a mad attempt to get out of the country. Gripping the ticket she had purchased for Budapest the day before, Catherine collapsed into a seat in a crowded carriage. As the train rumbled out of the city and into the countryside, rumors that German fighter planes followed overhead kept passengers in a state of raw anxiety. The engineer stopped often for no apparent purpose, and fearing a German attack, terrified people fled the compartments and cow-ered in ditches. Catherine joined them four times, and then decided she might as well die on a train as in the dirt. At the border, authorities debated among themselves over whether to allow the train to pass into Hungary. After an agonizing wait, the passen-gers cheered as the train chugged across the border.

Catherine longed to see Budapest, "a city of dreams, music, laughter, and coffee with whipped cream," but the next morning, she cringed at the way the threat of war had already cast its dark shadow. "They are afraid that due to the trade pact of theirs with

Germany that they will be bled white by Hitler, and nothing will be left for their own people."

Fearful of traveling through Germany, she planned a circuitous route back to Brussels through Yugoslavia, Italy, and France, which took over two weeks. During those harrowing days, England and France declared war on Germany, and a German U Boat torpedoed the British passenger ship, *Athenia*, which was en route to Montreal with over 1000 passengers. In Brussels, Catherine tried to persuade her mother to flee to Canada with her, but Emma refused. Catherine felt torn: How could she go back to America and leave her mother to face another war? Yet how could she abandon Harlem and the work she had started there? Emma smiled, made the sign of the Cross on Catherine's forehead, and whispered an old Russian blessing. Then she gave Catherine a treasured family icon of Our Lady of Smolensk, and they clung to each other in what would be their last embrace. Catherine wept inconsolably on the boat ride across the English Channel.

George was waiting for her at the hotel when she arrived in London. He had quit school and decided to return to Canada and enlist in the Royal Canadian Air Force. George's plans, the pain of leaving her mother, fear of what would happen to her brothers and their wives, and the dread of facing a perilous ocean voyage left Catherine numb. "My head and heart and soul are yet filled with what I have seen and heard, and what I myself have gone through," she wrote to Dorothy Day. "I cannot concentrate, somehow my ears are filled with the noise of tramping feet, and before my eyes, are multitudes of soldiers' green uniforms, gray uniforms, khaki ones, sky blue. . . They seem an endless chain that shuffles in a strange continuous patter, that vainly my tired brain tries to absorb."

It was gray and cold on the morning of October 6, when Catherine and George set sail aboard the RMS *Duchess of Richmond*. "There was an eerie feeling of danger," Catherine recalled. "It affected my son so much that when I was taking a bath he would stand in front of the closed door with a raincoat. . . He had read that some women in the *Athenia* disaster died because of exposure in the small boats. One had been taking a bath when the ship was torpedoed."

On October 14, after 9 days at sea, the ship docked in Quebec City. Back in Harlem, the people at Friendship House rejoiced at the news of Catherine's safe crossing. When her train pulled into Grand Central Station the following week, a crowd of staff members, volunteers, teenagers, friends and neighbors waited on the platform to greet her. Overwhelmed at the sight, Catherine sat down on the stairs and wept.

Chapter Notes

"All these make you feel ...": Diary #20, July 29, 1939, MHA.

"People in the train are definitely afraid...": Diary #20, Aug. 15, 1939, MHA.

"Little by little things sort themselves out...": Ibid.

"Sorrow and worries fill the land...": Diary #20, Aug. 16, 1939, MHA.

"The Bishop was really afraid to speak...": Diary #20, Aug. 18, 1939, MHA.

"The beauty of Danzig...": Diary #20, Aug. 24, 1939, MHA.

"what in hell...": Diary #20, Aug. 22, 1939, MHA.

"We belong to the Third Reich..." and f.: Ibid.

"I realized then how terrible...": Diary #20, Aug. 24, 1939, MHA.

"Again the strange frightening sensation of fear...": Diary #20, Aug. 23, 1939, MHA.

"I stood as one petrified...": Diary #20, Aug. 24, 1939, MHA.

"Only the ones in uniform ...": C de H, "Three Days in Danzig," *Commonweal*, Sept. 29, 1939.

"The first thing I noticed...": C de H, "An Interview in Lwow," *Commonweal*, Oct. 27, 1939.

"I am frankly, afraid...": Diary #20, Aug. 31, 1939, MHA.

"War is declared!!": Diary #20, Sept. 1, 1939, MHA.

"a city of dreams...": Diary #20, Sept. 2, 1939.

"My head and heart and soul...": C de H to Dorothy Day, Sept. 25, 1939, Marquette University Archives.

"There was an eerie feeling...": *History of the Apostolate*, p. 330.

24

Harlem
1939

I n early November, Father Mike Mulvoy came to Catherine's apartment with devastating news: The new Provincial of the Holy Ghost Fathers had decided to transfer him to Tuscaloosa, Alabama, where he would work with wealthy white college students. The news struck Catherine "like a thunderbolt coming out of the blue sky that left me weak." What would happen to Father Mulvoy's race relations bureau, his efforts to convince white employers and labor unions to hire blacks, his work for fair housing, and the labor school he started to offset Communist influences? Father Mulvoy seemed more concerned about Friendship House closing if the new pastor shared the sentiments of the Provincial, who frowned on Friendship House having such close affiliation with the priests and had ordered Fr. Mulvoy to move the Friendship House clothing room out of the rectory basement.

Catherine could not imagine Friendship House closing. Juvenile delinquency in the area was down 14%. Visitors and volunteers came in droves. Wealthy people like the Grace family of New York, and influential people like Bishop Richard Cushing of Boston, offered financial support. Betty Schneider had returned after graduating from college, and volunteered part time at Friendship House while studying for her Master's degree at Fordham. New staff workers joined, the most promising of whom was Jane O'Donnell, an extraordinarily beautiful and talented young woman with pale blond hair and violet eyes, who worked in the clothing room.

A few days before Father Mulvoy's departure, Catherine received more devastating news when a telegram from Graymoor arrived saying that Father Paul had died during the night. He was 78 years old. Mother Lurana had died several years before, and Catherine felt totally alone. "Another friend gone. Oh Lord!" She prayed that the new pastor would fill the void, but when he arrived, the horrified parishioners flocked to Catherine, with shocking accounts of how Father Murray bellowed from the pulpit: "I want you to know that I did not come here to find you jobs, to put clothes on your backs, or shoes on your feet. I came to save your souls!"

It soon became obvious that the new pastor held deep-seated prejudices. He called the people of Harlem "animals," and "savages in civilized clothes." He said black teens walked the road to hell. He closed the race relations bureau, and he forbade Catherine from allowing certain people to speak at Friendship House. "He seems to be the wrong man for the wrong place altogether," Catherine concluded. "If he could, he would stop us."

For the first time since the Toronto years, Catherine felt frightened. It seemed as if her prayers for an understanding pastor had gone unanswered, but as she was fond of saying, "God writes straight with crooked lines," and the crooked lines that carried her away from Father Mulvoy led straight to Father Paul Hanly Furfey, the renowned author and sociology professor from Catholic University. When Catherine asked Father Furfey to be her spiritual director, he agreed. He believed God had chosen Catherine to do important work, but he tempered that by warning it would require great sacrifice and suffering on her part:

> There are plenty of people ready to save the world in easy ways, but these easy ways don't work. There are a few people willing to save the world in difficult ways, but most of these lose heart and become discouraged. Then there are a few select souls who both realize that they can save the world only by suffering and have the tenacity to carry their self-sacrifice through. These are very rare souls, but their success is completely out of

proportion to their numbers. These are the people who convert the world.

Furfey believed voluntary poverty made Catherine different from the average social worker. He saw voluntary poverty as rooted in love — not the romantic type of love based on feelings — but a deeper love, grounded in faith, self-sacrifice, and genuine concern for the well-being of others. Love, he told her, should remain at the core of her existence, and everything else should revolve around that center. He encouraged Catherine to balance active work with quiet prayer and to offset her sense of sinfulness with her understanding of God's mercy. He advised her to temper her burning denunciations of social injustice with charity toward those she criticized. Even something as mundane as going to bed early, he insisted, is often a greater sacrifice than staying up late to get things done — especially if tiredness caused her to be irritable the next day. Spending more time chatting with the staff is better than worrying about organizational problems. As a rule of thumb, he suggested, it is always preferable to choose the loving thing to do rather than the most expedient. Everything should be sifted through the intellect and acted upon from conviction, not emotion. At the same time he warned her not to be afraid of making mistakes because mistakes are the price one pays for venturing into uncharted areas.

Catherine's letters to Furfey seem similar in style and tone to her diary entries from this period. She shared with him her shortcomings, her failures, her sense of sinfulness, her deepest longings, her strongest temptations. She chronicled the daily happenings in Friendship House: news that a spunky young girl named Mary Jerdo arrived, disagreements among staff and volunteers, plans to start a newspaper, Flewy's aches and pains, a report that her old friends from London, Frank Sheed and Maisie Ward, opened editorial offices in New York, the decision to rent another storefront, and the arrival of Olga LaPlante, who had come from Canada to join Friendship House in Harlem. She also consulted Furfey on problems with staff members, who accused her of barking orders, exploding in anger, using sarcasm to correct people, and disposing of people abruptly. "I am really utterly, unworthy spiritually to be their leader," she confessed.

Furfey disagreed. With the skill of a diplomat, he pointed out that the staff workers were young, idealistic, inexperienced, and took themselves very seriously. Many were wounded, and had come, not so much to help other people, as to be helped by Catherine. "They do have virtues, too," he added. "They are innocent and generous and brave in so many ways and they are earnest about doing the right thing and they have high ideals, and the future belongs to them for better or for worse. We just have to be infinitely patient with them and kind and charitable and understanding. . . Quite a program for us, isn't it? But if we can only live up to it, we'll get results."

Tall and handsome with a big Irish grin, Father Furfey was loved by the staff workers. "He was comfortable and he invited confidences," Ellen Tarry recalled.

Furfey recognized that the staff had placed Catherine on an unrealistically high pedestal, and whenever she teetered, they reacted as if she purposely violated their image of her. What the staff did not understand was that Catherine struggled with problems and tensions beyond Friendship House. In early May 1940, the Germans attacked Belgium, Holland and Luxembourg. This offensive culminated some weeks later with the fall of France and the evacuation of British troops at Dunkirk. The fighting in Belgium continued until King Leopold III surrendered. "My poor mother is there," Catherine wrote to Furfey.

> All is pain in my heart, my soul, my mind. "Weary" I think is the word for it. Father, Father, before me rises all the suffering that has been mine for so many years. Will there be no end? The war is here again when at 15 I went into it, with all it spelled for me, you know. The starting out again in strange, distant, different lands. . . the struggle for survival. . . the hurts and pains of making a living here. . . then Boris (my husband) with all the cruelty that goes with such scandals as he created. . .

then again destitution and again a struggle for life, mine and George's. . . Respite: a heaven of refuge in FH, the finding of myself in God. Then the story of Toronto, its petty persecution, the closing of FH there with its wild rumors. . . Spain, Poland. . . pain for others. . . Now this . . . And I cannot mention the spiritual fight through all these years, with temptation, aridity, despair that so often threw its shadow over me. Why that sea of pain in which my whole life is bathed?

When Catherine received a call from the chancery saying Archbishop Spellman wanted to see her, she confided to Furfey her fear that Friendship House might be closed. To her utter amazement, however, Spellman greeted her with a grin and glowing praise for her work. He had heard that during a recent lecture tour in New England, Catherine told audiences what a good bishop he was, and he was flattered by the compliment. "One lone woman plus an Archbishop comes pretty near to forming a majority!" Father Furfey joked.

While Furfey knew better than anyone else the extent of Catherine's faults and failings, he genuinely liked her. "You want to know why you are so overwhelming?" he once told her.

There is this spirit of restless energy. Other people can't quite hold your pace. You even seem to "relax" strenuously. I mean long walks, etc. Of course long walks are excellent, but they don't represent most people's idea of rest. Yes, you are very, very dynamic and it's hard for the rest of us to keep up with you. Then you have a certain emotional energy, too. Every idea which comes up in your conversation is overcharged with emotion. You speak about injustice in ordinary conversation and you burn with indignation. You speak of FH and you glow with visible affection. Yes, you are all energy. Sometimes you miss the nuances. You live on a plane of such driving energy that you overlook a whole world of tiny emotions which seem important to ordinary mortals. This leads to occasional misunderstandings. But you are overwhelming. There's no doubt about that. Therein lies your power over people. That is a great gift. Only sometimes you scare little people who can't keep up with you. What a woman! What a woman!

Eddie Doherty and Helen Worden, reporters from *Liberty Magazine*, sampled Catherine's emotional energy when they walked into Friendship House in September 1940, and announced that they were researching an article about Harlem, the wickedest city in the world. Infuriated at their arrogance, Catherine roared: "You have found filth in our stinking dark hallways?"

You have found misery in our dirty neglected streets, in our shocking obscene slums? You are surprised? You are horrified? You blame Harlem for all this? Who made Harlem wicked, if it is wicked? Go ask City Hall. Go ask the respectable Christians of Manhattan and the Bronx, Catholics included. Go ask the shopkeepers who fleece them. If Harlem is bad, Manhattan is a thousand times worse. . . Why don't you write about some of your southern cities, if you want something really wicked. . .

Eddie Doherty liked her spunk, and when Catherine asked Ellen Tarry to take the reporters out and show them the "real" Harlem, Eddie scribbled a check for $400 and tossed it on Catherine's desk.

"Will it bounce?" she asked sarcastically.

"It won't come back, but I will," Eddie laughed. Then he winked at the statue of Blessed Martin de Porres behind her desk. Eddie had written a story about Blessed Martin for *Liberty Magazine*, and had witnessed the miraculous recovery of a baby with a ruptured lung after a priest held a relic of the saint on the baby's chest. The connection between Blessed Martin and Friendship House made Eddie wonder if the mulatto miracle worker had drawn him there for a reason.

Only within the past few years had Eddie become a believer in miracles. Born in Chicago in 1890, he thought about becoming a priest, but changed his mind when he discovered girls. Eddie never finished high school, but with natural curiosity, an outgoing personality, and a flair for writing, he worked his way from copy boy to ace reporter. In 1914, he married his childhood sweetheart, who died in the Spanish flu epidemic of 1918, leaving him with a baby boy. Angry at God, Eddie stopped going to church, and nine months later, he eloped with Mildred Frisbey, a Chicago newspaper woman, who had no religion. When Mildred discovered she was pregnant, Eddie suggested that they have a priest validate the marriage, but when they went to the rectory, the cantankerous old pastor screamed, "Don't you know you're living in sin?"

"Then I'll go to hell!" Eddie shouted back, and he stormed out of the rectory, promising himself he would never set foot in another Catholic church.

Nearly twenty years later, Eddie's editor at *Liberty Magazine* asked him to write a profile of Father Charles Coughlin, a controversial radio priest from Detroit, who refused all interviews. Eddie wrangled an introduction, and when Coughlin found out Eddie was a fallen-away Catholic, he agreed to an interview on the condition that Eddie return to the Church. "No soul, no story," Coughlin said.

"Sold!" Eddie replied.

As agreed, Eddie went to Confession, but he could not receive Communion because his marriage to Mildred remained invalid in the eyes of the Church. "I went to Mass every Sunday, though at first I felt ridiculous and somewhat hypocritical. There was no particular feeling of fervor in me. I was going to church not to honor God, but to keep a word I had given — to pay on the installment plan, as it were, for the story of Father Coughlin."

It was during this time that Eddie wrote the story about Blessed Martin, and both he and Mildred began to pray to the dark-skinned saint. Through a series of events that they believed Blessed Martin orchestrated, Mildred found a doctor from California, who relieved her of the chronic back and shoulder pain she had suffered for years. A few months later, a friend offered the use of his hillside home on the outskirts of Los Angeles so that Eddie could undergo a series of treatments by the same doctor to relieve foot problems. Their happiness turned into a nightmare, however, on the afternoon of March 14, 1939, when Mildred stumbled while walking alone on a steep canyon road. When she didn't come home for dinner, Eddie reported her missing. The next day rescue workers found her body in the brush with her neck wedged between the branches of a mesquite tree. The county autopsy surgeon certified the cause of death as "asphyxiation by strangulation following an accidental fall."

Eddie didn't rage at God the way he had after his first wife's death. He pressed a relic of Blessed Martin over Mildred's heart and prayed, "Blessed Martin, ask God to keep her happy forever and ever." Five days after Mildred's funeral, Eddie knelt in the darkness of a confessional and whispered to a priest that he wanted to come back to the Church. Eighteen months later, the flamboyant Eddie Doherty, the "highest paid reporter in America," became a Friendship House volunteer. He called it "the rarest place I know. . . unique among all unique institutions. . . new, gloriously new. . . simple and unpretentious." He parked his red convertible outside, and showed neighborhood kids how the black canvas top went up and down at the push of a button. He sat at the long wooden table eating soup, bread, and tea, and talked about God, poverty, and people. After dinner, he stood to chant the words of the Divine Office. He carried food and clothes to families in wretched tenement flats, and he saw what Catherine meant when she spoke about finding the face of Christ in the poor. He chatted with staff workers, "as beautiful as you'll find in all New York," and he joked that a man had to be careful at Friendship House if he wanted to remain a widower.

"The women loved Eddie," Ellen Tarry recalled. "He was gentle and kind. He was handsome in an Irish sort of way. He was older, experienced. You had the feeling that Eddie was going to take care of you."

Ann Harrigan called him undeniably "charming and attractive" and confessed that she had an "abysmal" crush on him.

"Doherty *is* nice!!" Catherine wrote in her journal, and she confided to Father Furfey that: "A little temptation again crossed my horizon in the shape of a reporter from *Liberty*, a Mr. Doherty, who came to write about Harlem. . ."

Eddie found Catherine mystifying, but the woman who captured his heart was the delicately beautiful Jane O'Donnell. "I think I'm falling deeper and deeper there," he confessed to Catherine.

"I saw quite a bit of Eddie in Catherine's company," Ann Harrigan recalled, "and I could see what she was doing with Eddie. She was pushing Jane at him, and advising him, but actually I could see this guy was going to come back to her. . . I was really jealous, because I liked Eddie, too, and he never paid any mind to me!"

In May 1941, Jane O'Donnell shocked everyone when she decided to leave Friendship House and join a religious group called the Grail. No one missed Jane as much as Catherine and Eddie did. They began to commiserate, sometimes slipping out for a drink or watching the waves slap against the pier at Battery Park. An attraction formed, but they didn't mention it to each other. "Blood is so hot, so young yet in my veins," Catherine prayed. "I feel at times like sun, and air, and fun and love. . . Are these temptations! Are they against my vocation — the one you have seemingly given me?"

Flewy recognized the flames of passion, and she warned Eddie that if Catherine ever married, it would be a disaster. "She doesn't want to marry. She'd never dream of deserting us for any man. That would close Friendship House. That would be a tragedy. A tragedy, and a mortal sin!"

Flewy insisted that if Catherine ever married, she would eat her shirt and wear a barrel. "I believe you belong to God," she told Catherine.

In early August, Catherine went to St. Bonaventure University in upstate New York to lecture on racial justice. A young English professor named Thomas Merton heard the talk and asked if he could work at Friendship House for a few weeks.

"Sure," Catherine replied, "come on."

Merton's arrival in Harlem on August 15 triggered an unexpected spark of jealousy in Eddie. He didn't like the way Merton looked at Catherine. He didn't like the way they spoke French. He didn't like their intellectual discussions about God, which had an abstract quality totally foreign to Eddie. Worst of all, Merton wrote poetry for Catherine, deep, mystical poetry that Eddie couldn't comprehend.

"You don't like him, do you?" Flewy asked with a smirk.

"I don't know him," Eddie scowled.

At the end of August, Merton returned to St. Bonaventure, and Catherine went to Canada for a holiday. Waiting for her in Toronto was Nicholas Makletzoff, who had bought five acres of river-front property for $350 on the outskirts of Combermere, Ontario, a tiny village where he had vacationed since 1932. There was an abandoned cheese factory on the land, but Nicholas planned to tear it down, and build a magnificent house, a place where he and Catherine could retire when the annulment of her marriage to Boris came through. They could start their own fishing lodge, he told her. They could build cottages, and the main house with its breathtaking view of the river and the hills, would be a place where guests could have meals or just relax.

Catherine didn't tell Nicholas about Eddie. There was nothing to say. No talk of marriage. No future plans. It was an attraction. Nothing more.

In mid-September, United States Immigration blocked Catherine's return to Harlem because her mother and brothers lived in Belgium, a Nazi-occupied country. "God help us!" Ann Harrigan wrote in her diary. "Now the B can't get from Canada to N.Y. Harlem is in a mess and generally speaking, things are in one hell of a mess."

Resentment in Harlem festered as defense industries hired white women rather than black men to work in factories. Reports of police brutality and lynchings filtered in from throughout the country. Black Catholics spoke out against the way Catholic hospitals refused to treat black patients and the way Catholic priests resisted bringing Communion to the sick and elderly in tenements. Militant members of black nationalistic leagues called for riots. Monday night discussions at Friendship House became heated, and without Catherine to add insight, tempers flared.

When Catherine finally returned to Harlem on November 6, the staff threw a huge welcome home party. Missing from the festivities was Eddie Doherty, who had moved to Chicago in October to take a job at $10,000 a year with *The Chicago Sun*.

Catherine stayed in Harlem one week, and then left on a lecture tour, which included several stops in Chicago, where Eddie anxiously awaited her arrival. On November 30, a date they marked as a special anniversary, Eddie took Catherine to a country inn on the outskirts of Chicago, and begged her to marry him. Panic-stricken, Catherine ran from the restaurant in tears, and when Eddie caught up with her, she insisted that marriage was impossible.

"Yes, it must have cost a struggle to say *No* to Ed," Father Furfey admitted.

> He is one person who really could live with you in Harlem and you two could still carry on your work there after marriage. But of course it would hurt the work. You couldn't give yourself to him and the work both, with the same emotional intensity. But it must have been very hard. Ed is such a beautiful character.

By the time Catherine returned to Harlem in mid-December, the Japanese had bombed Pearl Harbor, and the United States had entered the war. The new year brought price controls, sugar rationing, and a ban on the sale of passenger cars and trucks. Friendship House staff workers rolled bandages and stockpiled canned food and water. New York City was designated a blackout area, and thick curtains shrouded the Friendship House windows. Darkness fell over Catherine, too, and she told Father Furfey she wanted to leave Friendship House for a while and disappear into the slums of a large city, where she would work as an immigrant, using the name Katie Hook, and reach out on an individual basis to poor white working girls, who had fallen away from God.

"You aren't really serious about being Katie Hook, are you?" Furfey replied.

> Every reason in the world tells you that Harlem is the place for you to stay. That is unquestionably your work . . . We have always felt, haven't we, that the weakest point in the FH organization is that the kids don't stay? Now you won't go and set them a bad example, would you, by running away from FH?

Furfey tried to divert her attention by encouraging her to write some intellectually focused articles on Friendship House, but it didn't calm her inner restlessness. In mid-March, she set out on another mid-west lecture tour that started in Chicago. "And to make matters worse," she told Furfey,

> I get there on St. Patrick's Day, the Saint of the Irish. I sort of have an idea that (St. Patrick) and (Blessed) Martin are almost conspiring to bring me and Eddie together, over and over again, though all I want is to be separated from him by at least a thousand miles.

Chapter Notes

"*like a thunderbolt...*": Diary #22, Nov. 8, 1939, MHA.
"*Another friend gone...*": Diary #22, Feb. 8, 1940, MHA. [Father Paul of Graymoor, 78 years old, died at 4 a.m. on Feb. 8, 1940. Mother Lurana died on April 15, 1935.]
"*I want you to know...*": Interview, Ellen Tarry.
"*animals*": Diary #22, May 11, 1940, MHA.
"*savages*": Diary #24, Sept. 22, 1940, MHA.
"*He seemed to be the wrong man...*" Ibid.
"*There are plenty of people...*": PHF to C de H, Mar. 6, 1940, MHA.
"*I am really utterly, unworthy...*": Diary #22, June 17, 1940, MHA.
"*They do have virtues, too...*": PHF to C de H, Feb. 1941, MHA.
"*He was comfortable...*": Interview, Ellen Tarry.

"My poor mother is there...": C de H to PHF, May 10, 1940, MHA.

"One lone woman...": PHF to C de H, May 15, 1942, MHA.

"You want to know why...": PHF to C de H, Dec. 17, 1942, MHA.

"You have found filth..." and f.: ED, *Cricket in My Heart*, p. 21. (Hereafter *Cricket*).

"Don't you know you're living in sin?" and f.: ED, *Gall & Honey*, p. 168.

"asphyxiation by strangulation...": "Doherty Burial to Be in Chicago," *Los Angeles Times*, Mar. 17, 1939.

"Blessed Martin, ask God to keep her happy...": *Gall & Honey*, p. 299.

"the rarest place I know...": ED, "Harlem's Holy House," *The Torch*, Feb., 1941.

"as beautiful as you'll find...": *Cricket*, p. 53.

"The women loved Eddie...": Interview, Ellen Tarry

"charming and attractive...": AH Diary, Nov. 18, 1940 and Nov. 25, 1940, AUND.

"Doherty is nice!!": Diary # 22, Oct. 1, 1940, MHA.

"A little temptation again crossed my horizon...": C de H to PHF, Oct. 5, 1940, MHA.

"I think I'm falling deeper...": ED to C de H, Jan. 11, 1941, MHA.

"I saw quite a bit of Eddie...": Interview, Ann Harrigan by Sister Louise Sharum, MHA.

"Blood is so hot...": Diary #24, July 23, 1941,, MHA.

"She doesn't want to marry...": *Cricket*, p. 56.

"I believe you belong to God...": Flewy to C de H, Sept. 19, 1941, MHA.

*"Sure,"*Catherine replied: Thomas Merton, *The Seven Storey Mountain*, p. 334. [Thomas Merton returned to Friendship House the following summer, and after a staff retreat, given by Fr. Furfey, Meton decided that his true vocation was with the Trappists.]

"You don't like him..." and f.: *Cricket*, p. 61.

"God help us!": AH Diary, Sept. 16, 1941, AUND

"Yes, it must have cost a struggle...": PHF to C de H, Dec. 5, 1941, MHA.

"You aren't really serious...": PHF to C de H, Feb,, 1942, MHA.

"And to make matters worse...": C de H to PHF, Mar. 12, 1942, MHA.

25

Chicago
1942

Eddie Doherty waited with a bouquet of flowers as Catherine's train steamed into the LaSalle Street station. He never missed a chance to ask Catherine to marry him. "She was the forbidden woman; I was the forbidden man," he recalled. "Still I could not help proposing to her." He showered her with flowers, telegrams, and long distance phone calls. He wrote articles about Friendship House and signed up as a speaker for the newly launched Friendship House Lecture Bureau. When Catherine struck out in her attempts to convince newspaper editors to write articles about discrimination, Eddie succeeded in persuading Marshall Field to let him write a series of articles for *The Chicago Sun* on the "Negro question" in the United States.

Nothing worked.

But Eddie had one more scheme. He decided to introduce Catherine to Bernard J. Sheil, the Auxiliary Bishop of Chicago, with the hope that Sheil would see the potential for a liaison between a saintly social worker and a star reporter. When they arrived at Sheil's elegant apartment on the top floor of St. Andrew's rectory, however, the Bishop seemed more interested in hearing about Catherine's work in Harlem. After she explained how she had dedicated her life to God and Friendship House, the Bishop agreed that marriage would never fit into the plan. "I felt awkward, foolish, stunned, lost," Eddie recalled.

For Catherine, the meeting with Sheil seemed providential. She now had the ear of a bishop, who was a passionate defender of human rights. As a young priest, Sheil served as a prison chaplain, and he saw that delinquent boys were not evil in themselves, but had become victims of an evil society filled with greed, avarice, selfishness, and intolerance, a society that shirked its responsibility to young people. He promised himself that some good would come from these tragic lives, and in 1930, he kept that promise by founding the Catholic Youth Organization in Chicago. The movement spread rapidly to other cities, including Harlem, where Catherine started the first black CYO.

Sheil agreed with Catherine's plans to expand Friendship House programs and to work toward social change. She explained how the staff wrote letters demanding an end to discrimination in Catholic high schools and colleges, labor unions, hospitals, and businesses and industries. She set up panels of Catholic lawyers to handle discrimination cases, and each week white staff workers from Friendship House tested the New York State Civil Rights Law by taking a black friend to lunch and reporting restaurants that refused to serve them. Catherine warned Sheil that restlessness in Harlem continued to grow and talk of race riots had become more heated. The year before, President Roosevelt had signed Executive Order 8802, prohibiting discrimination in defense industries, and by this Order, Roosevelt averted a planned March on Washington by unemployed black workers. The Friendship House Mothers Club wanted Catherine to go to President Roosevelt with a list of new concerns, but she suggested that Sheil might have greater influence with the president. The people's demands were simple: they wanted an end to segregation in the military, an order stopping the Red Cross from keeping separate blood banks for blacks and whites, tougher penalties for defense industries with discriminatory hiring, and a black member of the Cabinet.

In early May, Bishop Sheil met with Roosevelt, who seemed open to Sheil's concerns, but suggested that since this was a moral issue, perhaps the American Catholic Bishops should take the first step by issuing a statement on racial justice. Stung by Roosevelt's crafty reply, Sheil told Catherine he would pay her air fare and expenses if she would meet with Bishop Edwin J. O'Hara of

Kansas City, Missouri, who headed the American Bishops' Social Justice Committee, and Bishops Joseph F. Rummell in New Orleans and Gerald P. O'Hara of Savannah, Georgia, who spearheaded the Southern Clergy Conference.

The bishops admitted to Catherine that racial tensions had erupted in their dioceses, but they felt pressured by influential white bigots, who held prominent places in Catholic parishes. In Savannah, Catherine encountered this bigotry while lecturing to a Catholic women's group. Enraged at her demands for desegregation, the angry audience surged at the stage. "My blouse was in shreds, and I was black and blue from the blows of the women," she recalled. Custodians saved her by smuggling her out the back door in a trash can. The incident did not intimidate Catherine, and she continued to challenge bishops, nuns, and priests to take a stand.

"Baroness, we have to move slowly," they told her. "The time is not yet ripe."

"I have never read anywhere in the Gospel where Christ says to wait 20 years before living the Gospel," she retorted.

After these kinds of confrontations, she would return to her room and stare at a crucifix. "Pray, oh pray," she wrote to Dorothy Day, "that the human element in the Church does not fail my Negroes!!"

Impressed with Catherine's efforts, Bishop Sheil told her he wanted a Friendship House in Chicago as soon as possible.

"It seems to be the will of God," Catherine wrote to Father Furfey, and she started looking for a storefront in Chicago's Black Belt, an area bulging with over 300,000 people between 31st Street and 55th along State Street and Federal. On side streets, slum landlords sub-divided wood frame houses intended for one or two families into one-room apartments with a gas burner for cooking. A single house might hold up to 18 families, who had to share one or two common bathrooms. People unable to pay rent lived in wood sheds, coal bins, and garages. The putrid odor of dead rats and decaying garbage hung in the air. Animals at the Lincoln Park Zoo had better living conditions.

In June, Catherine found two storefronts, one for a library

meeting place, and the other for a youth center on 43rd Street, a busy thoroughfare with shops, saloons, cheap theaters, and the roar of the El overhead.

"The B, we learned, had promised to send 'Tarry' and 'Harrigan' before she bothered to tell Ann Harrigan or myself about it," Ellen recalled. "The last thing I wanted to do, at that time, was leave New York."

Ann Harrigan agreed. "Both Ellen and I were professional people. . . We had financial obligations to our families."

Catherine convinced Ann Harrigan and Ellen Tarry to give it a try, and Bishop Sheil sweetened the deal by offering to pay them each a salary of $6,000 per year, plus hire a black secretary to help them.

"Personally, I do not think that the mere existence of salaries is fatal," Father Furfey told Catherine, "but it would be fatal if your workers should begin to feel themselves as professional social workers instead of persons who are devoting themselves to the work for the pure love of it. It will certainly cause feeling when it becomes known in [Harlem] that the staff in Chicago is salaried, while the girls there are expected to work for the pure love of the movement."

Furfey worried about Bishop Sheil's influence over Catherine. Sheil offered all the trappings of power, luxury, fame, and worldliness that never existed in Friendship House. Furfey explained that Dorothy Day embraced a life of poverty as a way of influencing others, while Bishop Sheil used money and prestige. Neither was right or wrong, but each remained consistent in the way they lived. "You mustn't try to run with the hare and hunt with the hounds," he warned Catherine.

That September, Ann Harrigan and Ellen Tarry went to Chicago and began renovating the storefronts for a November grand opening. Because of the housing shortage, they rented an upstairs bedroom in a mortuary owned by Mrs. Sunshine Edwards on South Michigan Avenue. Catherine, who was staying at the Morrison Hotel at Bishop Sheil's expense, tried to help, but after Ellen and Ann wrote her a letter asking her to please let them do it on their own, Catherine backed off. Hurt at what she considered a rejection by her own staff, she busied herself with another project for Bishop Sheil, who wanted her to meet secretly with bishops and black leaders in an attempt to stop the newly revived plans for a March on Washington. When Father Furfey discovered Catherine's plans, he warned that white bigots were also trying to halt the March for their own hate-filled purposes, and if her name became aligned with theirs, it would be disastrous. "I don't trust Bishop Sheil on racial lines quite as implicitly as you do," Furfey told her.

> Please, please, please, don't spoil all your glorious work by making a mistake now. A very fine priest, a level-headed man who gets around the country a lot, was talking to me about you the other day. He said he didn't quite trust you because he was afraid you had too high a respect for expediency. He was afraid you might be persuaded to compromise with your principles under some circumstances. Naturally, I defended you, not without heat. Please don't let me down.

Catherine promised to shift Sheil to her lowest priority, but a few weeks later, Sheil asked Catherine to accompany him when he addressed the Annual Conference of Catholic Charities in Kansas City, and she agreed. He peppered his talk with phrases like "the Brotherhood of Man under the Fatherhood of God," which showed Catherine's influence. The following month, the American Bishops took a much weaker stand on racial justice, with no mention of the need for black equality in Catholic hospitals or schools.

That November, Catherine and Sheil attended the official opening of Friendship House. Reporters and photographers hovered around them, giving Catherine all the credit for starting the new Friendship House. Ann and Ellen never complained openly, but resentment brewed beneath the surface. Catherine was too busy with another project for Bishop Sheil to notice. She had proposed that Sheil start an adult education center to offset the

Abraham Lincoln School, where Chicago Communists trained laborers.

"She wrote out a whole plan and she convinced Bishop Sheil to sponsor it," recalled Nina Polcyn Moore, a Milwaukee teacher recruited by Catherine for the project. "When we came there, we discovered we were totally ill-equipped to run such a thing! But that was part of her grand scheme, you know. She thought a little piety substituted for a vast body of knowledge. That was just her method of operation. It was a rich adventure."

Registration for the Sheil School of Social Studies opened January 11, 1943, with classes scheduled to start on February 1. People called it a revolutionary new idea in adult education, but Father Furfey worried more than ever. "Promise me you won't ever lose interest in Friendship House," he pleaded.

Catherine assured him that everything ran smoothly with Nancy Grenell, a former advertising executive who gave up her career to join Friendship House, serving as director of Friendship House Harlem, and Ellen Tarry and Ann Harrigan as co-directors of the Chicago house. Catherine had not noticed the mounting tensions between Ann, who tended to be well-organized and authoritarian, and Ellen, who saw Friendship House as being more community oriented and flexible. By the end of December, Ellen quit and returned to New York. Ann felt bitterly resentful.

Back in New York, Catherine floundered in her own miseries. She told Eddie before she left Chicago in November that she didn't want to see him again. In December, she bid a painful good-bye to George, who left on an intelligence mission into Russia as military attaché to the Canadian Ambassador. Fears for her mother and brothers in Europe plagued her waking moments. Nightmares shattered her sleep.

Catherine returned to Chicago in February 1943, but within days of her arrival, she mysteriously disappeared. She hinted before she left that Bishop Sheil had another project for her, but she did not tell anyone where she went. Only Sheil knew that Catherine had secretly become Katie Hook.

Sheil had seen in Catherine the same restless temperament

he possessed, a temperament fueled by the need for constant change, constant excitement. "There are souls who are meant to start one thing and then God sends others to take care of their start," he told her.

It was exactly what Catherine wanted to hear. She packed a few things in a battered suitcase and took the El down to the Loop where she rented a drab room with stained wallpaper for $5 a week in a boarding house at 1111 South Wabash Avenue. She took a series of menial jobs as a day waitress in a diner called William's, on an assembly line making paper cups, as a chamber maid making beds at the YMCA, and finally, as a cocktail waitress at Millie's, the most notorious pickup joint on South State Street. Katie Hook talked freely to everyone she met, and people told her about themselves because she seemed to care. "The Baroness has died for a while," Catherine wrote. "Katie is on her own, alone, no glamour, no rapt audiences, no companionship of like spirits, no light and love of the FH crowd, nothing but work and a drab room and a little harvest of precious souls, wrung out of the desert that no priest ever crosses except to sin."

Catherine wrote weekly letters to Bishop Sheil, and occasional letters to Ann, Nancy and some of the others without revealing where she was or what she was doing. Eddie Doherty was the first to find Catherine, and on April 7, he took Ann Harrigan to see her. When they walked into Millie's, Ann reeled at what she called the "awful muck, dirty, stifling air & stench of sex gone mad." Within one hour, Catherine convinced Eddie to go to Hollywood, where a producer had made him a lucrative offer to write the screenplay for a movie based on an article he had written about the five Sullivan brothers, who died when their ship was torpedoed. She also promised Ann that her stint as Katie Hook was almost over, and assured her that she had already written to Father Furfey, apologizing for disappearing without telling him.

"I would have been happy if you had told me about this ahead of time," Furfey replied.

THEY CALLED HER THE BARONESS

It is perfectly well understood that I don't have any authority over you. I certainly never claimed any. When I became your spiritual director, I made that clear. You must make your own decisions. But the one thing I want as a spiritual director is the opportunity of knowing about major decisions ahead of time, so that I may at least express an opinion. That's all I want from you. I ~~want you always to listen to my advice~~. I certainly don't demand that you should follow it. Is this asking too much?

Catherine returned to the Chicago Friendship House at the end of April, and was back in New York by mid-May. Flewy told her it wasn't good for her to be away for so long. Vicious rumors circulated about Catherine being a pseudo-Catholic, who tried to undermine the Catholic Church by advocating racial equality. One woman wrote an 8-page letter to bishops across the country claiming Catherine was a Russian infiltrator and a fake Baroness, who had conspired with an agent of the British government to convince the Catholic hierarchy to silence radio priest Father Charles Coughlin. Catherine shrugged it all off as lies.

What did affect Catherine were love letters Eddie penned from his suite at the Beverly Hills Hotel. He begged her to marry him, and a new urgency flowed through his words. In what seemed like an uncanny coincidence, Rome granted Catherine's annulment from Boris on March 17, the feast of St. Patrick, who, Eddie insisted, had interceded on his behalf. "I love you and I want to marry you," he wrote.

I want to marry you openly and immediately in the Church or out of it.

I am sorry if bishops and priests whom I revere will feel hurt. But why should it always be you and me who "take it"?

Please write and tell Bishop Sheil you mean to marry me in NY in early June and ask him if he will officiate. If not, we'll marry anyway —

Katie, is your love for me big enough for this — open, lawful, simple, public marriage as soon as possible?

And to hell with the consequences? Or must I wait some
more?

Lady, this trip has done things to me in more ways than
one. The principal thing it has done is crystallize my
ideas about marrying you. It has increased my hunger
for you. And it has made me a trifle ashamed of the ease
with which I let other people come between me and you
— Fr. Furfey, Bishop Sheil, Nicholas, Anne, Nancy,
most anybody at all — trying to tell myself in a convinc-
ing way that this was the will of God.

I don't think it is now. I think it is His will that you and
I forget the rest of the world — defy the world if
necessary and follow our hearts.

Catherine pointed out that she had agreed to write a book for
Sheed & Ward about her experiences as Katie Hook. She had
article assignments, lecture dates, and she faced the challenge of
organizing a training school for Friendship House staff workers.
There was also a possibility that she might become Katie Hook
again. "Can I do all this and be your wife too?" she asked. "Can I?
Can I? Can I? Can I?"

On May 30, Eddie flew to New York and persuaded Catherine
to return with him to Chicago where Bishop Sheil could decide
their fate. This time, Eddie shocked Catherine and Sheil when he
knelt down and proposed to her in front of the Bishop, promising
that he would sell his property, give away his money, and live in
poverty if she would become his wife. Overwhelmed at the
realization that Eddie would give up everything to marry her,
Catherine wept. Sheil had one more condition, however: "If you
want to marry her, Friendship House must come first."

When Eddie agreed, Sheil offered to perform the ceremony
in his private chapel and host the wedding breakfast. They set the
date for the morning of Friday, June 25, but Catherine insisted that
it be kept secret. "I didn't tell anybody from Friendship House
about the wedding because I didn't know what the reactions
would be. I must admit that I was frightened about that."

The only wedding guests were Eddie's two brothers and two
sisters. Catherine wore a powder blue brocade suit with a match-

ing hat. That evening Eddie's mother, who had been unable to attend the wedding because of difficulty climbing stairs, cooked a roast beef dinner for them at the family homestead on North Sawyer. The phone never stopped ringing with Doherty relatives calling to extend their congratulations.

After three days of honeymooning at a Chicago hotel, Catherine left for a lecture tour and Eddie went back to his office at *The Chicago Sun*. His first call that morning was Ann Harrigan, who insisted that they meet after work in the lobby of the Morrison Hotel. When Eddie arrived, Ann told him she had already gone to Bishop Sheil and asked if Catherine and Eddie were married, but Sheil refused to answer. Eddie tried to hedge, but Ann was so upset that he finally confessed.

"The news of the marriage of the B to Eddie D has left a great ache in me," Ann wrote in her diary.

> Is it that the horizons of loneliness widen and ever widen? I might as well be in Timbuctoo — not to have let me know (that is what hurts & I am surprised at my pride). The whole Doherty family, every last one of them knew. This goddamn secrecy annoys me. But the shock of it disturbs my faith in the B. Isn't this an important enough thing to talk over with the heads of the 2 houses she's mothered? O God, I'm in such a fog — Have I given up my job for this? Now she steps out of the picture and leaves me holding the bag — and Nancy the same.
>
> We are just pawns in the hands of people like her and the Bishop — Human personalities don't count. That was my one big fear from the beginning with the B and then with the Bishop.

Ann called Nancy Grenell in Harlem. She also notified Father Furfey, who assured Ann that from now on, he considered her the head of Friendship House. A few weeks later, Ann left for New York, where she and Nancy broke the news to Flewy. "I was calm because I was numb like when you get cut it doesn't hurt for a few minutes," Flewy confessed.

Catherine purposely avoided Friendship House for a few weeks. She gave a few out of town lectures, and Eddie made plans for them to spend a few days at a country resort in Wisconsin. When they returned to Chicago, they found a studio apartment in a poor white neighborhood, which they rented for $7 a week.

On July 29, one month after the wedding, Catherine went to Harlem for the annual Staff retreat. That night, Catherine, Ann Harrigan, Nancy Grenell, and Father Furfey met privately to discuss the future of Friendship House. They told Catherine how hurt they had been by her secret marriage, and Catherine sobbed as she related the heart wrenching story of her first marriage to Boris, and how she had never known the kind of love Eddie gave her. It wasn't until she offered to resign from Friendship House that everyone in the room, including Father Furfey, broke down and wept. After five long hours, they decided Catherine could continue as Director General.

"All is well and my beloved FH has not left me," Catherine wrote to Eddie. "I am so very happy darling and I want you to share it."

It would be weeks before Catherine would see Eddie again. Long before she had even thought about marriage, Catherine, Ann, and Nancy had agreed to go to Canada for a working vacation in August. They planned to stay in the new house Nicholas Makletzoff had built on the Madawaska River, and Catherine would have to find some way of telling Nicholas, as gently as she could, that his plans for a life with her would never become reality.

Chapter Notes

"She was the forbidden woman...": *Cricket*, p. 76.

"I felt awkward...": *Ibid.*, p. 68.

a passionate defender...: For information on Sheil see Roger L. Treat, *Bishop Sheil and The CYO*, New York: Julian Messner, Inc., 1951; and Steven M. Avella, "The Rise and Fall of Bernard Sheil," *The Critic*, Spring, 1990.

"My blouse was in shreds...": *Fragments*, p. 148.

"Baroness, we have to move slowly...": *Ibid.*, p. 155.

"I have never read anywhere...": *Ibid.*, p. 155.

"Pray, oh pray...": C de H to Dorothy Day, May 26, 1942, Marquette University Archives.

"It seems to be the will of God...": C de H to PHF, May 6, 1942, MHA.

"The B, we learned, had promised ...": Tarry, *Third Door*, p. 194.

"Both Ellen and I were professional people...": AH, "Invading the South Side," *Commonweal*, May 19, 1944.

"Personally, I do not think...": PHF to C de H, May 29, 1942, MHA.

"You mustn't try to run...": PHF to C de H, June, 1942, MHA.

"I don't trust Bishop Sheil...": PHF to C de H, Sept. 19, 1942, MHA.

"the Brotherhood of Man...": "Delinquency and Racial Minority Groups," paper presented by Bishop Bernard J. Sheil before the Annual Conference of Catholic Charities, September 27-30, 1942, Kansas City, Mo. Archdiocese of Chicago Archives and Record Center.

"She wrote out a whole plan...": Interview, Nina Polcyn Moore.

"Promise me you won't...": PHF to C de H, Nov. 15, 1942, MHA.

"There are souls who are meant...": C de H to PHF, Apr. 4, 1974, MHA.

"The Baroness has died...": C de H to PHF, Mar. 30, 1943, MHA.

"awful muck...": AH Diary, Apr. 7, 1943, AUND.

"I would have been happy...": PHF to C de H, Apr. 3, 1943, MHA.

a pseudo-Catholic...: It was during this time period that Catherine began to de-emphasize her Orthodox heritage and deny that she had been received into the Catholic Church in London. On May 1, 1947, an unsigned general information bulletin was issued to Friendship House staff workers for the apparent purpose of addressing rumors. Under the topic Religion, Catherine is listed as Roman Catholic with the following note: "Often you will hear that she is a convert. This rumor started due to the specific laws governing the status of Roman Catholics in Tsarist Russia, which had no concordat with Rome, and if one party was Orthodox, the children were brought up Orthodox officially inasmuch as they had to attend religious classes in that faith. After the Revolution this was abolished, and all parties reverted to their original Faith, in their official documents." See "Catherine de Hueck, For General Information of Friendship House Staff Workers," May 1, 1947, Friendship House Papers, CHS.

In the years that followed, Catherine insisted that her father was Roman Catholic and her mother was Orthodox, and despite family objections, she publicly held that claim for the rest of her life.

a scathing 8-page letter...: Mary J. Leach to Your Excellency, Father, and Christian Friends, Mar. 10, 1943, Friendship House Papers, CHS.

her annulment from Boris...: The annulment was examined by the Supreme Sacred Congregation of the Holy Office in Rome on March 17, 1943, which decreed that the marriage was invalid on the basis of consanguinity. On March 18, 1943 Pope Pius XII approved the decision.

"I love you and I want to marry you...": ED to C de H, May 19, 1943, MHA.

She had agreed to write a book...: The book, entitled *Dear Bishop*, was published by Sheed & Ward in 1947.

"Can I do all this...": C de H to ED, May 23, 1943, MHA.

"If you want to marry her...": *Fragments*, p. 170.

"I didn't invite anybody from Friendship House...": Ibid.

"The news of the marriage....": AH diary, July 1, 1943, AUND.

"I was calm because I was numb...": Flewy to CD, July 24, 1943, MHA.

"All is well...": CD to ED, July 30, 1943, MHA.

26

Combermere

1943

Nicholas built a masterpiece on the banks of the Madawaska River. The living room had a stone fireplace, hardwood floors, and a wall of windows overlooking clear water, blue skies, green hills, graceful pines, and slender white birches. A narrow curved staircase wound its way upstairs to three bedrooms with gable ceilings and French windows. Nicholas was so proud of the house that Catherine didn't have the heart to tell him about her marriage. She didn't tell him the next day either, and the longer she waited the harder it became.

Eddie wrote daily urging her to just tell the truth. By the time Nicholas left on August 17, however, Catherine still had not told him, so she mailed him a long letter explaining everything.

"I feel very sorry for Nicholas," Flewy told Catherine when she returned to the States, "but he could not have fitted into the FH picture could he?"

Flewy struggled with her own mixed feelings about Catherine's marriage and she faced a barrage of questions and snide remarks from other people. Catherine explained to Flewy that the annulment was granted because she and Boris were first cousins, and because she was only 15 at the time of their marriage. As for George, she assured Flewy that the Church still regarded children of annulled marriages as legitimate. Catherine insisted that no one had the right to ask such personal questions, and she instructed Flewy to reply: "For us, it is enough that she had her annulment from Rome. . . and that a Catholic American Bishop married her with all the pomp and blessing of a nuptial Mass."

It did not stop the rumors.

Back in Chicago, people gossiped about Catherine and Eddie living in a white neighborhood far from Friendship House. Catherine insisted that she and Eddie could not find an apartment in the Black Belt because of the housing shortage, but she now believed that this was a sign God wanted her to start bringing blacks into a white area. On Friday nights, she and Eddie began hosting a study group in their apartment with people of all races, ages, and professions, which they named "The Outer Circle" of Friendship House.

Catherine also welcomed a steady stream of visitors, who came to the apartment at odd times of the day and night to talk to her individually and seek advice. Ann Harrigan referred to all of this as "the course FH is taking with the Baroness interested in other things."

> When the B puts on her lipstick at 5 o'clock I am jealous. Now Lord, she ups & is away from the hustle & bustle — I'm chained to it for 5 more hours. . . A pang of real envy goes thru my heart each time I think of her having Eddie to go to, to run to, to sob on his shoulder and to be gathered to his heart. I open the ice box and I see what I can get together for supper — & I am jealous of her flat — and yet — would I exchange? No, I guess not.

The situation also frustrated Father Furfey. He wrote Catherine a long letter accusing her of abandoning Friendship House and suggesting that she make up her mind where her loyalties lay. Catherine insisted that her involvement in Friendship House had not changed, but Furfey was not convinced: "You know those intuitions you have when you say you don't 'feel' right about something? Well, I have that same sort of intuition that you aren't as close to FH as you used to be — but I could be wrong, couldn't I?"

In February 1944, Friendship House held its first Convention, and staff delegates criticized Catherine so unmercifully that even Ann Harrigan admitted that Catherine seemed like "a saint in the making — All the weaknesses & criticisms of her work in Harlem she took humbly & admitted them — the greatness of this is apparent — very generously she openly confessed & promised to do different."

Something had changed beneath the surface of Catherine. Several years before, Father Furfey had urged her to give up meditation for a type of prayer called contemplation. He told her to sit silently, gazing on God, without any conscious thought or verbal prayer. She resisted at first because it seemed unnatural, but gradually, as she tried it for a few minutes each day, she discovered that in silence God touched her in a different way. She now spent up to one hour a day in contemplation, and she wondered if maybe she had entered a new spiritual dimension, which she could not formulate into words, and which Father Furfey did not seem to understand. A Capuchin friar, named Father Dominic, tried to reassure her. "What God does in a soul is spiritual, and this cannot be seen," he explained. "Gradually this may appear externally only as a result of the interior change. But the real spiritual we cannot see without a special revelation of God."

While it was still not clear to Catherine what God was asking of her, she finally admitted to herself and to Father Furfey that her role in Friendship House had changed. At the 1945 Convention, she defined her responsibilities as maintaining contacts with staff and directors, holding general conferences, visiting the sick and the needy, instructing converts and fallen away Catholics, lecturing and writing, and inspiring the staff to become saints. "The last 18 months have definitely been the treading of a new path," she prayed. "My job as I saw then and now was and is to integrate FH and my married life. . . What place does the latter occupy in the former!? How do they dovetail — what is the purpose of my marriage, for I firmly believe that it was your will that brought Eddie and marriage into my life."

In July 1945, Catherine begged Eddie to take a month-long vacation with her in Combermere, the one place in the world that reminded her of Russia. Eddie, who had just received an award as

contemplation

the best reporter at *The Chicago Sun,* had no interest in the quiet countryside, but after some cajoling, he finally agreed. "Neither of us had the least glimmer of an idea that this was to be the most important trip either one of us ever made," he recalled, "important not only to us but to thousands of others."

The train stopped at a small town called Barry's Bay, and they hitched a ride to Combermere in a mail truck, which deposited them in the yard behind Nicholas' house. "This was Katie's rustic mansion?" Eddie thought. "This unpainted, dull, grim, dejected forlorn wooden structure?" When Catherine walked him around to the front, however, Eddie stared in awe at the graceful beauty of the architecture. "If Nick will sell this house," he said to himself, "I'm going to buy it." He had no idea how much it would cost, and it never occurred to him that someone living in "voluntary poverty" should not own property. "I hadn't expected, or intended, to say anything about buying any place. But when I heard myself saying it, I knew I really meant it. I would do anything to own that house!"

Eddie didn't know that Nicholas was about to lose the house. He had borrowed $1,000 the year before from a woman who hoped to marry him, but Nicholas never proposed, and when he defaulted on the loan payments, the woman threatened to take "peaceful possession" of the property as outlined in the loan agreement. Catherine and Eddie offered to give Nicholas $5,000 for the house, pay off the $1,000 loan, and settle another outstanding construction debt of $635. Nicholas agreed, asking only for a small parcel of land on an adjacent island where he planned to build a log cabin for himself.

While they finalized arrangements for the sale in Combermere, an American pilot on the other side of the world dropped an atomic bomb on the city of Hiroshima, destroying 62,000 buildings and killing over 80,000 people in a single flash. A few days later a second bomb exploded on Nagasaki. By Wednesday, August 15, World War II ended. The church bell in Combermere tolled all day, and that evening, Catherine, Eddie, and Nicholas celebrated at a square dance at Mrs. Hudson's

Sunset Inn. When someone phoned to say the newly installed Bishop William Smith of Pembroke was in Combermere and wanted to meet Catherine, she and Eddie hurried back to the house to receive him. "He, more or less, broke the ice," Bishop Joseph Windle later noted. "He went to her."

Catherine told Bishop Smith that she wanted to use the newly purchased house in Combermere as a training center for Friendship House. They also discussed the possibility of keeping the house open year round as an apostolate to the rural poor. Catherine had already tried in small ways to reach out to poor families in Combermere, who struggled to farm the rocky soil. Some men had to leave home for months at a time to work in the logging industry or in the mines. Rustic houses had no electricity and no indoor plumbing. The closest hospital was nearly 70 miles away. "Well," Bishop Smith replied, "I don't know the diocese very well, but it is a rural area and there must be room for a rural apostolate. I have no objection at all to your starting from scratch if you want to do it."

Catherine and Eddie returned to Chicago in late August overflowing with news about the house in Combermere. It seemed to fit with the new direction Friendship House had taken. Bishop Sheil had already purchased another farm for them 300 miles north of Chicago near the small village of Marathon, Wisconsin, and Catherine envisioned thrilling possibilities for the expansion of Friendship House into rural areas. Ann Harrigan disagreed. She feared that the farm at Marathon and the property in Combermere would detract from the focus on racial justice. Catherine and Ann also disagreed over the acceptance, training, and assigning of staff workers. They argued about the dismissal of a staff worker that Ann wanted out, and Catherine wanted in. When Betty Schneider, who had left for a year to help her family, wanted to come back as a staff worker in the Chicago house, Catherine said yes; Ann said no. "The whole thing appears slightly hopeless," Ann admitted. "For I don't see that the B will change — & maybe she shouldn't — for she's the founder, & her ideas should prevail."

That fall, racial tensions in Chicago nearly exploded as black and white soldiers came home from war to face severe housing shortages. When a new housing project accepted the first black family, Father Dan Cantwell, the chaplain of Friendship House Chicago, agonized over the bitter reaction of white tenants. "I remember going out and trying to just be present, and oh, the hatred on people's faces, and in their eyes, and in their speech. Racial prejudice goes down deep."

Father Cantwell belonged to a new breed of passionate young priests, who received their formation under Msgr. Reynold J. Hillenbrand, Rector of Mundelein Seminary. A proponent of Catholic Action, Hillenbrand instilled in these young clerics the radical idea that God called not just nuns and priests, but all people to an active role in the Church, and that love of God must be linked with love of others. Father Cantwell was teaching sociology at Mundelein Seminary when Ann Harrigan gave a talk to the seminarians in the fall of 1942. Deeply moved by her description of racial injustice, he volunteered to be chaplain of Friendship House.

Father Cantwell liked Ann's fiery zeal, her intelligence, her quick wit, and her ability to argue her positions. When differences of opinion arose between Ann and Catherine, he tended to side with Ann. "I always regarded Catherine as a kind of John the Baptist," he admitted. "In that role she did a great job. She really stirred people. She was a very forceful woman. She had all the charm of her Russian background and her dialect. I found her hard to work with."

. What Father Cantwell called her "God talk" and what Catherine herself referred to as "directions from afar," sometimes seemed hard to swallow, especially when she tried to "organize" the houses in her bi-monthly staff letters, which included explicit instructions on everything from setting and serving a table, cooking with leftovers, talking to visitors, cataloging books, resolving disputes, and even how to clean a bathroom.

Increasingly, however, it was not Catherine's letters, or her opinions, or even her human failings that roused staff dissension.

It was the way Catherine's lifestyle differed radically from the lives of the staff workers. While they lived and worked in the slums, ate meals together, prayed together, wore used clothing, survived on $5 a month, and voluntarily accepted the counsels of poverty, chastity, and obedience, Catherine and Eddie lived apart. Catherine unconsciously made things worse by describing in staff letters how they would go to the Dohertys for holiday dinners. Her stories about hosting meetings at her apartment, entertaining visitors, writing books, and lecturing all over the country sounded very glamorous. Photos of her in furs and fancy dresses, and the way she puffed on a cigarette holder and called people, "Darling," made her seem more like a movie star than a saint.

"I don't think she ever understood the physical poverty that many of us had lived through in the Depression," reflected Belle Bates Mullen, the Assistant Director of Friendship House Harlem at the time. "I think this is what turned a number of young people off. Of course, Catherine's background was entirely different. She was from aristocracy. So what was poverty to her looked pretty good to some of us."

No one knew how much disposable income Catherine and Eddie had from his salary, and royalties on both of their books. Catherine insisted that they gave the money away and embraced the same standard of poverty as the people in Friendship House, but in her journal she admitted that her commitment to poverty remained unsettled: "I try desperately to be poor," she wrote, "yet in the depths of my soul, I am afraid of destitution in old age. I do not want to acknowledge that I buy things needed, like dresses, etc., once in a while with Eddie's money. I am confused in this and I have not clarified my stand yet..."

In November 1945, Catherine submitted a financial report to the staff. She listed the combined income for herself and Eddie as $12,800, and added a detailed summary of expenses that included rent, food, entertainment, laundry, taxes, charitable donations, and postage totaling $12,813, a net loss of $13.

The financial statement compounded the problem. Questions arose as to how Catherine could live apart and still insist in staff letters that there was only one way of life in Friendship House: "All who come to us, MUST ACCEPT *OUR WAY* of going to God. . . our work, our style."

As tensions mounted, Catherine, who was undergoing severe symptoms of menopause/learned that she also had a heart condition called myocarditis, which causes inflammation of the heart muscles and eventually leads to death as the heart loses its ability to pump blood. Her doctor predicted that Catherine had a 50% chance of surviving the year. He ordered rest and a drastic reduction of all activities. Eddie knew the truth, but Catherine insisted that no one else be told.

"What makes you talk as though you were an old woman?" Furfey asked her after receiving a long letter in which Catherine reminisced about the early days of Friendship House. Catherine did not reply. She had a list of things she wanted to organize before her death, and her first priority was grooming Ann Harrigan as the next Director General of Friendship House. "Let her persevere," Catherine prayed, "so that she should be the next Mother of FH, taking my place as she can so much better than I!"

Chapter Notes

"I feel very sorry for Nicholas...": Flewy to CD, Aug. 28, 1943, MHA.

"For us, it is enough...": CD to Flewy, Sept. 4, 1943, MHA.

"The Outer Circle": The idea of an "Outer Circle" proved so successful that Frank Sheed and Maisie Ward started a similar group in New York City connected to the Harlem Friendship House. See Maisie Ward, *Unfinished Business*, New York: Sheed & Ward, 1964.

"the course FH is taking...": AH to Fr. Cantwell, July 15, 1943, Cantwell Papers, CHS.

"When the B puts on her lipstick...": AH diary, Sept. 22, 1943, AUND.

"You know those intuitions you have...": PHF to CD, Dec. 4, 1943, MHA.

"a saint in the making...": AH diary, Feb. 3, 4, 5, 1944, AUND.

"What God does in a soul is spiritual...": Fr. Dominic to CD, May, 1945, MHA.

"The last 18 months...": Diary #33, Feb. 19, 1945, MHA.

"Neither of us...": *Cricket*, p. 123.

"This was Katie's rustic mansion?": *Cricket*, p. 126.

"If Nick will sell this house...": *Cricket*, p. 127.

"I hadn't expected....": *Cricket*, p. 128.

What Eddie didn't know...: Anna Larose to CD, Aug. 7, 1945, MHA.

"He, more or less, broke the ice...": Interview, Bishop Joseph R. Windle.

"Well," Bishop Smith replied...": Elisabeth Louise Sharum, *A Strange Fire Burning*, pp. 168-169.

"The whole thing appears slightly hopeless...": AH to Father Cantwell, Aug. 30, 1945, Cantwell Papers, CHS.

"I remember going out...": Interview, Msgr. Daniel M. Cantwell.

a new breed of passionate young priests: See Margery Frisby, *An Alley In Chicago*, Kansas City, Mo.: Sheed & Ward, 1991.

"I always regarded Catherine...": *Ibid*.

"organize" the houses...: "Work & Friendship House," May 1945, MHA.

"I don't think she ever understood...": Interview, Belle Bates Mullen.

"I try desperately to be poor...": Diary #33, Feb. 22, 1945, MHA.

"All who come to us, MUST ACCEPT OUR WAY...": "Staff Letter," May 15, 1945, MHA.

Myocarditis: Physicians today know that myocarditis can only be accurately diagnosed with a tissue biopsy, a procedure not available in the 1940's. Catherine's physician probably based his opinion on symptoms and apparently misdiagnosed her condition. Interview, Frank Barbarossa, M.D.

"What makes you talk ...": PHF to CD, Nov. 28, 1945, MHA.

"Let her persevere...": Diary #33, Nov. 6, 1945, MHA.

27

Chicago
1946

I n late January, the third annual Friendship House Convention opened, and for five days, delegates sat around a wooden table in the Chicago storefront discussing what direction Friendship House should take. By the end of the week, they agreed that Catherine could run a training program in Combermere on a trial basis that fall, and that she could establish what she called an Office of the Director General, which would publish *Friendship House News*, coordinate the interracial summer school at Marathon, accept or reject invitations to open new houses, appoint local directors, and assign staff. To some, it appeared as a power play on Catherine's part, but her intent was to set Friendship House on a firm foundation before her death. "I must keep this illness a secret from the FH crowd because it might upset them, frighten them, worry them."

Catherine's secrecy made matters worse. Ann Harrigan had no idea that Catherine planned to mold her into the next Director General, and she bristled at Catherine's sudden intrusion into her work. The tension affected everyone. Blanche Scholes, a University of Chicago graduate, who had been second in command in the Chicago Friendship House since 1944, admitted that "once in a while, I got caught between Ann and Catherine." On one occasion, Catherine asked Blanche to ship a box of children's clothes to Combermere for poor families, and Blanche, who had been to Combermere and had seen the poverty, did what Catherine asked. "Well, Ann just about blew her top," Blanche recalled.

Betty Schneider felt as if she "carried water on both shoulders." Catherine had assigned Betty to the Chicago house over Ann's objections, and Ann retaliated by making Betty report to one of the least experienced new staff members. "Ann made my life hell those first months," Betty admitted.

As pressures mounted, Ann complained about Catherine's authoritarian style of leadership, even though her own way of dealing with people sometimes seemed more rigid than Catherine's. "You know I am worried about Ann's approach," Catherine prayed, "And yet, she is so shiny, so much yours, so much better than I am, so obviously my better — and my successor — that I almost hesitate to voice my doubts."

Late that summer, Catherine left for Combermere. Ann, Monica Durkin, who was director of the farm at Marathon, and Mabel Knight, who had taken over as director of Friendship House Harlem after Nancy Grenell married, joined Catherine on September 1, for an intense two-week meeting to clarify unsettled issues. For the past year, they had struggled with shortages of money and staff while workloads increased. Ann and Mabel pointed out that the farm at Marathon was a drain on the resources, and they criticized Catherine's plans for an Office of the Director General, which they saw as another financial drain. By the time they left, Catherine felt confident that they had settled the issues. The others were not as sure.

Two weeks later, six new staff workers arrived in Combermere for the first Friendship House training school, and Catherine tried to instill in them a deep love of God that would carry them through the noise, the dirt, the lack of privacy, and the sacrifices of living and working with the poor. "I would try to teach them such simple things as work-habits, the joyousness of the service of the Lord, the history and ways of FH, all that in the simplicity of common living under one roof."

Every morning they walked to the parish church for Mass. After breakfast, they did chores — cooking, cleaning, washing, working in the garden, chopping wood, tending fires, cleaning oil lamps, pumping water — and Catherine showed them that discipline comes from doing small, seemingly unimportant things. In the afternoon, she lectured on topics ranging from communism and interracial techniques to Eastern spirituality.

Mary Galloway, 26 years old, had graduated from law school and had worked in St. Louis as a recreation counselor before coming to Friendship House. She constantly questioned Catherine. "I was so sincere that I really wanted to understand everything she had to say, but I think she thought it was a challenge at times. She gave us a very long lecture one time on how important it was to be for God, and that training and intelligence really don't matter. When she was through I said to her, 'Are training and intellectual interests a disability? Do they get in the way? Will they disrupt and be a problem?' And she said no. And I said, 'Okay. I'm in the right place!'"

Mary never realized that she was Catherine's favorite. In a confidential memo to Ann, Mabel, and Monica, Catherine described Mary as:

Brilliant, intelligent, burning with desire to serve God, absorbs knowledge, and brings it forth with the ease of a man on a flying trapeze. Devout, punctual, orderly, willing to do anything from scrub floors to make signs. A lawyer, a pianist, graduate of [Marymount] College, draws beautifully, paints, does charcoal drawing, sews, embroiders, and can put life in a party. Sings and dances beautifully. Too good to be true. Wears well under trials, loves the rural and interracial apostolates, good experience with recreation, draws even shy kids to her for story telling, captivates all she meets with a natural simple manner. A perfect lady.

When the training session ended in November, Mary continued her training under Ann Harrigan in Chicago. Within two weeks, Ann confronted her with the charge that she was going out on too many dates.

Ann struggled with problems of her own that fall. In October, she survived a private airplane crash with minor cuts and

bruises, but the trauma left her emotionally and physically shaken.)
When she returned to Chicago, she learned that Friendship House
faced eviction, and she had six months to find another location.
Catherine suggested that Ann live in the apartment at 8 West
Walton where Ann would rest and recuperate until she and Eddie
returned from Combermere in December. At first, Ann thanked
Catherine "for the chance to think and pray that it seems to
afford." After several weeks, however, Ann admitted in a long
letter to Nicholas Makletzoff that while she loved the "luxury" of
living Catherine's lifestyle, it only intensified her conviction that
Catherine had lost touch with Friendship House, its staff, and its
problems.

> The difficulty is that she is living one life — she has a
> husband, a home and security — & the rest of us are
> living a quite different one — with no husbands, homes
> or any security whatsoever — & there is no meeting of
> the minds — no common ground so to speak on this
> level. The whole idea of poverty, for example is com-
> pletely different for her and for us. Now, for example,
> we *actually face* nowhere to go. Even if she & Eddie were
> here, they would still have their house as a refuge — &
> Eddie could still make plenty of money. Not that I don't
> want to be poor. But this double standard is all wrong
> and my spiritual director says there will probably be a
> head-on battle some day, or else a 3d party will have to
> tell her — which is better I think. He himself could do it
> quite well. But I don't know. I hate to hurt her, because
> she *does* deceive herself so — & she doesn't realize her
> own motives.

By November, Ann openly complained to other directors
and staff about Catherine's authority. She objected to Catherine
and Eddie owning property in Canada. She pointed out that while
the training school in Combermere had cost over $1,000, it had not
prepared the new staff workers for life in the slums. "At one time
it occurred to me that she was 'organizing' directors against me

behind my back, but I got over that idea," Catherine noted. "She was just expressing herself."

In early December Catherine stopped in Harlem for a few days during a lecture tour, and she found a secret letter from Ann to Mabel, which proved beyond a doubt that Ann wanted to oust Catherine at the upcoming Convention. Catherine tried to calm the crisis by admitting to Ann, Mabel, and Monica that many of the current problems in Friendship House were caused by "my self, my methods, and my ways." She offered to concede everything: "I leave to you all the final decisions. Personally I desire above all the greater good of FH. If these questions are not resolved, then we shall wreck FH and whatever we do PLEASE DON'T LET US DO THIS."

For Ann, however, Catherine's peace offering did not settle the matter of her marriage or the poverty question. On December 19, Catherine agreed to meet with Ann and Msgr. Hillenbrand, the confessor for the Friendship House Chicago staff workers. Ann outlined her concerns about Catherine's lifestyle. Hillenbrand sided with Ann.

"To say that this hit me hard is to put it mildly," Catherine wrote.

> But I kept my peace and wit (I hope) and asked them point blank what was the answer. They remained silent. I then summed up the matter thus: "Since I am according to you both breaking a fundamental principle of FH — its rule of Factual poverty, then I do not belong there, and I would ask any Staff worker who did this to leave, I will have to ask myself to do likewise. The only answer, therefore, is my resignation."

Hillenbrand hedged. The general public saw Catherine and Friendship House as one, and her resignation might hurt the movement. He suggested that they discuss the matter in more depth at the Friendship House Convention in January.

Devastated, Catherine poured out the problem to Father Furfey, who advised her not to resign. He suggested that she consider turning over Eddie's salary to Friendship House and live on an allowance. "I am not sure that it is the best possible scheme. What I am sure of is that the movement would be helped enormously if your life could be made more like that of the average staff workers or director in its externals."

Catherine refused. Eddie had lost his job a few months before. He had no salary, and he had no privacy because their apartment had become another Friendship House with people coming and going just as when she lived in Harlem. Eddie had kept his promise to live in poverty by selling his house in Larchmont and giving away his car, his bank accounts, and his insurance policies.

> Now someone got a bee in her or their bonnets, and they want him, not only me, to do something else doubly as radical as he did before. Tomorrow if he agrees to that, they will find something else. . . Either they all trust me — us, or they don't. And that is the crux of the matter. Were I to do what you suggest it would last a year and then another question would pop up and we would be at it again. . . So that is my stand. Take me as I am, try to see that in me and Eddie you have a greater FH than without us. . . If you are ready to trust your spiritual mother to do what she taught you how to do. . . then OK . . . if not. . . then the question is on the floor. . . .

On Saturday, January 25, 1947, delegates to the fourth annual Friendship House Convention arrived in Marathon, Wisconsin. Each house sent its director, assistant director, and representatives chosen from staff and volunteers. There were four priests: Furfey, Cantwell, Hillenbrand, and Fred McTernan, the chaplain of Friendship House Harlem. On Monday morning, they scheduled two separate sessions: one for staff workers and volunteers, and a private session for Catherine, Ann, Mabel, Monica, and the priests. Ann presented her case against Catherine:

We came to FH to live in poverty, literal insecurity, and she no longer lives that way herself, & is trying to get us all to go along the same way. . . We came to dedicate our lives as *single* people — and she isn't — so she's trying to further confuse the issue by always insisting married people can be staff workers.

Her method is frightening. She talks to one person at a time & can she *talk*. You are absorbed in the *miasma* of her words. Then she talks to the next person & tells him that you agreed with her in this, whether you did or not, & you are led to do something frequently by thinking the other guys are all for it. You must be wrong if you are the only one holding on. . .

Yet here we are — about 20 of us who owe our lives to her in one sense of being in FH and working here — & yet who are being prevented from doing the work we came to do because the *integrity* is being undermined.

They resolved nothing in the morning session. In the afternoon session, everyone met together. "All the people jumped all over Catherine at that meeting," Blanche recalled. "We were sitting in the library of this old farm house in Marathon and everybody was telling Catherine how she was pulling away from the interracial apostolate, and she was doing this and that against poverty."

No one expected the hostile reactions from staff and volunteers, who had not been privy to the private morning discussions, and Ann Harrigan found it "sweet beyond anything I can say. . . The climax was Father Furfey's weeping when he said how she had lost something infinitely precious when she married, that these girls had something infinitely precious living & working as they did — that turned the tables."

Ann suggested that they form a Board of Directors, which would rule in a democratic way by voting on issues. "I presented my rebuttals, I think, logically and consecutively," Catherine recalled. "I felt that this was against the spirit of the mandate given to me."

The delegates outvoted Catherine on every point. By the end of the week, the delegates had appointed a Board of Directors, consisting of Catherine, Ann, Mabel, and Monica. They limited Catherine's term as Director General to three years, and after that, it would become an elected office. They declined the offer of the house in Combermere, and decided that Friendship House would focus on racial justice. Catherine could conduct staff training in Marathon that spring, but someone from the Board would monitor everything she said.

Catherine recalled how Father Carr had told her years before that when storms rage, she should stand perfectly still and let them pass. Catherine never lost her composure and she never cried in front of them. Instead, she went upstairs early at night to weep in her bed.

On the last night, after the business ended, the delegates made fudge and celebrated with square dancing and charades. Someone wrote a skit to break the tension, and in it they poked fun at Catherine and themselves in a good-natured way. Blanche recalled how Catherine laughed as people imitated her booming Russian voice, her inconsistencies and her exaggerations. "Now that's a big soul," Blanche thought, "to be able to go through everything she went through today, and to sit there and enjoy this skit."

Catherine later admitted that the pain was so excruciating she could not find words to describe it. Her spiritual children had shattered her vision of Friendship House, and what she had perceived as her mandate from God. They rejected her and then mocked her. "I maintain married couples can work at FH. . . They say 'No.' I maintain that their concept of poverty is narrow; they say mine is too deep and wide. I say FH started on a broad social field and will continue so. They say the interracial field is big enough. So it goes, and I am 'outside looking in' again, on my own child."

When Catherine returned to Chicago, she met with Bishop Sheil. As agreed at the Convention, Ann Harrigan accompanied her to make sure Catherine reported everything accurately. Out-raged, Sheil glared at Ann and called the situation "damn non-sense." He advised Catherine to get rid of the staff and start over, but Catherine told him she wanted to avoid scandal.

Eddie told Catherine to ignore Ann. "Just be yourself and let those oppose you who will. So long as you feel you are right it doesn't matter too much that other people are wrong... Just speak your mind and your heart, and be content — and take all the criticism, etc., as you always have with serenity."

It took every ounce of Catherine's courage to follow Eddie's advice, and few outside Friendship House saw the dissension. When there were obvious hints, such as Catherine's decision not to attend the Ninth Anniversary Celebration of Friendship House Harlem, the staff made excuses for her absence. Throughout March and April, she fulfilled most of her speaking engagements with her usual flair. She blasted the Jesuits at Georgetown for not admitting black students in undergraduate programs. She gave a series of talks in Washington, and took the train to Boston, where Cardinal Cushing asked about the possibility of her opening a Friendship House to work with Portuguese immigrants. Catherine referred him to Ann. During the Friendship House training pro-gram in Marathon that spring, Catherine presented three 90-minute sessions each day with Mabel Knight monitoring the classes.

"I wish there was something I could do or say that would console you in this business of the rift in FH," Eddie told her. "But I can think of nothing. Let us suppose it is the will of God that these things happen — that He is making it more and more evident to you, as well as to me, that we should make our headquarters in Canada."

Combermere seemed like the only option. Catherine's doc-tor feared that the palpitations and shortness of breath she expe-rienced were signs of heart failure, and he insisted that she reduce her activity and eliminate stress. "I have had time to think things out clearly," she wrote to Eddie,

And now I know the score, and what it adds up to! There
has been a showdown of sorts in FH and Ann won. What
is happening is that I have been rather roughly "ousted."
I am but a figurehead because Ann & Co are afraid,
unsure yet if they can swing FH with me alive in the
world somewhere and not on its causes or flag. But she
& Co are determined not to give me any voice anymore
in its ideals, its running, etc., etc. And they do it by the
simple unanswerable procedure of creating a Board
with the majority on their side always.

Canada I know is a graceful (I hope) retreat of mine all
along the line. Suits them fine. They save their faces by
simply saying for all to hear "She is different. She is a
Russian. She has 1,000 crazy ideas. Let her do as she
wishes. We will attend to the business at hand."

To sum up, and I have to sum it up and face it, face to
face, standing up, they have for all purposes "ousted"
me from FH. It is the pattern of my life. Every decade of
it or so there has been this radical change in it.

On April 28, Catherine suffered her final humiliation when
the Friendship House Board decided that any houses opened by
Catherine in Canada could retain the Friendship House name, but
would share nothing else in common with Friendship House
USA. As for staff workers, directors, finances, and conventions,
they would be distinct, like two brothers from the same mother,
both of whom have their own family establishments. If a staff
worker decided to transfer from Canada to U.S. or U.S. to Canada,
she would resign from one and apply to the other.

Betty Schneider, who always looked for peaceful compromises, found the situation terribly upsetting. "Let us leave all
things to the Holy Ghost," Catherine told her, "in time He will
show us who is right and who is wrong." [2]

On the morning of May 10, 1947, Catherine and Eddie
loaded clothes, books, a few pieces of furniture, Catherine's
Russian icons, some groceries, and two typewriters into the brand
new black Keyser, which Eddie bought with money borrowed

from Bishop Sheil. There were no going away parties, no sad farewells, no tokens of any one's appreciation. They went to Mass that morning at Holy Name Cathedral, and then Eddie stopped at a little store on Halstead Street where he bought Catherine a statue of Our Lady of Guadalupe, who had, in 1531, made roses bloom miraculously in winter.

"We're not Adam and Eve driven out of paradise by a lousy snake in the orchard," Eddie told Catherine as they drove down South Shore Drive. "We're Adam and Eve moving to a better Paradise." Then, in his own zany way, he launched into a takeoff on a popular Bing Crosby song: "Tural lural lural," he crooned, "Tural lural eyes. Plural rural murals. Combermere is Paradise."

Chapter Notes

"I must keep this illness a secret...": Diary #33, Jan. 7, 1946, MHA.

"once in a while, I got caught...": Interview, Blanche Scholes Lepinskie.

"carried water...": Interview, Betty Schneider.

"You know I am worried...": Diary #33, Mar. 5, 1946, MHA.

after Nancy Grenell married: Nancy Grenell's decision to marry a man of mixed race caused tension within Friendship House. In her lectures Catherine had repeatedly insisted that black men were not romantically interested in white women, and she assured parents of white staff workers that interracial marriage was out of the range of possibility. Catherine feared that Nancy's marriage would harm Friendship House, but Nancy held firm, and the marriage took place in November, 1944. Nancy stayed on as director of FH Harlem until April, 1945, when she resigned due to pregnancy, but she agreed to remain as a volunteer. Catherine was the godmother of Nancy's first child.

"I would try to teach them...": CD to PHF, Oct. 11, 1945, MHA.

"I was so sincere...": Interview, Mary Galloway James.

"Brilliant, intelligent...": CD to Directors, Oct. 1946, MHA.

"for the chance to think...": AH to CD, Oct. 24, 1946, MHA.

"The difficulty is...": AH to NM, Nov. 10, 1946, AUND.

"At one time it occurred to me...": CD to PHF, Dec. 20, 1946, MHA.

"myself, my methods and my ways...": CD to PHF, Dec. 1946, MHA.

"To say that this hit me hard...": CD to PHF, Dec. 20, 1946, MHA.

"I am not sure this is the best...": PHF to CD, Jan. 9, 1947, MHA.

"Now someone got a bee...": CD to PHF, Jan. 10, 1947, MHA.

"We came to FH...": AH Diary, Feb. 1, 1947, AUND.

"All the people jumped...": Interview, Blanche Scholes Lepinskie.

"sweet beyond anything...": AH Diary, Feb. 1, 1947, AUND.

"I presented my rebuttals...": *History of the Apostolate*, p. 474.

"Now that's a big soul...": Interview, Blanche Scholes Lepinskie.

"I maintain married couples can work...": Diary #58, May 18, 1947, MHA.

"damn nonsense...": *History of the Apostolate*, p. 478.

"Just be yourself...": ED to CD, Apr. 14, 1947, MHA.

"I wish there was something...": ED to CD, Apr. 15, 1947, MHA.

"I have had time to think...": CD to ED, Apr. 19, 1947, MHA.

As for staff workers, directors...: Minutes from FH Board of Directors Meeting, Apr. 28, 1947, AH Papers, AUND.

"Let us leave all things to the Holy Ghost...": CD to BS, Dec. 5, 1955, Friendship House Papers, CHS/MHA.

"We're not Adam and Eve...": *Cricket*, p. 170.

28

Combermere
1947

Catherine and Eddie arrived in Combermere at 4 o'clock on the afternoon of Saturday, May 17. While they would not admit it to each other, they both knew that Combermere was no paradise. Catherine felt as if she had failed to live up to the mandate God had given her, and she failed not just once, but twice. She trembled uncontrollably. "The only prayer I could say during the first day or month was, "Lord, have mercy on me and may Thy Holy Will be done."

Doubts plagued Eddie. "What are you going to do now?" a mocking voice inside of him taunted. "No job. No dough, unless your Russian has it. No friends. No apostolate. . . And probably not even a boiled potato or an onion in the house. Why don't you turn that damn machine around, and go back to a normal life in Chicago or New York?"

A few days later, George arrived in Combermere after a long, painful visit with Boris, who was dying from cancer in a Montreal hospital. Boris called Catherine long distance before she left Chicago, and with sobs interrupting his words, he told her how he confessed his sins to a priest. He begged Catherine to forgive him for all the pain he caused her during their marriage, and he promised to seek George's forgiveness for being a bad father.

On June 9, Boris died. George returned to Montreal for the funeral, but Catherine stayed in Combermere. She felt as if all the painful parts of her life had erupted and she became so emotionally distraught that she had to force herself to open the gate and walk out into the road. "I was afraid of people, strange as it may seem, for they could hurt me."

Flewy knew better than anyone else the extent of Catherine's weaknesses, yet she still believed that God had chosen Catherine for some great work. She came to Combermere that June to help her friend. She did housework, gardening, and laundry. "If a china tea pot was cracked, she uncracked it with some sort of glue," Eddie recalled. "If a door knob needed a screw, she found one and put it in. If a wall or a window sill or a chair needed painting, she painted it."

Flewy helped Catherine organize a lending library in the living room and a clothing room in the basement, and then spread the word that Catherine had free books and clothes. While country folks felt leery about the Dohertys with their big house, big car, and strange ways, Flewy settled into Combermere as if she had grown up in the woods. "She could visit all the homes in the vicinity, drinking one scalding cup of tea after another, talk about nothing all day, and make friends everywhere," Eddie joked.

Eventually, Catherine started to accompany Flewy, and in time, her fear of people melted away. On July 30, Catherine stood alone in the parish church, staring at the First Station of the Cross that depicted Jesus being unjustly condemned to death, and it occurred to her that maybe everything in Chicago had happened for a reason. "Now I know I must not blame anyone," she prayed, "and what is more, I must both bless them and pray for them, for maybe they knew not what they did. Who knows but you wanted me here to face myself and you in the great silence and pain of Combermere."

The summer passed quickly, and by late September, Catherine and Flewy had harvested the garden and finished the canning. Local women came to the back door for winter clothes and a cup of tea. After school, Catherine and Flewy held story hours for local children with homemade cookies and hot chocolate. They mailed books to families in outlying areas. When it became known that Catherine had nurse's training, people called at all hours of the day and night asking her to tend the sick and deliver babies.

That fall, Eddie returned to Chicago to research a book he was writing on Martin de Porres. On October 14, he sent Catherine a telegram saying his mother was dying: "Can you come? Love Eddie."

"I nearly collapsed entirely at the thought of having to travel so far and meet FH Chicago at the end," she admitted. But her love for Eddie overcame fear, and she arrived in time to stand by him at the funeral. While she was in Chicago, she visited Friendship House, and noted that "for all practical purposes Ann is the Director General of FH. . . But authority is resting heavy on her shoulders; she too is having a nervous breakdown and taking a leave of absence for three or maybe six months."

Ann returned for the 1948 Friendship House Convention in New York. She anticipated another power struggle with Catherine, but it was Mary Galloway and a group of staff workers, who tipped the balance by challenging Ann's authority and the Friendship House Board of Directors. They wanted a democratic constitution with every member of Friendship House having an equal vote and limitations placed on the power of the local directors. "Your chickens have come home to roost," Catherine told Ann.

Catherine decided that she would wait out the year so as not to cause scandal, and then resign from the Friendship House Board at the 1949 Convention. "As far as I am concerned it is a page of as yet an unwritten book that has closed itself," she told Eddie. "I am joyous at the thought that now I can without distractions offer ALL my works, pains, travail of starting over again."

The rural apostolate in Combermere was Catherine's third, and probably her final chance to follow what she believed was her mandate from God, and she made a steely commitment to herself that in Combermere, she would never back down or compromise as she had with Friendship House.

Catherine was back in Combermere only a few weeks when Eddie suffered a slight heart attack, and the doctor ordered a strict diet and bed rest. Still tormented with chronic chest pains herself, Catherine took on Eddie's chores with Flewy sharing the added load. When the Doherty family learned of their struggle, they sent money each month to pay for a local girl, named Rita Perrier, to help with cooking and cleaning. That summer, Rita's assistance became invaluable as a steady stream of people visited Catherine's new apostolate.

Father William Power, a young priest from Montreal, brought members of his youth groups to Combermere so they could see how Catherine tried to live a life of Christian love. "I wanted them to hear her ideas, learn of her background, and see who she had been and what she had done."

Catherine assigned the guests to work in the kitchen, in the gardens, and on maintenance. Romeo Maione considered her the most authoritarian woman he had ever met, but Catherine didn't care. If people didn't like the way things ran, she told them, they could leave. Maione kept coming back, and he later admitted that the experience broadened him. "It was the first time I had ever been in Compline where you had the singing of the office every night back and forth in two lines," he recalled. "After that we would go off in that back kitchen, and there we would discuss the theology of the lay apostolate, social action, the social problems, the racial problems. To me this was an eye-opener."

Nicholas Makletzoff also spent summers in Combermere. He lived in a log cabin on an island connected to Catherine and Eddie's property by a long wooden bridge. He ate meals with Catherine and Eddie, contributing whatever fish he caught that day, and in the evening, he challenged Flewy to board games or cards. Catherine knew Nicholas had dated Ann Harrigan, but the news that Nicholas, who was nearly 60 years old, married 38-year-old Ann that October, stunned Catherine as much as it did the other people in Friendship House. "Why she married this guy? I don't know," Nina Polcyn Moore reflected. "She was dying to get married. Maybe it was a victorious feeling that she got him. Then she dropped out of our lives."

After Ann left Friendship House, Catherine remained in the nebulous position of being the Director General in name only with no power. When staff members wrote to her about questions or controversy, she bluntly expressed her option and took sides in disputes, which created even more dissension. "Personally I feel the B is a great big factor in the unrest and confusion," Father Ed Dugan, the new chaplain in Harlem told Father Cantwell. "She seems to want to keep her finger in the pie and yet more and more she is withdrawing from the apostolate of FH."

"The B is a problem," Cantwell agreed. "Still I don't think we can afford to have a Convention where the B will be sort-a ousted from the movement."

When the two priests canceled the 1949 Convention, Catherine never carried through on her plans to resign from the Friendship House Board of Directors. During a lecture tour in early 1949, she visited the houses in Harlem, Chicago, and the newly opened house in Washington D.C., and she learned that another wave of staff workers, including Mary Galloway, had left to get married. Mabel Knight remained antagonistic, and Betty Schneider still tried to act as a mediator. As new staff workers arrived, they received mixed messages about Catherine. "I know many of you do not even know me in person, others disagree with me. . . automatically, simply because I SAID SO. . . others again because they truly feel that I am wrong. . . That is OK too. For after all is said and done. . . I am not infallible. . . and each of you is a free agent to accept and reject whatever I say. . . only I too can say it. . . and I do," Catherine wrote in an open letter to Friendship House staff and volunteers.

While Catherine's ties with Friendship House USA remained strained, in Combermere she moved energetically, starting teen dances, square dances, card parties for adults, and a 4H group. On Thursday evenings, she conducted a home nursing course with a dozen local women learning to dress wounds, take temperatures and blood pressure, administer medications, and change a bed with a patient in it. The newspaper, *Restoration*, which she and

Eddie launched in December 1947, because *Friendship House News* refused to print her articles about Combermere, reached a circulation of 1,000. They supported themselves with income from Catherine's lectures and royalties from Eddie's books.

In early 1949, four new people came to work with Catherine, but within a short time, they all left, claiming that Catherine lured them to Combermere as unpaid hired help. She insisted that she never forced anyone to come or to stay against their will, but rumors spread that Catherine was a charlatan. "I do not know why God sent this trial," she confessed. The incident reinforced Catherine's conviction not to ever compromise or back down. If God wanted her rural apostolate to exist, she told herself, God would provide for their needs.

That summer, Catherine launched her first summer school. Ten people enrolled, and a young woman named Pat Connors from Montreal stayed that fall to become a staff worker. Phil Larkin and Charlie Conroy, who were finishing their studies at St. Francis Xavier in Antigonish, promised to return the following summer. Catherine hoped that this might be a positive sign, but the future remained in darkness, and for the next six months, she continued to walk in blind faith.

The turning point came on St. Patrick's Day in 1950, when Catherine gave one of her most powerful lectures in a Montreal auditorium. "She was the only person on the stage and she filled the stage totally and completely," recalled Romeo Maione. Catherine's message was simple: God is a Spirit of Love. "That's what hit me," Maione admitted.

> What she always used to say is: Love is God. That's an incredible thing. It changes the whole of the Gospels. It changes the whole of theology. It changes the whole of the last judgment. You see, in the last judgment you're not going to be asked did you believe in me? Did you believe in God? Did you go to church? Did you say your Rosary? Were you spiritual? He's going to ask: Did you feed me? St. John says it, too: Wherever there is love,

there is God. And this, then, solves the whole problem of what is faith. Faith is believing that love is the energy of God. I don't know where the B got this. She must have got it from living it. But that's the hidden strength of the B — that she saw that love was the most important energy in the world.

Romeo Maione never joined the apostolate. Instead, he went on to become an international leader of the Young Christian Workers, and later credited Catherine for inspiring his vocation. Another person in the audience that night did join, however. Dorothy Phillips, a 35-year-old assistant personnel manager and accountant at Blue Cross and Blue Shield in Montreal, visited Combermere during her two-week summer vacation, and asked if she could stay.

Father John Thomas Callahan, a diocesan priest who served as chaplain of Mercy High School and hosted the weekly "Radio Rosary" in Rochester, New York, also visited Combermere for the first time in the summer of 1950. At first, Catherine considered him a "cold fish," but after he presented a powerful series of lectures, she changed her mind. Father Callahan returned at Christmas time, and spoke about his devotion to the Virgin Mary. "I talked of Her, and how she watched over my pilgrimage to Rome last summer. It was mostly narrative, and was not even intended as a formal talk about Her, and I was amazed at the response. I also in answer to some questions, talked about de Montfort, which started Eddie and Catherine Doherty on the way to this Act of Slavery."

St. Louis de Montfort's total consecration to Jesus through Mary was not a common devotion. It involved offering oneself as a slave of the Blessed Virgin, with the belief that she would lead people to a closer relationship with Jesus. "Know something?" Catherine told Father Cal, as they affectionately called him. "For 20 years I could not see this true devotion. Then YOU come along and presto it is as clear as day."

On February 2, 1951, Catherine and Eddie drove to Ottawa

where they knelt before a Statue of Our Lady of the Cape, and dedicated their lives to Jesus Christ by offering themselves as slaves of Mary. A few weeks later, Catherine asked Father Callahan if he would be her spiritual director. "I feel that yours is a big soul, really enlarged with the love of Christ," he replied, "and it takes a big man to lead a big soul, and that's where I'm a little scared." After praying about it for several months, Father Callahan finally agreed.

Pat Connors eventually left Combermere to enter a convent, but Catherine was not concerned because a stream of visitors and volunteers arrived in her wake. Dorothy Phillips officially became a staff worker. Louis Stoeckle, who decided to stay for "a few weeks" the previous November became a staff worker applicant, and Phil Larkin, who had graduated from college, arrived on June 19 to begin organizing local credit unions. In the midst of this activity, Catherine's spiritual life took another turn: "The presence of God is almost palpable, at times overwhelming me with a shaft of great light almost too strong to bear. Leaving me sort of numb," she told Father Callahan. One day she saw her life pass before her eyes with such a clarity that she recognized all of her sins. "And it shook me to the very marrow of my bones."

Father Callahan told her to simply report to him anything that happened, and then put it out of her mind. Sometime that summer, he sent her information about an upcoming Congress of Lay People in Rome, and suggested that Bishop Smith might send her as a delegate. The Bishop agreed to make Catherine an official delegate, but couldn't afford to pay her way, so Catherine started praying for the money. She was so certain that the money would come that she booked reservations on a steamship. Then she pushed it out of her mind, as Father Callahan suggested, and attended to the third annual summer school.

Mary Davis, a high school girl from Quebec, remembered Catherine's lectures during the summer sessions. "She talked about Catholic Action, and she talked about Russia, and the revolution, and Friendship House, and Communists. All day long she was teaching us. Whatever the priests taught us during those lectures paled beside what B was teaching."

Catherine housed women guests at the old O'Brien Hotel down the road, which she purchased later that year with money from lectures, and renamed in honor of St. Joseph. Men stayed in a cottage near the main house named after St. Peter. During the second week in August, Eddie lapsed into another attack of angina pectoris, which he jokingly called his "Aunt Jinah." Flewy didn't feel well either, and on the morning of August 8, Phil Larkin drove her into Barry's Bay to see the doctor. When they returned Catherine insisted that Flewy rest.

"There's nothing wrong with me," Flewy argued.

That night, when Dorothy Phillips came upstairs after the last summer school session, Flewy complained of indigestion, and then slumped over in bed. "Flewy's dying," Dorothy cried. Catherine, Eddie, and a visiting priest from Harlem rushed into the room.

"Flewy had a drawn look about her," Dorothy recalled, "but after the priest anointed her, her face broke into a smile. Then she died." Grief-stricken, Catherine wept inconsolably.

The next day, people from throughout the countryside paid their last respects at Flewy's wake. A little boy crowed like a rooster because that was one of Flewy's favorite tricks. Others talked about how Flewy hated cleaning oil lamps and how funny it was that electricity came to Combermere on the day of Flewy's wake. Three priests concelebrated her funeral at the parish church. Louis Stoeckle carved a wooden cross to mark her grave.

"The place is empty without her," Catherine told Father Callahan, but he saw Flewy's death as the end of an era, and predicted that new people would arrive to take her place. That fall, a local school teacher named Mamie Legris, who struggled with what a priest called a vocation problem, became an applicant. "I was 35, and at that time, mind you, the only vocation on earth was to be a nun or to get married or to be what they called an Old Maid."

"You should try this place," Catherine told her.

Mamie became the cook and the librarian. "We all kind of helped wherever there was a need," she recalled. "We had long meals. Eddie sat at one end of the table and she sat at the other end. She was always telling stories that had a punch to them."

Marité Langlois, a college graduate from Montreal, also arrived that fall and stayed after hearing Catherine speak.

> I had never heard anybody preach the Gospel like she did. She just bowled me over! On the natural order there was much that repelled me. We slept in an old house. Everything was makeshift, beds donated, mattresses old, orange crates for a stand to put your things in, sheets that didn't fit the bed. Everything was clean but poor, very poor. Meals too were very cheap and simple. Most of us were searching for God. Each of us had been drawn, and I would say that the B was the one who drew us here. Otherwise there was not much else. She moved me very deeply and in my heart I was certain this was to be my lifetime vocation.

With the influx of new staff workers, Catherine abandoned the idea of going to Rome for the Lay Congress. She still needed nearly $1,000, and saw no way of getting it. A few weeks later, however, Catherine and Eddie drove to the nearby city of Pembroke for a dental appointment, and stopped to see a family whose daughter, Mary, attended a boarding school run by nuns not far from Madonna House. The Omaniques had heard from Bishop Smith that Catherine wanted to go to Rome, and they had a proposition for her. They would pay all expenses provided that Catherine would take their daughter, Mary, along. "Nobody could show her Europe as you can," they begged.

Stunned, Catherine agreed. On September 17, she left Dorothy Phillips in charge, and sailed for Europe on the *Empress of Canada* with Mary Omanique. Eddie, who was researching a book on St. John Bosco, planned to leave for Europe two weeks later on a Pan Am flight with expenses paid by his publisher. They agreed that sometime in October, they would meet in Rome for a second honeymoon.

Chapter Notes

"The only prayer...": *IN ONE EAR*, p. 140.

"What are you going to do now?": *Cricket*, p. 173.

Boris called Catherine...: CD to ED, Apr. 10, 1947, MHA.

"I was afraid of people...": *History of the Apostolate*, p. 508.

"If a china tea pot was cracked...": *Cricket*, p. 186.

"She could visit all the homes...": *Ibid.*

"Now I know I must not blame anyone...": Diary #33, July 30, 1947, MHA.

"Can you come?": ED to CD, Oct. 14, 1947, MHA.

"I nearly collapsed entirely...": CD to PHF, June 20, 1948, MHA.

"for all practical purposes...": CD to PHF, Oct. 22, 1948, MHA.

"Your chickens have come home...": Interview, Mary Galloway James.

"As far as I am concerned...": CD to ED, Feb. 2, 1948, MHA.

"I wanted them to hear...": Interview, Bishop William E. Power.

"It was the first time...": Interview, Romeo and Betty Maione.

"Why she married this guy?": Interview, Nina Polcyn Moore.

"Personally I feel the B is...": Fr. Edward Dugan to Fr. Daniel Cantwell, Nov. 16, 1948, Cantwell Papers, CHS.

"The B is a problem...": Fr. Daniel Cantwell to Fr. Edward Dugan, Nov. 18, 1948, Cantwell Papers, CHS.

"I know many of you do not even know me...": "Staff Letter," Jan. 28, 1949, MHA.

"I do not know why...": *History of the Apostolate*, p. 706.

"She was the only person...": Interview, Romeo and Betty Maione.

"cold fish...": *History of the Apostolate*, p. 733.

"I talked of Her...": JC, "My Mary Book," unpublished spiritual journal, Feb. 17, 1951, MHA.

"Know something?": CD to JC, Jan. 28, 1951, MHA.

"I feel that yours is a big soul...": JC to CD, Mar. 26, 1951, MHA.

"The presence of God...": CD to JC, June 6, 1951, MHA.

"She talked about Catholic Action...": Interview, Mary Davis.

"There's nothing wrong with me...": Interview, Phil Larkin.

"She had a drawn look...": Interview, Dorothy Phillips.

"The place is empty without her...": CD to JC, Aug. 8, 1951, MHA.

"I was 35...": Interview, Mamie Legris.

"I had never heard anybody...": Interview, Marité Langlois, by Sr. Louise Sharum, June 14, 1974, MHA.

"Nobody could show her Europe...": *Cricket*, p. 212.

29

Rome
1951

C atherine and Mary Omanique arrived in Rome after a week of sightseeing in England, Belgium, Switzerland and Italy. While Mary explored the Eternal City, Catherine attended the First World Congress of the Lay Apostolate with 1,200 delegates from 74 countries sharing their experiences in bringing the Gospel message to others. What Catherine found most astounding was how these delegates all claimed that Christ had called them to a life of service. While techniques varied, love of God and love of neighbor formed the common denominator. "It gave everyone a sense of courage and banished all feelings of loneliness," she noted. "It was so apparent at the Congress, you really could say, 'Behold those Christians, how they love one another. . . .'"

Only one thing troubled Catherine. None of the other groups functioned as a democracy or had divisions as Friendship House had. Their spiritual lives seemed stronger, too, with the focus on following God's will. While many took simple vows of poverty, chastity, and obedience, almost all had a promise of stability with workers agreeing to stay for a designated time. I now see ALL my mistakes so clearly, in the light of St. Peter's Holy Ghost altar where I prayed so much for FH and all in it," she wrote to Betty Schneider, who had been elected National Director of Friendship House USA. "I know it is hard to turn the clock back. I won't even try. I will and have left all things to the Holy Ghost in this matter, but I still leave with you the thought of tightening up the stability."

On Sunday, October 14, Catherine met with Papal Secretary of State Monsignor Giovanni Baptista Montini, "a slight dark man with piercing eyes," who was destined to become Pope Paul VI. Montini suggested that Friendship House could solve their stability problem by becoming a secular institute, a relatively new structure for lay groups that the Vatican authorized. The following day, Montini arranged for Catherine to have an audience with Pope Pius XII, who blessed her and "all who belong to your apostolate in any way...." Then he placed his hands on Catherine's head, and prayed in Latin. "I felt healed. . . strong in God and in the frail man who was giving me of his strength so bountifully," she told Father Callahan.

When Catherine and Eddie met in Paris the following week, Eddie noticed that Catherine had changed. "She reminded me of the prima donnas I had met at depots in Chicago and New York and Los Angeles. There was an aura of triumph about her — or what I took to be triumph. And the radiance in her eyes, which had always greeted me when we met like this, was not for me alone. That was hard to take."

Catherine told Eddie what Montini said about secular institutes, and how she had changed her mind about staff workers taking vows of poverty, chastity, and obedience. She had also learned from her bitter lesson in Friendship House Chicago that she and Eddie would have to embrace the same lifestyle as the staff. Panic seized Eddie. He had no problem with poverty or obedience. But chastity?

"So when do we take these vows," he asked.

Catherine replied that they had to discuss the matter with the Friendship House staff in both Canada and the US.

"I'm in no hurry," Eddie joked, "Let God take his time. Don't rush Him. Now I can pray as St. Augustine did before he gave up his mistress and all other women — 'Lord, make me chaste; but not right away.'"

Eddie flew home from Paris. Catherine and Mary Omanique sailed on the RMS *Seythia*, and as Catherine looked out at the ocean, she felt as if God burned like fire in her soul. "The desire of bringing souls to Him is so immense that I would call it obsession, madness, if I did not know that it was a great undeserved grace," she wrote in her journal.

Catherine hoped that when she told Betty Schneider and Father Cantwell what Montini had said that they would resolve all differences, and Friendship House could apply to Rome as one united group for status as a secular institute. Betty and Father Cantwell did not agree, however. They rejected the idea of vows and wanted to avoid dealing with Rome because they had already submitted a Friendship House Constitution to Cardinal Stritch of Chicago for approval. "There is no reason why things shouldn't go ahead in Canada," Betty suggested, "and there you wouldn't have the same situation with the hierarchy as we do."

Catherine reeled in pain at what she perceived as another rejection by Friendship House staff. "It seems to be your will that I be thus pushed out from inside my spiritual family," she prayed, "alone to find this new unglamorous apostolate in rural Canada. Amen. Be it done to me according to Thy will."

Increasingly, Catherine had started referring to her apostolate as Madonna House, the name she had given to the house itself when Nicholas built it so many years before. Over the next few months, events unfolded at Madonna House in ways that Catherine never imagined possible. It started on April 20, 1952, when Father Callahan arrived for the annual staff retreat, and collapsed the next day from nervous exhaustion. The doctor ordered sedatives and bed rest, but Father Callahan continued to suffer heart palpitations and extreme nervous tension. On the afternoon of July 17, while Father Callahan relaxed outside in a lawn chair, something happened that he later described as "a deep inner conviction that God wanted me to remain at Madonna House as its permanent chaplain."

Father Callahan knew that he would face obstacles in seeking a release from the Diocese of Rochester, and in the process, he would have to endure the ridicule of those who could not understand how he could give up everything to follow this strange woman into the backwoods of Canada.

Catherine was thrilled at the prospect of having a permanent chaplain. Her spiritual life had moved into a highly mystical state, and she had come to rely on Father Callahan's ability to discern what was real and what was an illusion. Sometimes, after receiving Communion, she would lapse into spiritual ecstasy. It would appear as if she had fainted, but with all her bodily senses suspended, she felt her soul move into another dimension. "Time and space seemed to have ceased to exist. I at times 'know' without 'knowing' that indeed I live in eternity in the very Essence of it, Father, Son and Holy Ghost, yet through Mary who is within it." She described it to Father Callahan as a state of immense light, ineffable joy, and deep, penetrating peace, but the actual experience remained beyond words.

Father Callahan insisted that Catherine never speak of these mystical experiences. He had studied mystical theology in the seminary, and knew the extraordinary ways God worked in the souls called to the mystical life. He defined a mystic as "a soul that has passed through the barriers of time into a realm divine for purposes divine" and he called these experiences "the secrets of the King."

"We didn't know that when B was fainting that she was having ecstasies," one staff worker recalled. "It was like the Lord had scales on our eyes. She would come back from Communion, kneel down, and go flat on her face. As soon as she came to, she would get up and walk out. After Mass, Father Cal would walk out after her. Later they would come down for breakfast and go on as normal. She always told us, 'Don't let anybody near me when that happens. I'm just weak. Open the windows, air will come, and I'll be all right.'"

In early 1953, Father Callahan suggested that they build a two-story addition onto the main house that would include a large dining room downstairs to accommodate the increasing numbers of guests, and a chapel upstairs dedicated to the Immaculate Conception. "Madonna House is Our Lady's House," he wrote in his diary, "Her House of love: Her novitiate of Love."

On May 17, 1953, they broke ground for the new addition,

and the next day, a letter arrived from Archbishop Richard Cushing of Boston, offering to underwrite the cost of construction. The staff rejoiced at the new course Madonna House had taken under Father Callahan's direction, but the mood changed the following week, when two priests arrived unannounced from Rochester. "They're trying to take Father Cal away," a panicky staff worker surmised.

It was no secret that the Bishop of Rochester did not approve of Father Callahan's desire to remain at Madonna House. In June, 1953, Bishop James E. Kearney sent a telegram ordering Father Callahan to return to Rochester and assume the position of Chaplain at the Cenacle Convent.

Everyone at Madonna House reeled in shock. Eddie suffered heart pains and Catherine plunged into a flaming sea of pain. Even the contractor, who worked on the new addition, admitted that nothing seemed the same without Fr. Cal. In Rochester, Fr. Callahan endured severe anxiety attacks. "Just like a hollow, dull weight in the pit of the stomach," he told Catherine. On July 20, 1953, after less than 4 weeks, Father Callahan begged the Vice Chancellor for permission to return to Combermere. At 10:30 that night, Father Cal's sister and her husband drove him back to Canada.

The following week, Catherine received a letter from Father Gene Cullinane, CSB, an economics professor, who had given the opening talks at the Madonna House summer school that year. He told her something strange had happened to him in Combermere, and he now believed that God was calling him to leave the Basilian order and join Madonna House. "I felt God and experienced God as never before in my life," he confessed. "My eyes were opened and I saw holiness here as I had never seen it anywhere before. A consciousness of the supernatural took hold of me to such an extent that I believe I myself was transformed."

Father Gene understood that by leaving the Basilians he would trade comfort for austerity, security for insecurity, and the respect of his friends for a reputation as a fanatic and a traitor. He was convinced, however, that God asked this of him.

Stunned, Catherine recalled how several months before, she

felt as if God were telling her that he would send priests to Madonna House. Now it seemed to be happening, and the staff responded enthusiastically.

"Having priests here gave the place some semblance of respectability," recalled Mary Davis, the high school girl from Quebec City, who returned as a staff worker applicant that year. "Here's this woman who was so different from anyone else and the place was really suspect. And you'd wonder, 'Are people right?' All your inclinations are that she is for real. But you don't know if you're right. When a priest is here you knew it was all right."

Earlier in the year, Father Callahan paid Nicholas and Ann Makletzoff $5,000 for the log cabin on the island, which Catherine named St. Kate's. It became a dormitory for visiting priests.

The summer of 1953 brought an interesting assortment of new staff workers. Kathleen O'Herin, a registered nurse from Chicago, decided to become a staff worker after six months of helping Catherine provide nursing care to poverty stricken people in the back woods. Trudi Cortens, a spirited young woman from Winnipeg, arrived for a restful week in the country, and by the end of a grueling week of hard manual labor, decided to stay. A young woman from Detroit, and two young men from Boston and Montreal also asked to stay, but the most unlikely newcomer was a middle-aged school teacher from Hartford, Connecticut with chronic health problems. As soon as Mary Ruth walked through the door, she realized that she had come to the right place. "It was the whole idea of the Gospel being lived that attracted me very much. And the flexibility of it. It wasn't rigid. And furthermore, let's face it, she was the only person who would give me a chance!"

That fall, Catherine visited the Yukon Territory at the invitation of Bishop Jean Louis Coudert, who asked her to open a Madonna House in Whitehorse. The shack-like buildings in the shadow of icy mountains reminded Catherine of Murmansk, and she decided she could not in good conscience send young people into this icy wilderness. She changed her mind at Mass the next morning, November 17th, when the priest talked about St. Gregory the Wonder Worker, who purportedly moved a mountain on faith alone. "If St. Gregory could move mountains," she decided, "other Christians could too."

While Catherine was in Whitehorse, she saw an extraordinarily beautiful Indian woman wearing a caribou-hide parka, and carrying a baby in her arms. "The woman smiled at me, not saying a word," Catherine recalled. "She kept looking at me. I stood nailed to the snow-covered sidewalk. Gently, without haste, and with a last smile and a little inclination of her head, she walked away." One of the teachers from the Catholic school, who was with Catherine, pulled out a pad and sketched the woman. Later, Catherine showed the sketch to Bishop Coudert, who told her Indian women no longer dressed in that fashion. Catherine believed that the woman was Our Lady of the Yukon.

By the time she returned to Combermere that December, she felt herself floating in a strange state of awe and wonder. Life had taken so many twists since she and Eddie had arrived in Combermere in 1947. "The coming was, or seemed, like dying," she reflected.

> Madonna House was a new beginning, and yet it seemed no beginning at all — because no one believed but myself that it was to be anything at all but a nice place for me and Eddie to live off our writings. To most of the world I was a "quitter" of sorts, a traitor, that is, to my world of Catholic Action and Friendship House.
>
> And years — How many 3, 4, 5? — I sensed they were years of waiting. For what? For whom? I could not tell.
>
> Then Mary's slavery and Father (Cal's) sickness. A growth overnight — phenomenal. Staff workers arrival. Growth of Summer School, of everything physical, inward, outward like roses in June. Then the change inward Fr. (Cal) wants me to write about, and of which I can say so little. No, so few broken, halting words. June '52 — the discovery of a whole new horizon within myself. The life betwixt and between. Sights, sounds, gifts. Vows of poverty, obedience for life. Secrets of a heavenly King. A new life — and light, blinding, clear, on the apostolate, the truths of God; and love of Him and Mary that any

minute seems to grow so big it must burn me up, annihilate me! But never does, or did. . . .

So days merged into months, and a year and more went by. The strange lecture tour in Canada's west — after Bishop Coudert's visit to Madonna House. The acceptance of Whitehorse as a second foundation on the feast day of Gregory the Wonder Worker. Our Lady of the Yukon — Her immaculate parka all white!

And the return home — the physical weariness, exhaustion, colitis — and utter serenity and peace; and as if a huge parchment page was turned by an unseen hand — a new way of life started!

The year 1954 would indeed bring a new way of life, not just for Catherine, Eddie, and Father Callahan, but also for the priests and the young people, who would journey to the backwoods of Canada and join them.

Chapter Notes

"It gave everyone a sense of courage...": CD to JC, Oct. 21, 1951, MHA.
"I now see ALL my mistakes...": CD to BS, Oct. 14, 1951, Friendship House Papers, CHS.
"a slight dark man with piercing eyes": CD to JC, Oct. 21, 1951, MHA.
"She reminded me of the prima donnas..." and f.: *Cricket*, p. 241.
"all who belong...": "Pius XII Blesses FH," *RES*, Dec. 1951.
"There is no reason...": BS to CD, Feb. 28, 1952, MHA.
"It seems to be your will...": Diary #34, Mar. 5, 1952, MHA.
"a deep inner conviction...": JC, "Confidential Notebook," MHA.
"Time and space seemed to have ceased to exist...": Diary #34, Aug. 31, 1952, MHA.
"a soul that has passed through...": JC, "Confidential Notebook," MHA.
"We didn't know that when B was fainting...": Interview, Trudi Cortens.
"Madonna House is Our Lady's House...": JC, "Confidential Notebook," MHA.
"Just like a hollow, dull weight...": JC to CD, June 28, 1953, MHA.
"They're trying to take Father Cal...": Interview, Trudi Cortens.
"I felt God...": Fr. Eugene Cullinane to CD, July 25, 1953, MHA.
"Having priests here...": Interview, Mary Davis.
"If St. Gregory could move mountains...": *History of the Apostolate*, p. 792.
 [St. Gregory the Wonder Worker, or St. Gregory Thaumaturgus, should not be confused with Pope St. Gregory the Great.]
"She kept looking at me...": Ibid., p. 793.
"The coming was, or seemed...": Diary #37, Dec. 3, 1953, MHA.

30

Combermere

1954

On the evening of Wednesday, April 7, 1954, 17 people gathered in the Madonna House chapel. Since January they had studied and discussed the idea of secular institutes, and now each person voted secretly on whether Madonna House should become one. It meant a lifetime commitment under vows of poverty, chastity, and obedience — not just for staff workers — but for Catherine and Eddie. It also meant organizational restructuring, a new constitution, and severing ties with the people in Friendship House USA, who opposed the idea.

The ballots tallied 16 votes in favor of the secular institute, with Phil Larkin casting the only dissenting vote because he did not feel personally called to a lifetime commitment. Later that evening, the 16 staff members took promises of stability for one year, and Catherine gave each person a silver cross inscribed with the Latin words *PAX* and *CARITAS* — Peace and Love — which they had adopted as their motto.

"Those were exciting days," Mary Davis recalled.

During the weeks that followed, everyone helped pack the half-ton truck, named "Mickey," after St. Michael the Archangel, which Mamie Legris, Louis Stoeckle and Kathleen O'Herin would drive across Canada to open the new house in the Yukon Territory. It was gray and rainy after breakfast on the morning of May 8, when staff members gathered in the yard to bid them farewell. Father Callahan and a visiting Anglican minister gave their blessing, the Madonna House bell tolled, and the truck rolled out the driveway amid cheers and tears.

"It was almost beyond belief but it was tangible!" Catherine reflected. "They were on their way to the Yukon. . . and I knew the power of the Lord because of course I was nothingness itself. But he used that nothingness, and as he alone could, made it fruitful."

Kathleen O'Herin later noted that it demanded a tremendous leap of faith on Catherine's part to send her two most experienced staff workers and her only nurse to the Yukon. Later that year, an unusual assortment of people — each drawn through different circumstances and each with a needed talent — arrived to take their place.

Laurette Patenaude heard Catherine speak the year before in Edmonton. "You meet a lot of people, who are all trying to believe in God," she observed, "but what struck me about Catherine was that she wasn't trying. She really did believe." Laurette had a talent for cooking, and Catherine sent her to culinary schools to broaden her knowledge and skills.

Father John McGrath was camping in Algonquin Park when someone gave him Eddie's book, *My Hay Ain't In Yet*. Intrigued at the descriptions of Madonna House, he drove to Combermere the next day. When Catherine, Eddie, and Father Cal explained their plans to make Madonna House a secular institute, Father McGrath announced that he was a canon lawyer and could help them write a new constitution.

Sixteen-year-old Marie Javora enrolled in the Madonna House summer school that year. "When I came home, suddenly I was doing the dishes without being asked, and my mother was so astounded that she said, 'What happened to you!'" Marie was too young to join Madonna House, but ten years later after graduating as a registered nurse, she became a Madonna House staff worker. "Nothing else ever satisfied me. I had to come back here after that first experience."

The Rowland family visited in August 1954 with their daughter, Mary Kay, who ended up breaking off her wedding engagement to become a staff worker. "Catherine was always prodding, encouraging, training, drawing out each one's talents and gifts," she recalled. "She had a great gift of loving each individual very personally. She had this great facility for making connections — every day life with the Gospel, people with people, movement with movement, saints with the present time, the present and history of the Church, books pertinent to this or that. Catherine was concerned with everything large and small." She groomed Mary Kay to become a local director.

Elsie Whitty, a registered nurse from Scotland, arrived for tea one afternoon wearing white gloves and high heels because she heard Catherine was a Baroness. Appalled when Catherine bellowed a greeting from the back porch and then handed her a scalding mug as she walked in the door, Elsie remembered thinking, "A mug! This is an insult to tea!" After the initial shock, however, Elsie saw what the others had seen: the glow of love and life in the faces of Catherine, Eddie, and these young men and women. "When Catherine spoke, I could not believe what I was hearing," she confessed. "It went straight into my heart. I never experienced that before." Catherine sent her to school in England to become a certified midwife.

Therese Richaud, a practical nurse from Deer Horn, Manitoba, assisted Catherine and Elsie with nursing calls. They used Father Callahan's green station wagon, which they named St. Patrick, as an ambulance to transport people to the hospital.

During this time, Catherine also took in unmarried pregnant girls, but had to stop when rumors spread that the girls were Madonna House staff workers. She continued to take in other unusual guests, however, including recovering alcoholics, a senile old woman, a teenage boy whose father had died, a young girl from a large family who needed some personal attention, and several juvenile delinquents. Bishops sent priests in need of a rest. Doctors sent patients in need of outdoor exercise. To protect people's privacy, Catherine established an unwritten rule banning personal questions, and most staff workers never knew last names or where people came from unless the information was volunteered. The system worked so well that when staff members from Friendship House USA visited that summer, Mary Kay Rowland recalled meeting them, but had no idea tensions existed between them and Catherine.

Late that fall, Catherine accepted a written invitation from Archbishop John Hugh McDonald to open a house in Edmonton, Alberta, and on January 7, 1955, she sent Dorothy Phillips as the first director. By the time Marian Center officially opened five months later, Dorothy and her two staff members were feeding and clothing hundreds of transient men each week.

Madonna House seemed to branch out in directions that went beyond anything Catherine ever imagined. Throughout 1955, 15 more applicants arrived, among them Ronnie MacDonnell, who had a strong background in farming. Others had talents for writing, carpentry, electronics, and gardening. Inexperienced city kids tested people's patience. One young woman accidentally pulled out all the cucumber plants while weeding the garden. Two young men, who didn't realize potatoes grew underground, wandered for hours in search of potato bushes. Trudi Cortens recalls the day she accidentally shipped vitamins for the staff workers to a rural doctor and Catherine screamed so loud out of sheer frustration that people came running because they thought the garage had caught on fire.

Yet, no matter what happened, Catherine always stressed that what you *are* is more important then what you *do*. "Do you know that God loves us," she told them, "and he doesn't care what we do, he still loves us. Even if we don't love him, he loves us. Even if we're in 10,000 mortal sins, he loves us."

Smart, sophisticated Teresa Davis, who brought along her golf clubs thinking Madonna House was a religious resort, could not believe what she heard. "I graduated from St. Michael's in Toronto where I learned that you had to do lots of things for God to love you, but Catherine was saying, 'God is a passionate lover. He loves you madly. He does not care about your life, your background. And when somebody loves you passionately, and looks into your eyes and says, "I love you," will you spit in his eye?'"

Catherine groomed Teresa to become a local director.

"One of the things that struck me was that you didn't have to be educated and high class," recalled Laurette Patenaude. "You didn't have to be anybody to join Madonna House."

"It was wide open," Mary Kay Rowland agreed. "She filled us with fire and we stayed, not because of her, but because of the vision she gave us of loving God and serving the Church."

In October 1955, Father Emile Briere, who served as chaplain of the house in Edmonton, asked his bishop for a leave of absence and came to Combermere. Father Gene Cullinane had already received his release from the Basilians, and with three priests at Madonna House, thoughts of the priesthood tugged at Eddie. On October 30, 1955, Catherine and Eddie knelt before Father Callahan and Father Gene Cullinane to take their vows of celibacy. That night, before falling asleep, Eddie said to himself: "Now I must become a priest." On Christmas Day, he wrote a letter to Pope Pius XII with documentation on the deaths of his first two wives and his vow of celibacy with Catherine, hoping that he would receive permission to be ordained.

Eddie had not received an answer by the end of March, when 20-year-old Bob Pelton arrived. Handsome, intelligent, and a third year honor student at Yale University, Bob Pelton had already completed classes to become Catholic, but had not been received into the Church. After meeting Catherine and Father Callahan, he asked if he could take the final step at Madonna House. At 10:30 p.m. on Holy Saturday, he made a profession of faith in the Madonna House chapel with Catherine as his god-mother. When he received his First Communion, he felt as if the fire of the Holy Spirit poured through him. The next day, an idea struck him: "My vocation is to join Madonna House and be a priest."

Bob Pelton would become the first man ordained to the

priesthood specifically for Madonna House. It was an honor everyone thought Eddie might hold, but in the summer of 1957, the Vatican denied Eddie's request for ordination because he had been married too many times. Catherine thought back to a moment of intense prayer over a year before when she felt as if God told her that Eddie would become a priest. Doubts bombarded her, but she forced them out of her mind. "I realized," she confessed, "that if ever I was asked by God to be 'obedient' it is now. If ever I had to be 'indifferent' it is now. If ever I had to make a 'fiat' it is now."

That spring, Catherine and Father Callahan sent Father Gene Cullinane to serve as chaplain at Madonna House in the Yukon, but later that year, two new priests, Father Paul Bechard, a rural pastor from Saskatchewan, and Father Tom Rowland, a diocesan priest from Texas, arrived to take his place. The priests at Madonna House served as more than just spiritual directors for the staff and celebrants at daily Mass. They functioned as an integral part of the Madonna House community, spending long hours in manual labor with the Madonna House men, who were in the process of building Madonna House into a rural village unto itself. A few years before, Father Callahan bought a local farm on a small shallow lake and the Madonna House men built a family camp called Cana Colony for married couples and their children. Around the same time, he negotiated the sale of another 200-acre farm for Catherine and José de Vinck of New Jersey, who used the house as a family vacation spot and gave Madonna House permission to farm the land.

Madonna House bought a third farm in the spring of 1956, and used it for growing hay. That fall they found a fourth farm for sale. "The land wasn't good," Ronnie MacDonnell recalled. "The guy planted one field near the house with oats to hide the rocks. The back of the hill was the same thing." They bought the 350-acre farm anyway for $4,500, called it St. Benedict's Acres, and developed it into a dairy farm with cows and beef cattle, a Quebec oven for baking bread, and a cook house for canning fruits and vegetables. They learned to make their own cheese and butter, and eventually organized local farmers in a co-op to produce maple syrup and other farm products.

In the fall of 1958, Phil Larkin, who had married one of the Madonna House volunteers, sold his 150-acre farm to Madonna House because he wanted to move his family back to Prince Edward Island. Madonna House converted the Larkin farmhouse to dormitories, and used the fields for grazing sheep.

"I cannot yet grasp that *this* is it — not like Toronto, not like Harlem," Catherine confessed. "It really seems to have this time achieved order and unity of spirit."

Throughout the 1950's, Catherine had drifted further from Friendship House, which shifted from the religious-based organization she founded into a more professional group of civil rights activists, who concentrated on legislative and social change. In September 1956, Catherine notified Anne Foley, the National Director of Friendship House, that Madonna House no longer felt bound by the distinction between Friendship House USA and Friendship House Canada, and would soon cross the border to open a Madonna House in Arizona, where they would serve Mexican immigrants and Indians. "In fact," Catherine added, "I am waiting for the end of this Council meeting and its result to decide finally, once and for all, the question of my resignation from the Board.

> Our ideas are so divergent that it seems to be quite an anomaly — my being on the Board and a Council member, for by being on it I tacitly agree to what Friendship House stands for today. Frankly, I don't. So unless there is a change in its policies, I will after this Council meeting submit my resignation both from the Board and the Council, which I know will be easily acceptable to all of you.

On October 10, 1956, Catherine officially resigned.
Later that fall, the Archdiocese of Portland, Oregon asked if

Madonna House would take over the Friendship House in that city, which was under the direction of Mabel Knight, who had sided with Ann Harrigan during the 1947 Convention. When Catherine arrived in Portland to negotiate the terms, Mabel met her at the station. "She was very embarrassed," Catherine noted. "I treated her as if nothing had happened for the truth be known I have forgiven her everything. She finally sort of apologized for all that had transpired in the past, but I hushed her."

The following June, Catherine sent Mary Kay Rowland to convert Friendship House Portland into a Madonna House. Mabel Knight seriously considered joining Madonna House, but her health failed, and she died a short time later.

As contradictory as it seemed, the faster Madonna House grew, the more people came, the more land and buildings they acquired, the lonelier Catherine felt. Her position of leadership kept her from making close friendships with the staff workers. The vow of celibacy isolated her from Eddie. While Father Callahan could support her spiritually, he distanced himself emotionally. "I have always been very lonely," she prayed. "Now it seems as if I were the essence of loneliness itself!"

The answer to her prayer came one afternoon in June 1957, when Father Emile Briere felt as if God instilled in him a deep understanding of the difficulties Catherine and Father Callahan endured. "God was asking me to support them. That was so clear. Just support them. Be there, and understand deeply who they are."

From that point, Father Briere assumed a new role as a friend to Catherine and Father Callahan. Father Callahan invited him to sit in on Catherine's spiritual direction, and a new division of responsibility emerged: Catherine took charge of the women, Father Briere worked with the men, and Father Callahan assumed responsibility for the spiritual life of the community and the priests.

Hundreds of people visited Madonna House during those years, and by one estimate, nearly 40 percent of those who joined as staff workers eventually resigned. Some married. Others entered convents or became priests. Some could not accept the authoritarian structure of Madonna House. Catherine asked others to leave because they were disruptive or would not conform to the rules. "The next bus leaves at 10:30," became one of her well-known sayings to anyone who complained or wanted to challenge the Madonna House structure. She was particularly hard on anyone who tried to attach themselves to her emotionally, and it sometimes seemed as if she treated the people she favored more harshly than the ones she disliked.

"She was deathly afraid of having favorites," Mary Davis recalled, "so you got that close and no further. She always said, 'I cannot draw people to myself. I'll go to hell if I do. I have to lead them to God.' She told you very plainly, and she lived it out. Some people got mad and hurt."

Catherine's old friend, Father William Power, who eventually became the Bishop of Antigonish, Nova Scotia, suggested that some people felt hurt because Catherine was trying to make them turn a corner that they didn't want to go around. "Sometimes, you have to be confrontational," he observed, "and some people take that personally. I'm not saying that the woman was not capable of saying something that would hurt somebody, but if the B said something that she thought was for the good of the person, a lot could depend on the way that person received it. I would say that would be the case with 50% of the people who feel they were hurt."

In the fall of 1957, Catherine and Mamie Legris traveled to the Second World Congress of the Lay Apostolate in Rome where 2,000 delegates from 90 countries met, and Catherine returned more convinced than ever that Madonna House was moving in the right direction. Friendship House did not fare as well. The Harlem Friendship House closed in 1957. The following year, the house in Washington closed, and Jim Guinan, who was the director, came to Combermere as a staff worker. Betty Schneider left Friendship House shortly after Catherine resigned and pursued a career in teaching. By 1960, only the Chicago Friendship

House remained, but staff and volunteers continued to work passionately for racial justice, instituting unique projects such as home visits between black and white families that broke down barriers between the races and created bonds of trust that paved the way for the Civil Rights Movement. Staff workers received a small salary, and they saw their work as more than just a job, but not as the way of life Catherine envisioned. After the social upheaval of the 1960's, Friendship House in Chicago shifted its emphasis from racial justice to help for the homeless, the poor, and those suffering from drug and alcohol addictions.

Madonna House changed, too, and one of the most pronounced changes occurred after José de Vinck brought Father Joseph Raya, a Melkite priest, to Madonna House for a short visit in June 1958. From the moment Father Raya walked through the door, something about Madonna House touched him. "I saw a family!" he recalled. "She was making a family out of all these disparate people from all kinds of backgrounds!" When he saw the silver cross with PAX CARITAS inscribed on it that the staff workers wore, he wanted one. Father Cal explained that only staff workers, who had taken vows of poverty, chastity, and obedience, could wear the cross.

"All right," Father Raya exclaimed, "make me part of this!"

Father Callahan thought for a moment, and then he took the cross from around his own neck and put it on Father Raya, making him the first associate priest of Madonna House, which meant Father Raya would try to live the Madonna House spirituality at his own parish in Paterson, New Jersey, and later in Birmingham, Alabama. On subsequent visits, Catherine asked Father Raya to teach the staff about Eastern spirituality. Throughout the years she often spoke about Russian Easter and Christmas celebrations and traditions that she remembered from her childhood, but she refrained from talking too much about the Eastern Rites. "They've got enough trouble learning about the West," she would say. After Father Raya arrived, Catherine changed her mind. "He would teach the staff music and prayers," Father Briere recalled. "Then some of our priests became bi-ritual."

Father Raya's talks to the Madonna House staff enkindled Catherine's dream of working for the unification of the East and the West. Over the next 20 years, Catherine's dream would enlarge and spread, touching the minds and hearts of people all over the world.

Chapter Notes

"Those were exciting days...": Interview, Mary Davis.

"It was almost beyond belief...": Diary #39, May 8, 1954, MHA.

"You meet a lot of people...": Interview, Laurette Patenaude.

"When I came home...": Interview, Marie Javora.

"Catherine was always prodding...": Mary Kay Rowland to the author, June 10, 1994.

"A mug!" and f.: Interview, Elsie Whitty.

"Do you know that God loves us...": Interview, Teresa Davis.

"I graduated from St. Michael's...": *Ibid.*

"One of the things that struck me...": Interview, Laurette Patenaude.

"It was wide open...": Interview, Mary Kay Rowland.

On October 30...: After their vow of celibacy, Catherine continued to sleep in their old bedroom, and Eddie moved into a new bedroom that encompassed the upstairs portion of a new two-story addition, which also extended the kitchen downstairs. Several years later, Catherine moved out of the main house to live in the one-room log cabin Nicholas Makletzoff had built on the island. Father Callahan purchased the cabin for Madonna House in 1953.

"Now I must become a priest...": *Cricket*, p. 260.

"I know what my vocation is...": Interview, Fr. Robert Pelton.

"I realized...": Diary #40, July 29, 1956, MHA.

"The land wasn't good...": Interview, Ronnie MacDonnell.

"I cannot yet grasp...": Diary #40, Apr. 27, 1956, MHA.

"In fact I am waiting...": CD to Anne Foley, Sept. 13, 1956, MHA.

"She was very embarrassed...": Diary #37, Nov. 13, 1956, MHA.

"I have always been very lonely...": Diary #37, May 6, 1957, MHA.

"God was asking me to support them...": Interview, Fr. Emile Briere.

nearly 40 percent...: *Ibid.*

"The next bus leaves...": *Ibid.*

"She was deathly afraid...": Interview, Mary Davis.

"Sometimes, you have to be confrontational...": Interview, Bishop William E. Power.

"I saw a family..." and f: Interview, Archbishop Joseph Raya. [Father Raya was part of a Byzantine rite that started in Antioch, Syria, and Jerusalem during the early days of Christianity. After the Orthodox separated from Rome in 1054, some Melkite groups, such as the one Father Raya belonged to, remained faithful to the Pope.]

"They've got enough trouble...": Interview, Fr. Emile Briere.

"He would teach...": *Ibid.*

31

Combermere

1960

In April 1960, Father Paul Bechard and Eddie Doherty drove to Barry's Bay in one of the Madonna House vans to claim a large crate containing a six-foot bronze statue from Florence, Italy. The story of this statue started when Catherine, who invoked the Mother of God under titles such as Our Lady of the Kitchen or Our Lady of the Woods, started praying to Our Lady of Combermere. When someone asked what Our Lady of Combermere looked like, Catherine replied that she envisioned her as "descending from heaven, her arms outstretched, seeking souls, and blessing Madonna House."

A few years later, a Hungarian nun sketched a picture according to Catherine's description. "It wasn't as I had fancied," Catherine admitted, "but it was close."

Catherine had the picture framed, and Bishop Coudert suggested during one of his visits that they have prayer cards printed with the picture on one side and a prayer on the other. At the 1956 summer school, a Chicago woman prayed to Our Lady of Combermere for the conversion of her husband, and when he converted to Catholicism a short time later, the woman told Catherine that she wanted to raise money for a statue of Our Lady of Combermere. "I got somewhat panicky," Catherine confessed. "Could one put up a statue to Our Lady under a title not officially approved?"

At Catherine's urging, Father Callahan presented the problem to Bishop Smith of Pembroke, who sent the question to Rome.

Within two months, the Vatican granted permission to erect the statue. Now Madonna House faced the problem of finding someone to sculpt it. The answer came as Catherine paged through *Sign Magazine* one afternoon and saw a photo of a statue by Frances Rich of Santa Barbara, with the caption: "The Questing Madonna." Catherine stared at the picture in astonishment. It was identical to her mental image of Our Lady of Combermere. Catherine wrote to Frances Rich at once, asking for permission to have a local artist copy the statue, perhaps in wood, with a flowing cape for "Mary should have a longer cape for these cold shores of ours."

Three days later, Frances Rich replied:

> Your letter moved me very much. The result is I am writing at once to ask you what you can afford to spend for the new sculpture, the Madonna of Combermere? It must be somehow. . . and I can see that the cloak must be longer. . . So, close your eyes to worry about anything but what you can afford to pay. . . we must work this out.

The entire process took two years, and Madonna House paid only the cost of materials, labor and shipping, which amounted to about $3,000. On May 17, 1960, 13 years after Catherine and Eddie arrived in Combermere, the statue was erected in a pine grove overlooking the Madawaska River. Several years before, while swimming in the river, Catherine and Eddie had both seen an outline of Our Lady on this exact spot, and it seemed to be the appropriate place for the statue.

This was no ordinary statue. Our Lady of Combermere seemed alive with movement, grace, and passion, as if running with arms outstretched to embrace someone. Her cloak and skirt flare out after her. Her head tilts slightly to the left; her delicate, yet strong facial features express concern, compassion, and unconditional love.

During a special ceremony on June 8, 1960, Bishop Smith

blessed the statue. "I know that as the years go by great graces will flow out all over this diocese, all over Canada and the United States, and all over the rest of the world through Our Lady of Combermere, and the great work to which these people have dedicated their lives," he proclaimed. Then he reminisced about his first meeting with Catherine and Eddie on August 15, 1945. "I gave verbal approbation to the work. . . Of course nobody then envisioned what the future would hold. I did not realize that in 15 years such great things would be accomplished here."

Excited whispers whiffed through the crowd: "It was the first time that we had such words of approval from anybody that mattered," Mary Davis recalled. "We were just flying high that day."

That evening, Bishop Smith gave full approval to the women's division of Madonna House, and provisional approval to the men's and priest's division. "Catherine came close to fainting!" Father Briere laughed.

Madonna House now had over 60 staff workers and applicants with field houses in the Yukon; Edmonton; Portland, Oregon; Winslow, Arizona; and Balmorehea, Texas. Catherine had accepted invitations to open new houses on the Island of Carriacou in the British West Indies, where they would work with the poor, and in the diocese of Richmond, Virginia, where they would organize an apostolate and retreat center for families. That summer, hundreds of people visited Combermere. Six applicants made promises of poverty, chastity and obedience. Five others entered the applicant training program. Madonna House had finally become the unique way of life Catherine envisioned. She called it "the beautiful and awesome spirit of the Gospel applied to daily living, without compromise." She spoke of childlike simplicity, of recognizing the duty of the moment, of doing little things exceedingly well, of loving God passionately — all components of Catholic spirituality — yet people claimed Catherine possessed a spirit different from any they had seen in North America.

Father Raya agreed. While Catherine followed the laws and precepts of the Roman Catholic Church, beneath the surface, she possessed an Eastern mentality that made her different in a way North Americans could not understand. "That's why she was in so many ways persecuted," Father Raya insisted. "She spoke their language. She tried to feel what they felt, but she did not. I can detect it. Give me anything she wrote and I will tell you the difference between what she writes and what is behind her writing. There's always a vision, always an atmosphere, a spirit blowing that was different."

During these years, Catherine had recurring thoughts of Russian spiritual traditions. "I had laid them carefully aside, evidently wrapped up in the linen of memories, and perhaps I was afraid to unwrap them. I was afraid because I was living in a culture, a land, a civilization that seemed to be too far removed from such spiritual traditions. However, sometimes God unwraps the linens that contain memories and brings them forth to look at, to meditate upon, and to pray about."

She started writing about childhood experiences to illustrate the difference between the West, which she called intellectual, logical, legalistic, and concrete, and the East, which she described as intuitive, abstract, and simpler in a way that deals with the heart rather than the mind. She remembered the Russian *stranniks* who made pilgrimages to shrines; the *staretzi*, who grew wise with the wisdom of God; the *urodivoi*, who gave away their possessions and became fools for Christ; the *humiliati*, whom people scorned as the dregs of society; the *poustiniks*, who lived alone like hermits in a simple dwelling called a *poustinia*, the Russian word for desert. *Poustiniks* went into the desert to seek God in silence and solitude, in prayer and fasting. Unlike hermits, however, a *poustinik* advised, consoled and assisted people who came to them in need. Catherine recalled how her mother took her to see a *poustinik* in Russia. "How well do you love your enemies?" the old man asked her.

In the summer of 1961, Catherine decided to convert one of

the old farmhouses at Madonna House into a *poustinia.* "It was truly a spiritual matter that I was dealing with," she admitted. "I was about to bring the fruit of another country, another civilization, another background, into this new land! Who would understand it? How could I present it to them?"

The *poustinia* contained only a hard bed, a desk and chair, a Bible, a large cross without a corpus, drinking water, and a loaf of bread. Staff workers went into the *poustinia* to fast and pray in silence for a day or two. "Slowly, very slowly, the idea began to spread to our missions," she noted. "Some found corners or rooms that they could use in their houses. Others built little shacks; others used empty rooms in convents or retreat houses."

As guests and volunteers expressed an interest, Madonna House built small cabins in the woods for use as *poustinias.*

In the fall of 1961, Catherine asked Nicholas Makletzoff to draw plans for an outdoor shrine with an onion dome like the ones she remembered along the roadsides in Russia. Men from Madonna House constructed the shrine on the island near Catherine's cabin. Inside, Catherine hung a framed icon of the *Bogorodizita,* the Russian name for the Mother of God, with a vigil light burning day and night for the Bishops attending the Second Vatican Council. Facing the Russian shrine was a small western-style shrine with a statue of Our Lady. For Catherine, the two shrines became a symbol of unity between East and West.

"With her vision and her stamina, I'm sure she was convinced of one day putting East and West together," Father Raya observed.

This vision of unity was threatened, however, by what Catherine saw as madness on the part of people, who were destroying themselves and the world around them. During the winter of 1962, she read Rachel Carson's *The Silent Spring.* Madonna House immediately abandoned chemical fertilizers and pesticides, and turned to organic farming. "If we continue to interfere with nature," Catherine warned, "the next to go will be the trees, then the grass, then the wild flowers. And even without the atomic bombs, we shall live in a desert of our own making. And we shall kill ourselves slowly by the thousand poisons that we administer to ourselves through pesticides, chemical fertilizers, tranquilizers, euphoriants, and what have you."

Her words breathed fire. She warned that selfishness and greed consumed the world and people had reached the blasphemous point of worshipping no one but themselves.

> Truly this is a tragedy beyond words . . . to become a dark disciple . . . to make a god of oneself. No wonder, therefore, that mental illness and emotional disturbance fill modern man, and send him scurrying like a cornered rat to all kinds of escapes including tranquilizers.
>
> Emptiness and boredom are his milieu. They spur him, now to a frantic frenzy of useless activity, now to a withdrawal from all reality.
>
> Symbolically this adds up to a man-made hell. . .

Catherine believed the only hope for the salvation of the world was love—love of God and love of everything God created, including other people. It had to be the kind of love that would stamp out pride, greed, and selfishness, the kind of love that would heal and restore emotionally battered people. "The longer I live, the clearer I see that the answer to our personal, collective, national, and international problems is bridge-making between human beings — not allowing any human being to be an island unto himself — but connecting each with the other, with bridges of love."

Catherine, Father Briere, and Father Callahan believed that Madonna House was a bridge that could restore people to God. They met every night during those years to discuss the rapid evolution of Madonna House. "If there was any difficulty we voted and settled the question," Father Briere recalled. "We tried to get unanimity on everything but there was so much going on. People had to be trained. What about this one? What does she need? What does he need? Everything was in the making."

The biggest event in 1963, and the one Eddie Doherty called "Our Greatest Day," occurred on May 31, with the ordination of Bob Pelton. As the opening procession started down the center aisle of the parish church, the Madonna House choir sang, "Behold the High Priest," and Bob Pelton appeared in the long white alb Father Callahan had worn at his ordination 24 years before. "I looked at Catherine and scarcely recognized her," Eddie recalled. "She looked like a woman carved in an attitude of prayer."

During the banquet that followed, Catherine presented to Bishop Smith the three young women who would open the newest Madonna House in Pakistan. The bishop admitted that nothing pleased him more than to see the spirit of Madonna House carried throughout the world.

In the fall of 1964, Catherine and Father Cal sent Father Pelton to study in Rome where the Second Vatican Council was in progress. The rapid changes in the Church rocked the Catholic world, and the Madonna House community felt the impact. "Up to 1960, we were the lunatic fringe," recalled Father Briere. "There was no canonical explanation for what we were doing." With each session of Vatican II, however, it became increasingly apparent that the spirit of Madonna House with its emphasis on men and women living the Gospel with their lives, identifying with the poor, serving others in a spirit of love, and striving for personal sanctification embraced the same concepts that the Council documents emphasized. Priests and nuns flocked to Madonna House to sample this new kind of religious life. The touch of Eastern spirituality under the gentle guidance of Father Raya made it even more appealing.

In the summer of 1965, Father Raya and a friend entered the dining room during dinner with life-size, hand painted icons, which would be hung on either side of the altar in the Madonna House chapel. "All I saw was Christ and his Blessed Mother walking in the door!" Catherine recalled. "Time stopped. I couldn't breathe. I sat like a statue, unmoving. Perhaps I should say that time reversed itself. For here, into our Canadian apostolic headquarters, Christ of Russia and his Mother, the *Bogorodizita*, literally walked toward me in those icons. Like a flashback, in a second, I was back in my homeland, and tears were welling up in my eyes. A lifetime passed before me. Memories crowded."

With the memories came prayers for family members, living and dead, who were gone from her physically, but remained alive in her heart. Theodore died in Emma's arms in Finland in 1923 from a heart attack. Emma died from asphyxiation in 1948 after milk overflowed on her gas stove and extinguished the flame. Catherine's brother, Serge, and his family still lived in Brussels. André and his family moved to Cuba after World War II, where he worked at the University of Havana as a Judo instructor.

Catherine's half-brother, Vsevolod, was arrested in Russia during the Stalin purges of the 1930's, and was presumed dead. His wife, Lusia, their daughter, Ksenia, two small granddaughters and a grandson were banished to Siberia, but escaped during World War II, and ended up in a German refugee camp. After the war, they emigrated to New York with the help of a nun, who had read about their plight in an article Catherine wrote.

Following Boris' death in 1947, Claudia sold the house they owned and barely touched the money from Boris' estate, choosing instead to live like a pauper in a rooming house near McGill University in Montreal. When she died, she left over half a million dollars to charitable organizations.

George married and launched a successful career as an insurance executive, eventually starting his own international insurance consulting firm. He visited Combermere with his children throughout the years, but still harbored deep bitterness toward his mother and Madonna House that would rise to the surface with the angry accusation that Catherine had neglected him as a child and was responsible for the breakup of her marriage to Boris. "Day in and day out, I have you before my eyes, in my heart and soul," Catherine pleaded. "You are part of me always. . . I seem to understand you, almost feel your moods. . . almost see you living. . . sharing in so much of you, and doubting that you know it."

George did not understand.

There were also aspects of Catherine's life that she did not understand. For 40 years she had asked God: why had he chosen her — a refugee from Russia, a stranger in a new land — to found a lay apostolate? It seemed as if so many Canadians and Americans could have done a better job relating to people without the cultural barriers, the misunderstandings, the rejections, the failures. Priests told her through the years that God always chooses the weakest so that his power can confound the worldly wise, but the night Father Raya brought the icons, Catherine heard another answer deep in her soul: "Perhaps he wanted a humble little bridge between the Latin rites and the Eastern rites, for here I was brought up in the Latin Rite and the Eastern Rite. . . Now, here were the Lord, Christ of Russia and the *Bogorodizita* coming into our chapel for the Fourth session of the Council, which in Madonna House has been so specially dedicated to the reunion of the East and West. Now, there [the icons] were installed, blessing the Western world in an Easterly way, bringing about, by their very presence unity — based on love, prayer, and on understanding of one another."

By the end of Vatican II, Madonna House welcomed wave after wave of nuns, priests, and restless young people, who searched for meaning in their lives. Father Briere recalled how Catherine and the staff spent hours trying to answer their questions: "Did Christ really die? Did he really rise from the dead? Is God for real? Who believes in Mary anymore? She is not a valid model for women. Why can't women be ordained?"

Sometime in the late 1960's, Catherine, Father Callahan, and Father Briere met to discuss what course Madonna House should take through the chaos of a changing Church. "Let's center on the essentials," Catherine suggested. "The Gospels and the Little Mandate."

Father Callahan, who had the final authority on Liturgy at Madonna House agreed: "We will follow the Bishop of Pembroke."

"Those were two very important decisions," Father Briere recalled. "If we hadn't done that we would have gone in ten different directions. We would have split up into little groups wanting this and little groups wanting that. We would have gone all over the place."

By taking this stance, within a very short time, the reputation of Madonna House shifted from liberal to conservative, yet in essence, they had not changed at all. They stood still, as Father Carr had long ago advised Catherine to do in any raging storm, and while Madonna House stood silently, the Catholic world shifted around them.

Perhaps the greatest irony during this time is that while priests left in droves to marry, Eddie Doherty, a married man who had taken a vow of celibacy, still wanted to be ordained. After the installation of Pope John XXIII, Eddie resubmitted his request for ordination, but the Vatican rejected him again. When the Council approved a married diaconate, Eddie applied to become a deacon, but received a reply from Rome saying that Canada had not yet established a diaconate program.

"If I were a bishop, I would ordain you," Father Raya told him.

Six months later, on October 20, 1968, to the surprise of Eddie and everyone else in Combermere, Father Joseph Raya was named Archbishop of Acca, Haifa, Nazareth and all Galilee. In November, he made a farewell visit to Combermere. Wearing the robes and crown of an Archbishop, he installed Father Callahan as an Archimandrite, the Eastern Rite equivalent of a Superior in a monastery. "Now we are welded together, my diocese and your apostolate!" he proclaimed. "We are spiritually welded; we are physically welded."

Later that day, the new Archbishop assured Eddie that he would keep his promise and ordain him a priest.

Bishop Smith of Pembroke granted Eddie permission to transfer from the Latin Rite to the Melkite Rite, and in the spring of 1969, 78-year-old Eddie flew to Israel where he began training for the priesthood. When Eddie suggested that his ordination take place in the chapel of the Little Sisters of Jesus in Nazareth, the nuns told him that nearly 80 years before Charles de Foucauld prayed that someday, a sinner like himself would be ordained a priest in that chapel. Eddie Doherty, the tough Chicago reporter, who had "sold" his soul for a story and married a Baroness, became the answer to Charles de Foucauld's prayers on August 15, 1969.

During the ceremony, Archbishop Raya called Eddie forward, blessed him, and watched as Eddie made a pilgrimage around the altar three times. Then Eddie knelt. With the Gospel book resting on Eddie's head, Archbishop Raya invoked the Holy Spirit and ordained him a priest. The nuns vested Eddie in the Byzantine robes they had sewed for the occasion. Catherine did not attend Eddie's ordination because the staff took promises in Combermere on that day, and she felt it was her duty to receive the new staff workers into the apostolate. As Father Eddie Doherty began the long journey back to Combermere, he wondered, "What will I say to Catherine? What will she say to me?"

It was after 11 p.m. when the car carrying Eddie pulled into the Madonna House driveway. Catherine waited alone near the doorway to the main house. When Eddie entered, she kissed his hands, and said, "Your blessing, Father." Eddie placed his hand on her forehead and said, "The grace of Jesus Christ, the love of God the Father, and the fellowship of the Holy Spirit be with you now and always and forever and ever." Then he made the sign of the cross three times.

"It was difficult at first for Catherine to accept Eddie as a priest," Father Briere recalled. "She had always held priests in high esteem as if they were Christ himself, and here was this man, her husband, who suddenly moved into this role. It was a long time before she went to one of Eddie's Masses."

Gradually, however, Father Eddie, as he came to be known, grew into his priesthood, and Catherine realized that this new dimension of Eddie's life showered blessings on Madonna House and on her. That Christmas Eddie gave Catherine a card with the note: "At last I have a perfect gift for you. I shall offer the first Christmas Mass for you and your intentions at Midnight. For this I was born, that I should have Divine love and human love to give you, my beloved."

In February, 1970, Nicholas Makletzoff died. He was the only person left in North America to whom Catherine could say, "Do you remember Russia?"

Madonna House had adopted the flavor of Russian spirituality with icons, a Russian shrine, and *poustinias*, but after Nicholas died, Catherine started dreaming about a Russian chapel made out of logs with an onion dome. Her dream came true on May 17, 1972 when Bishop Joseph Windle, who had replaced Bishop Smith as the head of the Diocese of Pembroke, consecrated Our Lady of the Woods chapel, which the men of Madonna House constructed in a clearing surrounded by tall pines.

While some people criticized Catherine as a power hungry empire builder, who bought up property and used staff workers to erect buildings and statues for her own glory, she sloughed it off. "As I look from my island to the mainland I see structures belonging to Madonna House, but structures, physical ones, though needed don't attract me. I really see a Christian community of love growing on the shores of the beautiful Madawaska."

Eddie agreed. Madonna House was not a place, he insisted. Madonna House was a family joined in a bond of love for the glory of God. "Love transfigured them, made their eyes shine, made them sing, made them laugh. . . ."

Chapter Notes

"descending from heaven...": History of the Apostolate, p. 814.

"It wasn't as I had fancied...": Ibid.

"I got somewhat panicky...": Ibid.

"Mary should have a longer cape...": CD to Frances Rich, May 24, 1957, MHA.

"Your letter moved me...": Frances Rich to CD, May 27, 1957, MHA.

Several years before, while swimming...: *Katia*, p. 143.

"I know that as the years go by..." and f.: "Our Lady of Combermere," *RES*, July 1960.

"It was the first time...": Interview, Mary Davis.

"Catherine came close to fainting": Fr. Emile Briere, "God, How Much You Love Me," *RES*, Nov. 1990.

"the beautiful and awesome spirit...": *Dearly Beloved*, Vol. 1, p. 120.

"And that's why...": Interview, Archbishop Joseph Raya.

"I had laid them carefully aside": CD, *Poustinia*, p. 49-50, (Hereafter *Poustinia*).

"It was truly a spiritual matter...": Ibid.

"Slowly, very slowly...": *Poustinia*, p. 57-58.

"With her vision and her stamina...": Interview, Archbishop Joseph Raya.

"If we continue to interfere with nature...": "I Live on an Island," *RES*, Jan. 1963.

"Truly this is a tragedy beyond words...": "Man-Made Hells and the Lay Apostolate," *RES*, Apr. 1962.

"The longer I live...": "Love Builds Bridges," *RES*, Mar. 1963.

"If there was any difficulty...": Interview, Fr. Emile Briere.

"Our Greatest Day": "Our Greatest Day," *RES*, July 1963.

"I looked at Catherine...": Ibid.

"Up to 1960...": Interview, Fr. Emile Briere.

"All I saw was Christ and his Blessed Mother...": "I Live on an Island," *RES*, Aug. 1965.

"Day in and day out...": CD to G de H, Dec. 7, 1956, MHA.

"Perhaps he wanted...": "I Live on an Island," *RES*, Aug. 1965.

"Did Christ really die?" and f.: Fr. Emile Briere, "God, How Much You Love Me," *RES*, Nov. 1990.

"Let's center on the essentials..." and f.: Interview, Fr. Emile Briere.

"If I were a bishop...": ED, "Love Letter...," *RES*, July 1969; *Cricket*, pp. 262-263.

"Now we are welded...": ED, "Love Letter...," *RES*, Dec. 1968.

"What will I say to Catherine...": *Cricket*, p. 279.

"Your blessing, Father," and f.: *Ibid.*, p. 282.

"It was difficult...": Interview, Fr. Emile Briere.

"At last I have a perfect gift...": ED to CD, Dec. 25, 1969, MHA.

"As I look from my island...": "These Twenty-Five Years," *RES*, May 1972.

"Love transfigured them...": ED, "Desert Windows," *RES*, May 1972.

32

Winslow, Arizona

1975

In February 1975, Catherine received an emergency phone call saying that 84-year-old Eddie, who spent winters in Winslow, Arizona, had suffered a heart seizure and had been rushed to the hospital with fluid in his lungs. By the time Catherine and Father Briere arrived the next morning, Eddie was drifting in and out of consciousness. Doctors offered little hope. Yet, as soon as Eddie realized Catherine was in the room, he suddenly came alive. By late afternoon, his condition stabilized.

"I'll expect you in Combermere on St. Patrick's Day," Catherine told him.

On March 17th, Eddie came home with cheering staff workers greeting his arrival, but everyone, including Catherine, knew that Eddie had come home to die. Five weeks later, he developed a bowel obstruction and underwent surgery at Victoria Hospital in the nearby town of Renfrew. This time, Eddie did not bounce back. At midnight, on Saturday, May 3, Catherine and Father Briere hurried to the hospital because Eddie had slipped into a coma. At 2 a.m., Father Briere celebrated Mass at Eddie's bedside, and when he spoke the words of the consecration, Eddie repeated them out loud: "This is my Body. This is my Blood."

Catherine, 79 years old, was so overwrought that Father Briere took her back to the motel to rest. She was still sleeping the next morning at 10:34 a.m. when Eddie died.

"There was no doubt in my mind that Father Eddie was now reunited with the Lord he loved so passionately and so well,"

Catherine confessed. "I said to myself, 'Now you have reached journey's end. . . your long journey is finished.' But even as the thought came to me I realized that it was far from finished. In a manner of speaking it had just begun — begun in a new dimension."

For two days, Eddie's body lay in a simple pine coffin in the Madonna House Russian chapel with staff members keeping a constant vigil. On May 7, Father Callahan celebrated the funeral Mass with over 40 priests and 300 people in attendance. Archbishop Raya gave the eulogy. They buried Eddie in the parish graveyard near Flewy. Marking his grave was a wooden cross carved with the words, "All my words for The Word."

Catherine pushed aside the pain of Eddie's death and plunged into her work. Their new house in Gravelbourg, Saskatchewan opened that summer. That fall, she ran the local directors meetings in Combermere. Earlier in the year, her best-selling book, *Poustinia: Christian Spirituality of the East for Western Man*, was published, thrusting her into the spotlight, and creating a new demand for lectures. In October she gave a joint lecture with her old friend Frank Sheed in Toronto, and she visited Ann Harrigan. The trip resurrected ghosts of people and places that she had buried years before. Frank Sheed still reeled in pain over the death of his wife, Maisie, and he looked very old to Catherine. Ann Harrigan remained distant, and Catherine stuffed whatever pain she felt down into that place inside of her where layers of pain from over the years had already started to fester.

By Christmas 1975, the immensity of Catherine's unresolved pain overwhelmed her, and she collapsed in a state of near exhaustion. Her doctor insisted that part of the problem stemmed from her son, George, who had become interested in genealogy and started searching for extended family members all over the world. Like a man on a bulldozer, George unearthed painful details about Catherine's early life, the war, the revolution, her exile from Russia, and her life with Boris. He interviewed de Hueck relatives, who gave him old photos, letters, and documents. He contacted Claudia, and some of Boris' other mistresses. As George tried to fit the pieces together, he discovered discrepancies with dates, ages, people, places, and events. He challenged Catherine about her date of birth, the religion of her parents, the date of her wedding to Boris, and circumstances surrounding her marriage. It never occurred to him that he sliced open the most painful parts of her life, and that his questions burned like acid in the open wound.

During this time, Sister Elizabeth Louise Sharum, a Benedictine nun, working on her doctorate in history, chose Friendship House as a dissertation topic. Through interviews and archival research, Sister Sharum uncovered shocking details about the demise of Friendship House Toronto and Catherine's downfall in Chicago. By the end of January, Catherine grew so distraught that her doctor ordered complete bed rest and no contact with George or Sister Sharum. Catherine wrote George one last agonizing note: "It has nothing to do with 'being ashamed of'," she told him, "it simply is the fact that it stirs up traumatic memories. . . I wake up at night screaming, moaning, perspiring . . . So please, Georgy Porgy, leave me alone."

Catherine's doctor explained to George that as Catherine grew older, her body could not keep up with the pace she had set for herself. The exhumed details of her life, combined with delayed grief over Eddie's death, left her emotionally and physically exhausted. "Even though for several years she had nightmares off and on about the Communist persecution, she was able to put herself together and keep functioning and overcome those stressful situations," the doctor wrote. "It seems that with her exhaustion, it is hard for her to face past painful memories and it would not be helpful to her at this time to face past memories in a forceful way."

Within two months, Catherine improved dramatically. "I know something happened to her," the doctor noted, "especially in the area of being able to slow down and look at herself and face the problems, especially of old age and the death of Father Eddie.

During the last few days she has spoken very little of her rejections of her youth and looks very peaceful and not as irritable as before."

Catherine felt well enough on Wednesday, April 6, to travel to Ottawa for the investiture of the prestigious Order of Canada, the highest award given to a Canadian citizen, which was conferred by Jules Leger, the Governor General of Canada with the approval of Queen Elizabeth II.

> About me he said that I had given my adopted country my life, that I had served the poor zealously, constantly, and that I had extended the service to the poor internationally. . . You know, I can't express in words exactly what happened, but finally, *I was accepted* by my new country. Russia rejected me. Canada wasn't exactly happy to have me in the early days but they bore with me, I guess, and then suddenly and unexpectedly. . . I was accepted in a very beautiful and loving way. . . You have to be a refugee to understand what happened/ I can't say anymore, "I am a stranger in a strange land." Isn't that beautiful?

The following month, Catherine reeled in pain over the news that her brother, Serge, suffered a fatal heart attack in Brussels. "There are no words," she wrote in a telegram to her sister-in-law. "So I will not say anything. Pain and joy live in silence, I am silent with you in prayer."

Serge and his wife Joan had visited Combermere a few years before. After touring Madonna House, Serge told Catherine, "You have reproduced our childhood here. This is just like a Russian estate. God bless you for bringing a little bit of Russia to a foreign land."

The Russian culture and spirituality Catherine brought to Canada eventually spread to foreign lands through staff workers, field houses, articles and books. In the summer of 1976, Catherine received the Jules Favre Foundation Award from the Academie Francaise for the French edition of *Poustinia*, and publishers rushed to translate the book into Italian, Flemish, Chinese, Japanese, Portuguese, Spanish, Vietnamese, Polish, Russian, and German.

Catherine spent the winter of 1976 in Arizona. A few months before, she had an unusual dream in which her mother appeared and told her God wanted her to write. "In a period of one month, from March 1 to April 4, Catherine wrote her book *Sobornost* on the Eastern concept of unity between mind and heart," Father Briere recalled. "One month later, she wrote her memoirs, *Fragments of My Life*. In July, she wrote *Strannik*, a book about the pilgrimage into the heart of God. By August, she finished *Dear Father*, a book of letters to priests. This was an amazing literary output in so short a time!"

Throughout this period, Father Briere remained her companion and protector. He saw himself as a Simon of Cyrene, who helped carry her cross. "The prophet, the visionary, climbs the mountain alone," he reflected, "But a friend can accompany the prophet and enter into a similar silence and solitude, making the loneliness bearable, changing it even into companionship."

Father Briere cushioned the impact when Catherine's relationships with staff workers became strained. "Tell them in their own language what I'm trying to say!" she would bellow in sheer frustration, and Father Briere would try to reiterate what she meant. When Catherine seemed impatient or out of sorts, he took people aside and explained that she was ill or that she had been awake most of the night. Some people claimed Catherine could be insensitive, and at times, cruel in her dealings with the staff, but Father Briere insisted that she was like a person with no skin. "So what happens when you don't have any skin? You react to things. A person may simply give you a friendly tap on the shoulder and you scream. She was under that kind of tension all the time. I didn't see it so much as insensitivity as pain."

Jean Fox, who worked closely with Catherine as the Assistant Director of Women, described Catherine as very direct and honest. "Most people could not take that because their unhealed psyche was afflicted and they said, 'Oh, B doesn't love me.' And they would go off in a corner and cry. Those who persevered eventually got through that. At the beginning very few could take it, and she didn't care because she had something to do for God. But everybody whose heart was open knew that this woman loved you. You knew, not with your mind, but something inside said, 'This woman really loves me.' There are staff here now who have been able to work through extraordinarily difficult woundings because they held on to that kernel of truth that the B understood them in a way that no one else had ever understood them."

It was during this time that Catherine instituted what she called "listening houses," places where people would come because "God is spoken here."

"Why should anybody want to have a listening house?" she wrote.

> Because people today are lonely beyond any loneliness that has embittered mankind in years past! They are not only lonely. They are sort of alienated. They don't communicate with others easily. In fact some not at all! Perhaps it is due to our technological society. Perhaps it is due to our concern with self. Or to put it more plainly, our "selfishness." We seem to be interested only in ourselves, in our own well-being, our own amusement, recreation and what have you.
>
> All around us are millions of people who, figuratively speaking, with outstretched hands, cry to heaven, "I am so alone, Lord. So terribly alone. . . ."
>
> Yes, Madonna House has watched this happen and we have decided to open listening houses. The government has taken over welfare. It has taken over hospitals. It has taken over, in a word, what we used to call "the corporal works of mercy," but it has not noticed the terrible loneliness of man nor his alienation.

"Catherine envisioned the Madonna House staff workers bringing the invisible presence of God to people in the listening houses," explained Jean Fox, who opened the first successful listening house in Portland, Oregon. "Slowly, people found out about these houses and came to talk. We would just sit there and listen to them. This woman used to come and she talked about her children, about baseball, about losing weight. One day she sat down at the kitchen table and said, 'I don't understand this house. I come in the door and I am laden with problems, burdens that I cannot resolve, and when I leave I have peace in my heart.' That wasn't us. It wasn't she. It was the presence of God operating through very little, ordinary, humble, weak people, who were simply trying to be faithful to this incredible life that we've been given."

By 1978, Madonna House established listening houses in Ottawa, Cleveland, Gravelbourg, and the Yukon Territory. Two more listening houses in Raleigh, North Carolina and Moncton, New Brunswick were in the process of being opened. A short time later, the Bishop of Washington D.C. invited Catherine to open a listening house near Capitol Hill because he recognized that the spiritual poverty in that city exceeded the physical poverty.

"Factually, [a listening house] doesn't 'do' anything," Catherine admitted, "and yet it does very much."

While she believed that listening was powerful and demanding work, she also struggled with the way manual labor had become depersonalized and cut off from nature through the mindless use of machinery. "Our Canadian and USA youth does not know how to work without machines," she reflected. "They do not visualize how it can be done even. They do not visualize this because they do not know much about nature. One must teach nature."

"Every year, she had a new project," recalled Madonna House farm manager Albert Osterberger. "It's time to get set up to irrigate our vegetables. It's time to build a windmill. It's time to get a team of bred mares because you have to start farming with horses."

A trained mechanical engineer, Albert struggled with Catherine's insistence on what he considered antiquated farming techniques, but he soon discovered that by decreasing their dependence on machinery, they accrued practical benefits such as a reduction in their use of gasoline and an increase in farm productivity. It also had a strange healing effect on the farm staff, who found themselves, as Catherine predicted, in direct contact with animals and nature. The first time they plowed a field with horses, the silence astounded them. "When horses walk on soft ground there is very little noise," Albert explained, "and the silence, when compared to the noise of tractors, seemed breathtaking."

"Catherine was one of the strongest proponents that grace builds on nature," Jean Fox recalled. "Our natures are almost destroyed through war, and through the breakdown of western civilization. Here, she gathered up these fragments, and in blind faith, in total faith, she began creating the kitchen, the handicraft center, the farm, the carpentry shop, every department in Madonna House."

"Catherine created this family," Father Bob Pelton noted, "but it is not she around whom we are gathered. It is the Lord Jesus."

Staff worker Susanne Stubbs agreed. "When we speak about Catherine to strangers, I often fear that they imagine that because of her charisma, we have almost made her into a cult figure, and all who have followed her have only been changed by the human side of her personality. I can say for myself, and, I believe for many others as well, that I did not and never would lay down my life for Catherine Doherty. Twenty years ago, I decided to lay down my life for Jesus Christ."

The year 1980 marked the 50th anniversary of Catherine's decision to give her life to God, and the Madonna House staff wanted a huge celebration. Catherine insisted, however, that they plan no special activities. "Why don't you go and see the Pope for your golden jubilee?" someone suggested.

The following spring, Catherine and Father Briere arrived in Rome. Irene Posnoff of Brussels, who worked with Radio Free Europe to smuggle Christian literature into the Soviet Union, and Father Heber de Lima of Brazil, who had written a popular biography of Catherine in Portuguese several years before, came to call at Catherine's hotel. Radio Vatican interviewed her in Russian for a special broadcast beamed into the Soviet Union, and she met with the foundress of the Little Sisters of Jesus. "We were there for a week," Father Briere recalled, "and then we saw the Pope."

On the morning of Saturday, March 14, they arrived at the private chapel of Pope John Paul II. Catherine sat quietly on the right side of the chapel, while Father Briere talked with a priest from the Vatican. As time for Mass drew closer, Catherine wondered where Father Briere had gone. "Then suddenly I saw that he was concelebrating with the Pope. I started crying. I couldn't believe my eyes that our own priest, Fr. Briere, was concelebrating with the Pope."

Afterward, Father Briere introduced Catherine to the Pontiff, telling him that she had spent 50 years of her life in the service of God. The Pope kissed her, and they spoke briefly in French. Then he kissed her again.

A few hours later, Catherine and Father Briere arrived in Paris. "For two weeks the phone rang off the hook," Father Briere recalled. "The French edition of *Poustinia* had been received so well that people came from all over France to call on Catherine."

During a lecture to a huge crowd at the church of St. Gervais, she talked about love. She also appeared on a television interview show, and had a private audience with the newly designated Archbishop of Paris, Jean-Marie Lustiger, who invited her to open a Madonna House in the city. She ended her tour with a question and answer session at another crowded church, and then, it was on to London where Lady Priscilla Collins, her British publisher, organized a cocktail party in her honor. During her visit, the British Broadcasting Company produced a special program on *Poustinia*, which aired during Holy Week.

On April 5, Catherine and Father Briere flew back to Canada. During the four weeks they were abroad, 84-year-old Catherine maintained a pace that would have exhausted someone 60 years younger. Dorothy Day, who was a year younger than Catherine, had died the previous November, and although Catherine delighted in teasing the staff by saying, "*If* I die. . . ," she must have sensed her time was near.

On the morning of August 18, 1981, a staff member found Catherine unconscious on the floor of her cabin. She was not expected to live through the day. Father Briere kept a vigil at her bedside. "I guess this is it," Father Callahan said when he heard her labored breathing. At 2 o'clock that afternoon, however, Catherine's breathing returned to normal, and she opened her eyes. "Help me turn," she said to Father Briere. A few days later, Catherine told him that just before she woke, she felt herself sinking, but suddenly it seemed as if the hand of God lifted her up, and a voice said, "Not yet."

Catherine was too ill in November 1981 to attend the convocation at St. Michael's College in Toronto, where the Basilian Fathers conferred upon her an honorary degree in Sacred Letters. During the ceremony, Cardinal Emmett Carter of Toronto publicly apologized for the "very grave, long-standing injustice" that Catherine had been subjected to in Toronto in the 1930's, and he invited Catherine to come back to the city and open a Madonna House there. It was a vindication the likes of which no one thought Catherine would ever receive, but when Father Gene Cullinane told her what the Cardinal had said, she smiled as if somewhere in the depths of herself she had always known justice would prevail. "With God," she whispered, "one just has to wait!"

By mid-December, Catherine rallied again, and within six weeks she regained enough energy to walk across the bridge every day for lunch in the Madonna House dining room. Her stride wasn't as strong as before, and she stopped more often to savor the wonders of nature around her. Catherine had entered another dimension of life, and during the next two years, peaceful contentment filled her days. Catherine, Father Callahan, and Father Briere had all been freed to a certain extent from the every day responsibilities of Madonna House, and they seemed to delight in watching the staff. There were over 125 staff workers now, with 16 field houses, and 16 Madonna House priests. People traveled from all over North America, South America, Europe, Asia, Africa and Australia to visit Combermere. Some shared their skills, like the meat cutters from New Jersey who butchered the sheep and cattle every fall, the Indian who taught them how to tan deer hide, crafts women who showed them how to create objects of beauty with their hands, dentists, doctors, bakers, housewives, journalists, musicians, filmmakers, and flight attendants. Some came out of curiosity; some came out of a hunger for God. They came to pray, to touch others, to experience a simpler life, to find quiet in a chaotic world.

"The minute I walked onto the Madonna House grounds, the sense of peace and love pervaded me," one woman recalled. "It was not something tangible. I just had a sense of peace and love. I felt at home there."

Days at Madonna House flowed with a quiet rhythm. Everyone rises at seven, meets for morning prayer in the chapel at eight with breakfast afterward, and then begins morning chores. The main meal is at noon, followed by spiritual reading. Then everyone returns to afternoon chores, which might include gardening, housecleaning, carpentry, mechanical repairs, weaving, or woodworking. At 3:30, they stop for tea, and then resume work from four until five, with Mass in the Russian chapel at 5:15. Dinner follows, and the rest of the evening is free, with occasional special programs or meetings planned.

"You must suffer much," a young man observed after being at Madonna House only two days. "You cannot create this kind of atmosphere without struggle. It must be a hidden suffering though; because I don't see it in your daily life."

"The hard work is purifying me," a young woman said, "but essentially I am being trained to love. And to accept love."

In 1982 Catherine wrote *Molchanie: The Silence of God*, which invites the reader on a mystical journey inward to meet Christ. Later that year, Catherine wrote *Doubts, Loneliness, Rejection*, a series of meditations on how faith alone can sustain a human being through the darkness of anguish. In 1983, *Urodivoi*, which means "Fools for God," explores humility as the foundation of the spiritual journey.

Sometime in the spring of 1983, Catherine gave one of her last talks to the staff. She reminded them that Madonna House had been founded on feeding the hungry, clothing the naked, visiting the sick, and helping refugees. These activities would always be with them, but, she warned, they must always be open to the needs of others and be willing to grow and change. "Never grow rigid. Be willing to move with the needs of the time. Ask yourself, 'What is the duty of the present moment?' At Madonna House simple things become holy. Do those simple tasks in a way that makes them holy."

After the talk, Catherine went to the basement to sort books, but her days of speaking and sorting were coming to an end. By January 1984, she was so frail that someone had to drive her to the main house for lunch, and weeks would go by when no one would see her. Over the years, Father Callahan had become more reclusive also. During the nice weather, he spent hours fishing, which was one of the few activities that relaxed him, and he would take along one or two of the younger staff members. Few realized that Father Callahan's heart was steadily failing. On the night of March 31, 1984, he was rushed to Barry's Bay Hospital with chest pains. The medical staff stabilized him, and one week later, on the morning of Saturday, April 7, he told his doctor, "Today is Our Lady's Day. I have asked her to bring me home today. Do you think that would be possible?"

"I don't see why not," the doctor replied. After the doctor left the room to fill out the necessary release forms, Father Callahan slumped over in his bed and died instantly. Everyone said Our Lady came to take him home.

No one expected that Father Callahan would die before Catherine, and when Father Briere broke the news, she replied, "I'm next. And then you." Father Callahan's wake was held in the

Madonna House Russian chapel. On Tuesday, April 10, Bishop Joseph Windle celebrated the funeral Mass with Archbishop Raya concelebrating. Later that evening, the priests of Madonna House elected Father Bob Pelton by acclamation to be the new Director of Priests.

A few months later, Ann Harrigan Makletzoff died in Toronto after a long, painful struggle with cancer. When Ann was first diagnosed, she wrote to tell Catherine of her illness: "Time is running out. I want to take your hand and tell you I'm sorry for whatever I may have done to cause you grief or suffering."

Catherine replied, "There is nothing in my heart but love for you darling, always has been. What is gone is done and long forgotten. I truly love you very much dear heart and you haven't been out of my simple prayers for very long through all these years."

Over the next few years, Catherine and Ann both expressed in letters a desire to meet in person and renew their friendship. "I received many insights, graces really that came to me during the long, sleepless nights," Ann wrote to Catherine in 1980, "enlightenment about myself and my life, painful though some of them were, but full of hope and promise of great things to come. I realize, e.g., that I had never expressly invited you to visit us — although you would always have been welcome. But what an oversight, which I sincerely regret.

"Now I am wishing you'd visit us whenever you get to Toronto (& soon, I hope). We are both getting on and before we die we should renew our friendship, talk about the present, and what we have to look forward to now at this time in our lives."

"Yes, dear heart, you are perfectly right," Catherine replied. "We should renew our friendship and I will come when I am in Toronto, which is not very often, but still I want so very much to come."

A meeting was finally arranged in Combermere. Afterward, Blanche Scholes Lepinskie asked Ann about the encounter, and Ann replied, "Well, we embraced."

"I don't think Ann had the feeling that there had been a real reconciliation," Blanche admitted.

"It turned into a nothing visit," one of the Madonna House priests agreed, "and may have brought the two women more heartache still."

In June 1984, when Ann hovered in the last stages of her illness, Catherine called her on the telephone, and they made one last attempt at reconciliation. Before she died, Ann confessed to Trudi Cortens: "I spent my life accenting too much Catherine's faults and not giving her enough credit for her virtues."

Catherine lapsed into the final stages of her own illness in the summer of 1984. Nurses attended her around the clock. People came and held her hand. Sometimes she recognized them; sometimes she did not. At times she seemed peaceful, and at other times, she was tortured with pain, choking, and seizures. Nothing remained of her youthful vigor, her passion, her physical beauty. "Lips that once bore words inspiring to thousands must often remain silent in the struggle just to breathe. Hands that worked quickly and efficiently to serve countless needs can now only cling to another hand for consolation. Vigilant eyes that surveyed in a glance the pulsing life of a whole apostolate are often closed in light, restless sleep."

The only thing that still emanated from Catherine was love. She loved with the simple tenderness of a child, a living icon, and some said that during this time of utter helplessness Catherine taught them the greatest lessons they ever learned.

"It seemed like a curse that God would let this woman, who was such a giant become so degraded before our eyes in a human way," admitted Albert Osterberger. "But I remember one time one Sunday I was there and I knew that B really loved me. I knew that. It was in the air."

"It was for herself and the staff a time of deep reconciliation and forgiveness," Father Briere explained. "This is a very human family with people who have strong personalities that rub against each other. We all tried to love one another a little bit better through this."

For years, people had asked: What will happen to Madonna House when Catherine dies? She would answer very simply: "If this is of God, it will continue. If it is not, it will cease to exist."

At 5:30, on the morning of Saturday, December 14, 1985, the moment of truth arrived. Catherine de Hueck Doherty, 89 years old, was dead.

Chapter Notes

"I'll expect you in Combermere...": Interview, Fr. Emile Briere.

"This is my Body...": *Ibid.*

"There was no doubt in my mind...": "Journey's End," *RES*, June 1975.

"It has nothing to do with 'being ashamed of'...": CD to G de H, Jan. 25, 1976, MHA.

"Even though for several years...": Carlos Miura, MD to G de H, Feb. 2, 1976, MHA.

"I know something happened...": Carlos Miura, MD to G de H, Mar. 15, 1976, MHA.

"About me he said...": "Staff Letter," Awards file, MHA.

"There are no words...": *Dearly Beloved*, Vol. III, p. 97.

"You have reproduced our childhood...": *Ibid.*, p. 98.

"In a period of one month...": Interview, Fr. Emile Briere.

"The prophet, the visionary...": *Katia*, p. 172.

"Tell them in their own language..." and f.: Interview, Fr. Emile Briere.

"Most people could not take that...": Interview, Jean Fox.

"God is spoken here": "Listening Houses," *RES*, July 1978.

"Why should anybody want to have a listening house?": *Ibid.*

"Catherine envisioned the Madonna House staff...": Interview, Jean Fox.

"Factually, [a listening house] doesn't 'do' anything...": "Listening Houses," *RES*, Mar. 1982.

"Our Canadian and USA youth...": Diary #58, n.d., MHA.

"Every year, she had a new project...": Interview, Albert Osterberger.

"When horses walk...": *Ibid.*

"Catherine was one of the strongest proponents...": Interview, Jean Fox.

"Catherine created this family...": "Madonna House," produced by Karen Madsen Pascal, Windborne Creations, Ltd., Markham, Ontario, Nov. 1983.

"When we speak about Catherine...": "La Porte Ouvrte," produced by Roger Leclerc, Société Radio Canada-Canadian Broadcasting Company, Montréal, Québec, Mar. 1987.

"We were there for a week...": Interview, Fr. Emile Briere.

"Then suddenly I saw...": "Trip to Europe," *RES*, May 1981.

"For two weeks...": Interview, Fr. Emile Briere.

"If I die...": Interview, Kathy Rodman.

"I guess this is it" and f.: Interview, Father Emile Briere.

"With God," she whispered: "Memo," Awards file, n.d., MHA.

"The minute I walked...": Interview, Kathy Skipper.

"You must suffer much...": "Combermere Diary," *RES*, Sept. 1981.

"The hard work is purifying me...": *Ibid*.

"Never grow rigid...": "Combermere Diary," *RES*, April 1983.

"Today is Our Lady's Day..." and f: Fr. Gene Cullinane, "Homecoming," *RES*, May 1984.

"I'm next. And then you.": Interview, Father Emile Briere.

"Time is running out...": AHM to CD, n.d., MHA.

"There is nothing in my heart but love...": CD to AHM, July 4, 1975, MHA.

"I received many insights...": AHM to CD, June 13, 1980, MHA.

"Yes, dear heart...": CD to AHM, July 15, 1980, MHA.

"Well, we embraced..." and f.: Interview, Blanche Scholes Lepinskie.

"It turned into a nothing visit": Fr. Ric Starks to author, Mar. 1, 1990.

Catherine called her: Interview, Fr. Emile Briere.

"I spent my life...": Interview, Trudi Cortens. [Ann Harrigan Makletzoff died in Toronto on June 11, 1984.]

"Lips that once bore words...": Fr. David May, "A Word of Encouragement for Us All," *RES*, Aug. - Sept., 1984.

"It seemed like a curse...": Interview, Albert Osterberger.

"It was for herself and the staff...": Interview, Father Emile Briere.

33

Combermere

1985

As news of Catherine's death spread through Madonna House, staff workers crowded into her little cabin. Father Pelton recited the prayers for the dead. Archbishop Raya, dressed in Byzantine robes, prostrated himself as Father Briere and another priest concelebrated Mass. For the next three days, Catherine's body lay in the Russian chapel that she loved so much. "She did not become hard as corpses do," Bishop Windle recalled. "Her skin remained sort of soft, and if you put your hand in her hand — well, imagination has a lot to do with these things — but you'd think that she was holding your hand."

On Sunday morning, after breakfast, Archbishop Raya stood in the Madonna House dining room and publicly thanked George de Hueck for the gift of his mother.

"What I want is that you remember especially how human my mother was," George replied, "and what a great struggle she went through to become the woman you knew her to be."

On Tuesday, December 18, the men of Madonna House carried Catherine's pine casket to the parish church where it was covered with a white cloth, symbolizing the white garment she wore after baptism. Her life had come full circle. "This woman of great faith does not have faith any more," proclaimed Archbishop Donat Chiasson of Moncton, New Brunswick, the main celebrant of the funeral Mass. "The candlelight of her faith was blown out because her day was dawning. She does not have hope any more because if she sees the face of God what else could she hope for?

This woman has loved much and now she enters into the city of Love unlimited."

During the homily, Father Bob Pelton drew the analogy between Catherine's life and a seed that started small, grew, produced fruit, died, and then started over again as a seed. "It is rare to see someone become a seed more than once or twice," Father Pelton explained. "Catherine was a seed many times — as a child, as a refugee, again in a time of personal and vocational crisis, again when her work in Toronto failed, again in Harlem, and once again here in Combermere. The seed took root here, and a tree began to grow. It was not a visibly magnificent tree. It was a humble tree, but with infinitely deep roots. It put out many branches, and it is already bearing much fruit."

A seed. Catherine would have liked that image.

"I was a seed of wheat. You were the sower," she once wrote.

You buried me in the deep, dark furrow one day so long ago. I died a thousand deaths within that earth so dark, so rich, so warm, so cold, and yet I lived.

Twice I believed that it was time to bring forth fruit. But twice the storms of hatred, of scorn, froze the furrow and the earth.

Then, when it seemed to me I died my thousandth death, the rain, the sun came. And beneath its warm rays I brought forth my seeds and laid them in your hands to die again and multiply.

They buried Catherine in the parish graveyard near Eddie and Flewy. Marking her grave was a wooden cross carved with the words, "She loved the poor."

In the years that followed Catherine's death, Madonna House grew and flourished with over 200 staff workers and field houses on five continents, including a house in Russia and plans for opening new houses in Asia. While some religious communities have not seen a postulant in years, Madonna House attracts nearly a dozen applicants and hundreds of visiting volunteers annually from all over the world. They strive to live Catherine's mandate of preaching the Gospel with their lives, without compromise, and with a spirit of unconditional love.

After Catherine's death, her son, George, kept returning to Madonna House every year, still bitter, still searching for some way to stop the pain that gnawed inside of him. "I do love you in my own strange fashion," Catherine had written to him over 30 years before. "How much? I think you will find out after my death." In September, 1990, George sat in his mother's cabin, reading her diaries and correspondence from the painful years of his childhood. For the first time, George saw the truth about his parents' marriage and his own troubled past. He trembled uncontrollably as the wounds that had festered inside of him for more than 60 years broke open, allowing anger and resentment to drain out. He finally understood how much his mother loved him. Eight months later, 69-year-old George de Hueck died from a heart attack.

In late 1990, Bishop Windle granted permission to begin investigations into whether or not the Catholic Church should consider Catherine a candidate for sainthood. During the process, the details of her life are examined and her writings scrutinized. Testimonies are already being gathered from family members, friends, and acquaintances. Some have gone on record saying Catherine was a deeply compassionate woman, on fire with love of God, a poet, a prophet, a modern day saint, who could look into people's souls, and teach, comfort and inspire. Others say she was stubborn, inconsistent, short-tempered, rude, manipulative, overbearing, and power-hungry to the point where she stifled people, suppressed disagreement, and stamped out intellectual curiosity. Some speculate her annulled marriage will knock her out of the running for canonization. Others say her marital difficulties and her experiences as a single parent speak to Catholics today, who are struggling with the pain of broken families.

"She was flesh and blood," says Father Robert Wild, who is coordinating the investigation into Catherine's life. "She struggled to be kind to people. She was misunderstood. She was emotion-

ally and spiritually battered. But she kept getting up every day
and trying again. It's encouraging to all of us that you don't have
to be perfect, if you're willing to ask God's help."

Still, the question remains. Does Catherine de Hueck Doherty
meet the criteria for sainthood? And by what criteria should she
be judged?

"My own hunch," writes Kenneth L. Woodward, author of
*Making Saints: How the Catholic Church Determines Who Becomes a
Saint, Who Doesn't and Why*, "is that the story of a saint is always
a love story. It is a story of a God who loves, and of the beloved
who learns how to reciprocate and share that 'harsh and dreadful
love.' It is a story that includes misunderstanding, deception,
betrayal, concealment, reversal, and revelation of character. It is,
if the saints are to be trusted, our story. But to be a saint is not to
be a solitary lover. It is to enter into deeper communion with
everyone and everything that exists."

And what would Catherine say? She would probably reiterate the same thing she always told interviewers when they asked
about the future: "If it is of God, then it will happen. . . If it is not,
it won't."

In the meantime, the people of Madonna House continue, in
their own simple way, to try and live, willingly and joyfully, the
spiritual legacy Catherine left behind. It is a legacy that Catherine
believed was a personal mandate from God, a mandate asking her
to surrender everything and follow the Spirit into the hearts of
people everywhere, relying only on the simple trust that God
would be with her. The following is the "Little Mandate," the
words of Jesus, a synopsis of the Gospel message, that came to her:

> Arise — go! Sell all you possess. . .
> give it directly, personally to the poor.
> Take up My cross (their cross) and follow Me —
> going to the poor — being poor —
> being one with them — one with Me.
> Little — be always little ... simple — poor — childlike.

Preach the Gospel WITH YOUR LIFE — WITHOUT
COMPROMISE —
Listen to the Spirit — He will lead you.
Do little things exceedingly well for love of Me.
Love — love — love, never counting the cost.
Go into the marketplace and stay with Me... pray... fast...
pray always. . . fast.
Be hidden — be a light to your neighbor's feet.
Go without fears into the depths of men's hearts. . .
I shall be with you.
Pray always. I WILL BE YOUR REST.

Chapter Notes

"She did not become hard...": Interview, Bishop Joseph Windle.

"What I want is that you remember...": Text of funeral homily, Fr. Robert Pelton,
Dec. 18, 1985, MHA.

"This woman of great faith...": Text of funeral Mass, Archbishop Donat Chiasson,
Dec. 18, 1985, MHA.

"It is rare to see...": Text of funeral homily, Fr. Robert Pelton, Dec. 18, 1985, MHA.

"I was a seed...": CD, *Soul of My Soul*, Notre Dame, Indiana: Ave Maria Press, 1985,
p. 128.

"I do love you...": CD to G de H, Apr. 18, 1957, MHA.

"She was flesh and blood...": Bob Harvey, "Aiming to Immortalize," *Ottawa Citizen*,
Jan. 19, 1991.

"My own hunch...": Kenneth L. Woodward, *Making Saints*, p. 406.

"If it is of God...": Interview, Fr. Emile Briere.

"Arise — go...": *Little Mandate*, MHA.

Abbreviations for Chapter Notes

AH	Ann Harrigan
AHM	Ann Harrigan Makletzoff
BS	Betty Schneider
C de H	Catherine de Hueck
CD	Catherine Doherty
ED	Eddie Doherty
G de H	George de Hueck
JC	Fr. John Callahan
JMF	Fr. John Milway Filion
NM	Nicholas Makletzoff
PHF	Fr. Paul Hanly Furfey

ACA	Archdiocese of Chicago Archives & Record Center
ARCAT	Archives of the Catholic Archdiocese of Toronto
AUND	Archives of the University of Notre Dame
CHS	Chicago Historical Society
FAA	Friars of the Atonement Archives
MHA	Madonna House Archives

RES	Restoration, published in Combermere, Ontario by Madonna House
Diary	The personal and spiritual diaries of Catherine de Hueck Doherty are listed by number with a date of entry.

THE KOLYSCHKINE FAMILY

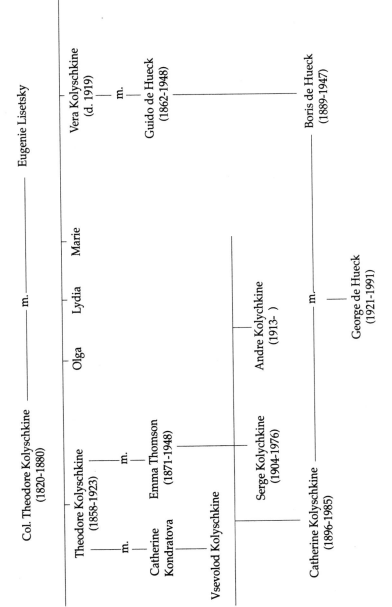

Col. Theodore Kolyschkine —— m. —— Eugenie Lisetsky
(1820-1880)

Theodore Kolyschkine — m. — Emma Thomson   Olga Lydia Marie   Vera Kolyschkine
(1858-1923)   (1871-1948)   (d. 1919)

Catherine
Kondratova — m. —   m.

Vsevolod Kolyschkine

Serge Kolyschkine   Andre Kolychkine   Guido de Hueck
(1904-1976)   (1913-)   (1862-1948)

Catherine Kolyschkine — m. — Boris de Hueck
(1896-1985)   (1889-1947)

George de Hueck
(1921-1991)

SELECTED BIBLIOGRAPHY

Books by Catherine de Hueck Doherty

Apostolic Farming, Combermere, Ontario: Madonna House Publications, 1991.

Dear Bishop, New York: Sheed & Ward, 1947.

Dear Father, Combermere, Ontario: Madonna House Publications, 1988.

Dearly Beloved: Letters to the Children of My Spirit, Vol. I, II, III, Combermere, Ontario: Madonna House Publications, 1990.

Dear Seminarian, Milwaukee: Bruce Publishing Co., 1950.

Doubts, Loneliness, Rejection, New York: Alba House, 1981.

Fragments of My Life, Notre Dame, Indiana: Ave Maria Press, 1979.

Friendship House, New York: Sheed & Ward, 1946.

The Gospel of a Poor Woman, Denville, New Jersey: Dimension Books Inc., 1981.

The Gospel Without Compromise, Combermere, Ontario: Madonna House Publications, 1989.

I Live On an Island, Notre Dame, Indiana: Ave Maria Press, 1979.

Journey Inward, New York: Alba House, 1984.

Lubov, Locust Valley, New York: Living Flame Press, 1985.

Molchanie, New York: Crossroad Publishing Co., 1984.

My Heart and I, Petersham, Mass.: St. Bede's Publications, 1987.

My Russian Yesterdays, New Canadian Edition, Combermere, Ontario: Madonna House Publications, 1990.

Not Without Parables, Notre Dame, Indiana: Ave Maria Press, 1977.

Our Lady's Unknown Mysteries, Combermere, Ontario: Madonna House Publications, 1990.

People of the Towel & Water, Combermere, Ontario: Madonna House Publications, 1991.

Poustinia: Christian Spirituality of the East for Western Man, Notre
          Dame, Indiana: Ave Maria Press, 1975.
Sobornost: Eastern Unity of Mind and Heart for Western Man, Notre
          Dame, Indiana, Ave Maria Press, 1977.
Soul of My Soul, Notre Dame, Indiana: Ave Maria Press, 1985.
Strannik: The Call to Pilgrimage for Western Man, Notre Dame,
          Indiana: Ave Maria Press, 1978.
Urodivoi, New York: Crossroad Publishing Co., 1983.

Books by Other Authors

Arseniev, Nicholas. *Russian Piety*, London: The Faith Press Ltd.,
          1964.
Baedeker, Karl. *The Dominion of Canada, Handbook for Travelers*, New
          York: Charles Scribner's Sons, 1922.
_____. *Egypt, Handbook for Travelers*, New York: Charles
          Scribner's Sons, 1902.
_____. *Palestine and Syria, Handbook for Travelers*, New York:
          Charles Scribner's Sons, 1898.
_____. *Paris & Environs, Handbook for Travelers*, New York:
          Charles Scribner's Sons, 1907.
_____. *Russia, A Handbook for Travelers* (A facsimile of the
          original 1914 edition), New York: Arno Press/Random
          House, 1971.
Boyle, George. *Pioneer in Purple*, Montreal: Palm Publishers, 1951.
Brebner, J. Bartlet. *Canada, A Modern History*, Ann Arbor: The
          University of Michigan Press, 1970.
Briere, Emile. *I Met the Humbled Christ in Russia*, Denville, New
          Jersey: Dimension Books, Inc., 1976. (Read and anno-
          tated by Catherine de Hueck Doherty, March 1982.)
_____. *Katia, A Personal Vision of Catherine de Hueck Doherty*,
          Sherbrooke, Quebec: Editions Paulines, 1988.
Charkravorty, B.C. *Rabindranath Tagore: His Mind and Art*, New
          Delhi: Young India Publications, 1971.
Doherty, Eddie. *A Cricket in My Heart*, San Antonio, Texas: Blue
          House Press, 1990.
_____. *Gall and Honey, The Story of a Newspaperman*,
          Combermere, Ontario: Madonna House Publications,
          1989.

_____. *My Hay Ain't In Yet*, Milwaukee: Bruce Publishing Company, 1952.

_____. *Tumbleweed*, New Canadian Edition, Combermere, Ontario: Madonna House Publications, 1988.

Farmborough, Florence. *Nurse at the Russian Front, A Diary 1914-18*, London: Constable and Company, Ltd., 1974.

Fisher, Claude Laing. *James Cardinal McGuigan, Archbishop of Toronto*, Toronto: McClelland & Stewart, Ltd., 1948.

Footman, David. *Civil War in Russia*, London: Faber & Faber, 1961.

Fortescue, Adrian. *The Orthodox Eastern Church*, London: Catholic Truth Society, 1907.

Frisby, Margery. *An Alley In Chicago*, Kansas City, Mo.: Sheed & Ward, 1991.

Furfey, Paul Hanly, *Fire on the Earth*, New York: The Macmillan Company, 1936.

Gannon, David. *Father Paul of Graymoor*, New York: The Macmillan Company, 1951.

Gody, Lou, editor in chief. *The WPA Guide to New York City*, Prepared by the Federal Writer's Project of the Works Progress Administration in New York City, 1939, facsimile published by Pantheon Books, Random House, 1982.

Gordon, David. *Quartered in Hell, The Story of the American North Russia Expeditionary Force 1918-1919*, Missoula MT: The Doughboy Historical Society and G.O.S., Inc., 1982.

Gorky, Maxim. *Untimely Thoughts*, Translated by Herman Ermolaev, New York: Paul S. Eriksson, Inc., 1968.

Gould, Joseph E. *The Chautauqua Movement*, State University of New York: University Publishers, 1961.

Hannula, J.O. *Finland's War of Independence*, London: Faber and Faber Limited, 1939.

Henderson, Larry. *Egypt and the Sudan*, New York: Thomas Nelson Inc., 1971.

Kerensky, Alexander. *Russia and History's Turning Point*, New York: Duell, Solan and Pearce, 1965.

Kochan, Lionel. *The Russian Revolution*, New York: The John Day Company, 1970.

Latourette, Kenneth Scott. *World Service*, New York: Young Men's Christian Association Press, 1957.

Lawrence, Louise de Kiriline. *Another Winter, Another Spring: A Love Remembered*, New York: McGraw-Hill, 1977.

Lincoln, W. Bruce. *In War's Dark Shadow, The Russians Before the Great War*, New York: Dial Press, 1983.

Marie, Grand Duchess of Russia. *Education of a Princess, A Memoir*, New York: The Viking Press, 1930.

Massie, Suzanne. *Land of the Firebird: The Beauty of Old Russia*, New York: Simon and Schuster, 1980. (Read and annotated by Catherine de Hueck Doherty and Rev. Emile Briere, January 1982.)

Mawdsley, Evan. *The Russian Civil War*, Boston: Allen & Unwin, 1987.

MacLaren, Gay. *Morally We Roll Along*, Boston: Little, Brown and Company, 1938.

McCorkell, Edmund J. *Henry Carr — Revolutionary*, Toronto: Griffin House, 1969.

Merton, Thomas. *The Seven Storey Mountain*, New York: Harcourt, Brace and Company, 1948.

Miliukov, Paul. *Outlines of Russian Culture, Part I: Religion and the Church*, University of Pennsylvania Press, 1942.

Morrison, Theodore. *Chautauqua, A Center for Education, Religion, and the Arts in America*, Chicago: University of Chicago Press, 1974.

Parker, W.H.. *An Historical Geography of Russia*, Chicago: Aldine Publishing Company, 1968.

Pitirim, Archbishop of Volokolamsk, et al. *The Orthodox Church in Russia*, The Bendome Press, New York, 1982.

Schmemann, Alexander. *Of Water and the Spirit*, Crestwood, New York: St. Vladimir's Seminary Press, 1974.

_____. *Sacraments and Orthodoxy*, New York: Herder and Herder, 1965.

Sheed, Frank. *The Church and I*, New York: Doubleday & Company, Inc., 1974.

Scott, Marian. *Chautauqua Caravan*, New York: D. Appleton-Century Company, 1939.

Shrive, Frank J. *Observations of a P.B.O (Poor Bloody Observer)*, Erin, Ontario: The Boston Mills Press, 1981.

Smith, C. Jay. *Finland and the Russian Revolution, 1917-1922*, Athens: University of Georgia Press, 1958.

Tarry, Ellen. *The Third Door: Autobiography of an American Negro Woman*, New York: David McKay Company, Inc., 1955.

Taunton, Ethelred. *The Law of the Church: Cyclopaedia of Canon Law for English-speaking Countries*, London: Kegan Paul, Trench, Trubner & Co., Ltd., 1906.

Treat, Roger L. *Bishop Sheil and The CYO*, New York: Julian Messner, Inc., 1951.

Tretjakewitsch, Léon. *Bishop Michel d'Herbigny SJ and Russia, A Pre-Ecumenical Approach to Christian Unity*, Würzburg: Augustinus-Verlag, 1990.

Trotsky, Leon. *Lenin*, New York: G.P. Putnam's Sons, 1971.

_____. *The History of the Russian Revolution, Vol I. The Overthrow of Tsarism*, Translated by Max Eastman, New York, Simon & Schuster, 1932.

_____. *The Russian Revolution*, New York: Doubleday, 1959.

Ward, Maisie. *Unfinished Business*, New York: Sheed & Ward, 1964.

Washburn, Stanley. *On the Russian Front in World War I, Memoirs of an American War Correspondent*, New York: Robert Speller and Sons, Publisher, Inc. 1982.

Westwood, J.N. *A History of Russian Railways*, London: George Allen and Unwin Ltd., 1964.

Wild, Robert. *Journey to the Lonely Christ, The Little Mandate of Catherine de Hueck Doherty*, New York: Alba House, 1987.

_____. *Journey in the Risen Christ, The Little Mandate of Catherine de Hueck Doherty*, New York: Alba House, 1992.

_____. *Love, Love, Love, The Little Mandate of Catherine de Hueck Doherty*, New York: Alba House, 1989.

Woodward, Kenneth L. *Making Saints: How the Catholic Church Determines Who Becomes a Saint, Who Doesn't and Why*, New York: Simon and Schuster, 1990.

Zatko, James J. *Decent into Darkness: The Destruction of the Roman Catholic Church in Russia, 1917-1923*, Notre Dame, Indiana: University of Notre Dame Press, 1965.

Zernov, Nicholas. *The Russians and their Church*, Third Edition, Crestwood, New York: St. Vladimir's Seminary Press, 1978.

Miscellenous Sources

Alvarex, Fred, S.A. *Historical Sites of Graymoor,* Garrison, New York: Heritage Commission, 1985.

De Hueck, George T.M., Editor, *Family Notes, A Journal of the Hueck Families,* Volumes I - VII, Privately published by the Hueck Family Association, Mobile, Alabama.

Doherty, Catherine de Hueck, *The History of the Apostolate,* unpublished manuscript, Vol. I, II, III, Madonna House Archives.

Doherty, Catherine de Hueck, "Little Mandate — How It Came To Be," transcribed tape, April 27, 1968, Madonna House Archives.

Doherty, Catherine de Hueck, *Stories for Staff Workers that go. . . "IN ONE EAR AND OUT ANOTHER",* unpublished collection of transcribed tapes, Madonna House Archives.

Gibbons, Rev. Marion Leo. *Domicile of Wife Unlawfully Separated from Her Husband, A Historical Synopsis and Canonical Commentary,* Washington D.C.: The Catholic University of America Press, 1947.

Kolychkine, Serge, "Unpublished Family History," Madonna House Archives.

Legree, Joseph C. *Lift Up Your Arms: A History of the Roman Catholic Diocese of Pembroke,* Combermere, Ontario, 1988.

Sharum, Elisabeth Louise, *A Strange Fire Burning: A History of the Friendship House Movement, A Dissertation in History,* Texas Tech University, May, 1977.

Videotapes

"Catherine de Hueck Doherty," *Christopher Closeup,* produced by The Christophers, New York City, 1978.

"The Lady They Call the B," *World Religions,* produced by Mike McManus, TVOntario, Dec. 7, 1973.

"La Porte Ouvrte," produced by Roger Leclerc, Société Radio Canada-Canadian Broadcasting Company, Montréal, Québec, Mar. 1987.

"Madonna House," produced by Karen Madsen Pascal, Windborne Creations, Ltd., Markham, Ontario, Nov. 1983.

Name Index